Advance Praise for *Queer Nature*

When heteronormativity prescribes a binary to everything it touches—something is either *natural* or *unnatural*—what a salve to reclaim and celebrate nature in its sprawling wonder and unfettered queerness. This is an invitation to readers who've long felt excluded from representations of the natural and pastoral. No longer stripped of its wildness and subtext, the nature reflected in these poems is the breadth of human experience: its complexities and aches, its trauma and desires, its richness and possibilities. *Queer Nature* understands nature resists constraint and simplification. It is boundless and borderless. It belongs to everyone.

RUTH AWAD, AUTHOR OF *SET TO MUSIC A WILDFIRE*

Imagine my delight and pride in being a part of this anthology! Imagine your pleasure as you immerse yourself in this beauty of queerness! This is a must-have book for all.

CHRYSTOS, AUTHOR OF *FIRE POWER, IN HER I AM,* AND *NOT VANISHING*

This anthology makes visible the astonishing range and impact of queer poets. Page after page shimmers with emotional and intellectual pleasures—these poems will make you think, weep, sing, and sigh with relief. Michael Walsh's remarkable curation reminds us what's natural has always been queer and what's queer is always natural.

EDUARDO C. CORRAL, AUTHOR OF *GUILLOTINE* AND *SLOW LIGHTNING*

Queer Nature grew from one queer farm boy's longing for poetry that spoke to his complex love for the natural world he loved but to which, he was taught, love like his did not belong. Like a dowsing rod, this longing led Michael Walsh to an underground poetic river, a heretofore obscure but essential American lyric tradition of conceiving, celebrating, and mourning nature. Gathering poets of innumerable ethnicities, histories, styles, and sexual and gender identifications, this book gives us access to a desperately needed aquifer of language that help us reimagine, revitalize, and repair our connection to the world we are destroying.

JOY LADIN, AUTHOR OF *THE FUTURE IS TRYING TO TELL US SOMETHING*:
NEW AND SELECTED POEMS AND *THE BOOK OF ANNA*

Queer Nature is a vital anthology, generous in scope and elegantly cultivated by editor Michael Walsh. As I began reading *Queer Nature*, I started highlighting passages that illuminated for me new paths of understanding. Now the whole book is neon, glowing: *Queer Nature*—a moon, *Queer Nature*—a firefly, *Queer Nature*—a fish in the dark abyss shining its own extraordinary light. Reader, if you hold this surprising and luminous anthology close, it just might guide you home.

ALICIA MOUNTAIN, PHD, AUTHOR OF *HIGH GROUND COWARD*

Queer people have had, are having, and will continue to have complicated relationships to nature, which is why this anthology of poems marks an important and nuanced contribution to our understanding of the nature poem. The real joy of *Queer Nature,* though, is the diversity of poems assembled here and their multifaceted renderings of nature, which challenge any simplistic understanding of the pastoral. By gathering these poems from the past 150 years in this long overdue and critically important anthology, Michael Walsh has accomplished an incredible thing.

JACQUES J. RANCOURT, AUTHOR OF *BROCKEN SPECTRE* AND *NOVENA*

The poems in *Queer Nature* investigate the ways we inhabit ourselves and our landscapes—everywhere unfurling, throwing roots, spores. Here, the ground is rich with worm and bone. Here, the concerns are both urgent and eternal. How do we locate the places where we can survive? How do we create them? And, ultimately, how will we create and recreate ourselves so we can thrive?

RICHARD SIKEN, AUTHOR OF *CRUSH* AND *WAR OF THE FOXES*

I fell in love on nearly every page of *Queer Nature.* Sure, there is suffering to consider in our long journey into the light of acceptance and recognition, but what tumbles out of these poems again and again are affirmations of love and the reek of hope. This anthology is a homecoming. Readers will recognize many of these voices and be moved by the magnitude of the rich populous of queer eco-centric nature poets gathered here. I am less lonely, less terrified of my queerness, as I pour through these pages. This is a magnificent collection.

AMBER FLORA THOMAS, AUTHOR OF *EYE OF WATER. POEMS*

The poems in this remarkable collection work in both tandem and contradiction to make the irrefutable sound of queer ecologies. An aching intervention into the violent logics that position queerness as the antithesis of a natural world, *Queer Nature* says otherwise. The poems congeal, illuminating again and again that queer is nature. Queer is the animal. Queer are the hands "moved like rivers." Queer is the genre of the poem itself—its small and infinite ecosystem.

STACEY WAITE, AUTHOR OF *BUTCH GEOGRAPHY*

QUEER NATURE

QUEER NATURE

{A POETRY ANTHOLOGY}

Edited by
MICHAEL WALSH

AUTUMN
HOUSE PRESS

This project is supported in part by the National Endowment for the Arts as well as the Amazon Literary Partnership Poetry Fund and the Academy of American Poets. Autumn House is grateful for this generous support.

Autumn House Press receives state arts funding support through a grant from the Pennsylvania Council on the Arts, a state agency funded by the Commonwealth of Pennsylvania, and the National Endowment for the Arts, a federal agency.

ISBN: 978-1-63768-038-4
Library of Congress Control Number: 2022933426

Book & cover design by Joel W. Coggins

CONTENTS

I GREW UP in the hilly fields of a Minnesota dairy farm, and no matter where I live as an adult, those fields and pastures are the homeland I carry inside me, complete with cows, insects, crops, and prairie plants. That farm, as well as my life there, was hard, messy, and dirty, but still, I loved it. I believe we all have at least one such place that we carry, and I also believe that poetry, perhaps more than any other medium, can locate it, can recreate it. But for years, I couldn't find a poem that celebrated this gritty place; instead, I found lines about bountiful, golden harvests and bouncing baby calves. These depictions didn't tell my truths, which made finding them and developing them in my own poetry that much harder. In addition, as a gay farm kid, I was aware that if an animal doesn't reproduce, it's unnatural and useless. This commonplace rural wisdom impeded my ability to express the queer version of the homeland I carry. For a long time, I couldn't figure out how I fit in, but still, I loved it, even if the story I was being told about what was right and worth appreciating in nature excluded the most important parts of me.

So, what did it mean in nature for a boy attracted to other boys? At that age, it suggested to me that nature had made a big mistake. Did I belong in nature at all? I wanted to, but everything around me seemed to suggest that there was simply no place, no use for me. Discovering poetry as a teenager and dedicating myself to its study as a freshman in college, I quickly and easily found celebratory pastorals redolent with flora and fauna as well as transcendent contemplations of life and death linked to animals and the passage of seasons, but these poetic conventions investigated the birds, the bees, and quite often, deer. I read everything by Robert Bly and James Wright, two poets with whom I share a landscape, but not an orientation or corresponding attitude toward nature. The speakers in their lyric poems evoked harmony with their natural surroundings, a harmony I didn't recognize in my marrow. It wasn't until much later that I found poems that responded to nature in a way that spoke to that homeland inside me: Ed Madden's filthy poem "Viscous" conjuring rotting hay bales and drying semen; Amber Flora Thomas's "Field Song" evoking the damage the human body does to a field of wheat. Both poems moved beyond the golden glory of harvests and depicted a nuanced, sometimes antagonistic, relationship with nature. In other words, before finding poems like these, I didn't find my queer life in the place where I had lived so long and knew best or in the poems I loved most. These poems opened a door, and they allowed me to see beyond the clichéd and expected; they showed me how queer nature can really be.

Because queer and trans poets have been writing about nature for as long as everyone else, the problem is with the canon of nature poetry. The lack of representation hindered my artistic development as an adult as much as my romantic relationship skills were hindered by all my teenage years in the closet. My experience wasn't unique; many of the poets in this anthology probably encountered the same issue, the same feeling of alienation. And in 2015, I decided I wanted to address this obvious gap.

Gathering queer and trans American poets from the nineteenth century through the twenty-first, such as John Ashbery, Richard Blanco, Jericho Brown, Natalie Diaz, Emily Dickinson, Thom Gunn, Audre Lorde, Mary Oliver, Kay Ryan, Adrienne Rich, and May Swenson, I approached this anthology with a sense of generosity regarding what the form and content of the nature poem could be and tried to suspend my skepticism for what couldn't or wouldn't fit. Many of these poems make statements, implicit or outright, on the following topics in addition to nature: appetite, body, death, desire, gender, habitat, home, hope, love, metamorphosis, monstrosity, nation, race, and of course, sex. As I searched, I also became more aware of how the construction of farms and cities had destroyed and displaced nature. Poems embodying this truth needed to be more chaotic, dirty, and nuanced than those I encountered. Finally, and perhaps most importantly, I didn't want to restrict the nature poem to the outdoors or to the "wilderness," a colonial term, in recognition of how built places are communities, habitats, and contested sites, as one notices in such poems as "Closing the Gay Bar outside Gas City" by Bruce Snider and "Taking a Visitor to See the Ruins" by Paula Gunn Allen.

Neither did I want to restrict the nature poem to feminine and masculine concepts imposed upon the more-than-human world, especially through the myth of Adam and Eve. In contrast, the Medusa, "the Queen under the Hill" of this anthology, is a better ancestor because her phallic snakes recombine the male and female and allow her to represent the human and more-than-human world. She is shameless. Many of these poems defy assumptions of feminine and masculine and write powerfully at this intersection of the human and more-than-human. In particular, some poems exemplify the defiances and inversions of gender that define their speakers but that are also commonplace in nature: most plants are monoecious (containing both male and female parts) and make ready and apt images for queer and trans poetics. In "Boy with Flowers" by Ely Shipley, the speaker refuses flowers when an aunt genders them as female-only and finds solace after top surgery in the final lines:

"[e]ach sewn tight with stitches, each a naked stem, flaring with thorns." In conversation, Cameron Awkward-Rich's poem, "The Little Girl Is Busy Asking Questions about Desire," describes a girl becoming a tree, which serves as a metaphor for the speaker's transition from female to male. All through this anthology, plants and flowers represent queer sources of joy and mystery. In "Bottle Gentian," KateLynn Hibbard speaks to a hardy prairie flower of its quiet and closed strangeness—a botanical introvert from the more-than-human world. Of course, in Allen Ginsberg's "Sunflower Sutra," the rambunctious speaker addresses a withered sunflower and asks, "Poor dead flower? when did you forget you were a flower?" and compels readers with uplifting admonitions such as "we're golden sunflowers inside, blessed by our own seed & hairy naked accomplishment." In ecstatic, extraverted exchange, the drag queen speaker in Benjamin Garcia's "Ode to the Corpse Flower" declares, "I am the week-old ham hock whore of horticulture" and sings "fuck Whitman fuck Pound // give me Emily D." Dead, alive, or filthy, flowers help many of us articulate identities.

Of particular delight were poems that fully infused the queer into nature in new and unexpected ways. Some poems exist in their own weird biomes and according to their own terms. For example, Kay Ryan's philosophical poem "How a Thought Thinks" transforms a thought into a mole-like creature chewing underground—a queer contrast to the lofty thought processes celebrated in European philosophy. In "Enskyment," Antler evokes the incantatory joy of being interred in the sky until, after downpours, all that's left of one's life is petrichor—a liberation from the metaphysics of earth and sky. Don't we all yearn for an explanation that will unbury us, once and for all? With the rain, we evaporate. In *Queer Nature*, this poem is only one example of how water is implicit to queer, poetic transformation.

As a force of contradiction, mutability, and impossibility, water is described in these poems as black, brown, burning, clean, disturbed, divided, fresh, laughing, knocking, murky, oily, open, and parted. In "Fairy Tale," sam sax writes of a boy who becomes an infectious steam, queer and dormant, inside his lovers from the baths. As a contrast, in "Sex" by Nikki Finney, steam redeems, rather than infects, lovemaking. Just as water is representative of the mutable, powerful, and transformative, so are bodies of water, including waterfalls and rivers. "Diving into the Wreck" by Adrienne Rich, one of the landmark poems of twentieth-century literature, deserves special mention as an origin myth and the likely wellspring of so many other poems. Her speaker describes the arduous and solo dive into the sea, an androgenizing process in which the animal, elemental, and unnatural must work together for the diver to recover knowledge that was never recorded.

If you are a queer or trans person occupying a built place or landscape and people question your right to existence, you might find yourself asking versions of two questions that have echoed throughout my years of editing this anthology: *Who belongs here and why? Who and what gets to be natural?* I have included poems that confound assumptions or offer possible answers to those questions. In his poem "Outing, Iowa," Oliver Baez Bendorf offers an alternate, queer framework for the rural and reclaims rural geographies from scarecrow stories. In "Amphibians" Joseph O. Legaspi contemplates the mutuality of amphibians and immigrants through metaphors of land, water, skin, and breath. Answering both in a different way, Kamilah Aisha Moon's powerful poem "Shared Plight" shows us the natural history of New York City in which Black people exist as animals to be hunted and a natural history of America in which Black towns are unwanted herds to be eradicated. Becoming the animal can be transcendence or dehumanization, dependent upon what person or system is transforming whom and why. Included, too, are many affirmations of our belonging in the world. "Coal" by Audre Lorde is a lyric of ancestral Black power, one derived from the metaphor of potent, elemental energy stored by and within the earth. Finally, the speaker of "Hermit Crab" by Stephanie Burt transforms her shell into a metaphor for her trans identity.

Years of delight and discovery went into editing these poems. Over and over, I returned most often to considerations of homes and biomes unlike mine, shell or wide-open ocean, and placed them in contrast to the Garden of Eden. I considered how we have never been unnatural. No matter how many times that story asserts its authority, we predate Adam and Eve. We have always been intrinsic to the world, and in this anthology, we are claiming a place.

In that spirit, *Queer Nature* makes its own place for this first, wild gathering of queer and trans poets. In these pages, you will find the birds, the bees, and, quite often, deer. Gay bars, riverbanks, bedrooms, fields, and forests are a few of the habitats in which these poems lament and sing. The inspirations and wisdoms these poets have to share, I leave to each of their individual geniuses and queer thoughts.

MICHAEL WALSH
De Soto, WI

QUEER NATURE

Wilderness of Flesh

I nuzzle the wheat
field of your armpit, whisper
how I like the fragrance,
sour as a rotted
onion.
                    The wilderness
            of flesh we both
inhabit rests deep in the quarry
of your skull, in the scat
fertilizing your chest,

& the sound that pours from
the brook of your throat
swells like a magpie's
shriek, or a bullfrog
belching after
                    home, & tonight—
            even if we flit in
& out of sleep like cardinals
winding through an ash
grove—our separate skins

will dissolve in the dark
musk of our mutual tug

& pull, our bodies nothing
less than a stick & stone
set to flint.

What Use Is Knowing Anything If No One Is Around

What use is knowing anything if no one is around
to watch you know it? Plants reinvent sugar daily
and hardly anyone applauds. Once as a boy I sat
in a corner covering my ears, singing Quranic verse

after Quranic verse. Each syllable was perfect, but only
the lonely rumble in my head gave praise. This is why
we put mirrors in birdcages, why we turn on lamps

to double our shadows. I love my body more
than other bodies. When I sleep next to a man, he becomes
an extension of my own brilliance. Or rather, he becomes
an echo of my own anticlimax. I was delivered

from dying like a gift card sent in lieu of a pound
of flesh. My escape was mundane, voidable. Now
I feed faith to faith, suffer human noise, complain
about this or that heartache. The spirit lives in between

the parts of a name. It is vulnerable only to silence
and forgetting. I am vulnerable to hammers, fire,
and any number of poisons. The dream, then: to erupt
into a sturdier form, like a wild lotus bursting into

its tantrum of blades. There has always been a swarm
of hungry ghosts orbiting my body—even now,
I can feel them plotting in their luminous diamonds

of fog, each eying a rib or a thighbone. They are
arranging their plans like worms preparing
to rise through the soil. They are ready to die
with their kind, dry and stiff above the wet earth.

The River's Address

Slow in the evening light through tree-covered streets
sounds develop unenvelopable—

Troubadour, river-citizen, can you navigate the sound's course
to my far shore's ecstasy?

Be gray here, be broken and strafed, fully roused and drawn here,
like a compass needle, find yourself bound and unintelligible.

You followed the shrift north from the city into the mountains,
to the place you eddy, churn, spell out the moon's tidal courses.

River-chaser, compass-worn, here the source spills to the sea,
and here the waters wend from the sea back to the source.

Unsire yourself—instead of street-maps and sounding depths
trace your name, trace the trees, trace the night into your mind.

Close your eyes and listen to the sound—try to remember—
or try to forget—here is the place you could turn and return.

Taking a Visitor to See the Ruins

for Joe Bruchac

He's still telling about the time he came west
and was visiting me. I knew he
wanted to see some of the things

everybody sees when they're in the wilds of New Mexico.
So when we'd had our morning coffee
after he'd arrived, I said,

Would you like to see some old Indian ruins?
His eyes brightened with excitement,
he was thinking, no doubt

of places like the ones he'd known where he came from,
sacred caves filled with falseface masks,
ruins long abandoned, built secure

into the sacred lands; or of pueblos
once home to vanished people but peopled still
by their ghosts, connected still with the bone-old land.

Sure, he said. I'd like that a lot.
Come on, I said, and we got in my car,
drove a few blocks east, toward the towering peaks

of the Sandias. We stopped at a tall
high-security apartment building made of stone,
went up a walk past the pond and pressed the buzzer.

They answered and we went in,
past the empty pool room, past the empty party room,
up five flights in the elevator, down the abandoned hall.

Joe, I said, when we'd gotten inside the apartment,
I'd like you to meet the old Indian ruins
I promised.

My mother, Mrs. Francis, and my grandmother, Mrs. Gottlieb.
His eyes grew large, and then he laughed
looking shocked at the two

women he'd just met. Silent for a second, they laughed too.
And he's still telling the tale of the old
Indian ruins he visited in New Mexico,

the two who still live pueblo style in high-security dwellings
way up there where the enemy can't reach them
just like in the olden times.

A Vegetarian Goes to H Mart

to finger the refrigerated meats. something about forbidden
fruit, how the flesh gives beneath my fingertips,
makes me lick my lips with pleasure. my gorge rises
as I imagine tearing into the muscle & sinew
of raw pork belly, sucking the juice off the bone, bursting
with carnality. I grit my teeth through the revulsion
because one can never truly shed animal instinct.
in the seafood aisle, my lungs fill with the stench
of fish, a potpourri of fresh death. I don't turn away
from the milky eyes & viscous tentacles
of a neatly-packaged octopus because my people
aren't afraid to look death in the face. we eat our fish
with the heads still on & pick the bones out of our teeth
at the dinner table. some call it impolite, but I call it
lack of pretense. a thousand vacant eyes
look back at me, open-mouthed as if to say
someday, you too will be gutted.
until then, I feast.

Enskyment

Imagine being buried in air,
      in the light blue earth of the sky,
Slowly lowered into thin atmospheres
      on pulleys of evaporation
While shovels of clouds shovel clouds over you
      and you hear far away
The last spadefuls of steeples and fireworks
      and clapping and laughter
And birdsong and forests and mountains
      all scooped on your immense grave of sky!

Imagine those heavenly maggots:
      lost kites, lost balloons,
Seeds we make wishes on,
      butterflies, fireflies,
Wingspreads of vultures,
      and all the nibbling stars.
And branches of trees really roots and roothairs?
      And rainbows really the tunnels of moles?
And earthworms peeping from their holes
      really birdbeaks probing the earth?

What exquisite decay!
All the warmth the sun gives as it melts you!
All those tons of cirrus, stratus, cumulonimbus!
      Skyquakes of lightning!
Your flesh unpetalling in downpours!
Your body become all sunset and ozone,
      delicate rumbles of vanishing thunder!
Till the aroma of sky after rain
      and earth after rain
Is all that's left of your corpse!

Encountering the Medusa

"Who in me says I'm ugly, makes me feel guilty;
who is it in my soul that needs you so desperately?"

—James Hillman, *Revisioning Psychology*, 139

Regular visitor she's become
can't seem to shake her
      out of my hair
everywhere I turn she's there
      her cold piercing stare
one glimpse and I freeze.

It's no use reciting my list
when I make the slightest move
with my hand
           they hiss and writhe
           the snakes in her hair
           stop me in my tracks
           bring the sweat every time

Too familiar she's become
you'd think I'd get used to it
I look in the mirror
           see her numinous glare
           know the daemon is there
           what a nightmare

I want to take a machete
hack off her head
      slip it on
turn my enemies to stone
      deaden desire

She was a horse
moved with the speed of lightning
till something frightened her
someone laid a curse on her
         paralyzed her

let's go, Ice Maiden, *move it*
make something, do something
                anything
Don't just sit there
letting emptiness gnaw   your bones
           Move it.

No use, I'm stuck in her grip
       ice cold
in the mirror
       her glittering eye
she can't move forward
I can't move backwards
frozen in this borderland
       this no-man's-land
        forever inbetween
dry whisper of scales
       fill my ears

They thresh and hiss
            the snakes in my hair
            my cold piercing stare
            I'll turn you to stone.

Atrophied Prescript:

When I say this is ~~nature~~ writing, I mean that I am an animal and that there is no outside in which one can stand to call this ecology "~~nature~~."

This body, this I ecological, cannot step outside the words "freak," "hybrid," "impostor," "pervert," "unfortunate monstrosity."
I let the words compose the way I go in the world.

The words surround from within.
The within roars from its trash organs.
The filth floats in the flood folding.
From the flood language inhabits us, infiltrating our thoughts and bodies, coercing ideas and movements, choreographing our little deaths. A flood language, a slime virus: it feeds on us, it needs us, and it lives in us. The reverse too: we feed on it, we need it, and we live in it. Language is a miasmic force engulfing. The miasma of the aroused genitals our air. Slipping obscurity. The hegemony rising up from the sexed gonads, the steam from the hot fruit entering and composing the architecture of the room. This is a text about rooms. This is a text about bodies in space. This is a text of creature textures variegating through envelopes and letters. The world an organic epistolary, composed of letters, pasted and folding into the folds and fissures inside bodies and rooms.

Asleep You Become a Continent

(Francisco X. Alarcón)

asleep you become a continent—
undiscovered, mysterious, long,
your legs mountain ranges
encircling valleys, ravines

night slips past your eyelids,
your breath the swaying of the sea,
sprawled across the bed like
a dolphin washed ashore, your mouth

is the mouth of a sated volcano,
O fragrant timber, how *do* you burn?
you are so near, and yet so far

as you doze like a lily at my side,
I undo myself and invoke the moon—
I'm a dog watching over your sleep

Farmer's Almanac

I never knew what to say in my uncle's presence, as if my softness
stirred a broken thing. After he died,
my cousin found his stash of hidden magazines, the boys
coated in a shine that escaped him. The ground
on which he stood, sinking imperceptibly.
Where the crops had been planted,
the trace of wheels was blooming upside down.

The last time I saw him, he told me
something about the road I had followed, as if it were moving
just ahead of me. I leaned against the door
of that house he grew up in, the house
he had to die to leave. I leaned against
the unknowable eruptions,

walking towards me as a child. A barrenness
elevates the brightness
of those who survive. Their thin green arrows,
pointing to the scarcity.
What I want to say is this—
drought is the neighbor of religion. A mirror
held up to distant fire.

Godzilla's Lament

What would it feel like if I loved
    this body? Really
    loved it, like these

fat folds were swaddling. Like I had
    ballerina's feet. Without
    the gnarl. Like I'd

earned the right to take this much
    space. Like I was
    a beacon, a craze, &

folk flocked to me, flies to honey,
    maggots to rotting flesh.
    Like I wasn't

worried about death, wasn't prey, wasn't
    an aftermath.
    Like I was
    a monster

Late Echo

Alone with our madness and favorite flower
We see that there really is nothing left to write about.
Or rather, it is necessary to write about the same old things
In the same way, repeating the same things over and over
For love to continue and be gradually different.

Beehives and ants have to be re-examined eternally
And the color of the day put in
Hundreds of times and varied from summer to winter
For it to get slowed down to the pace of an authentic
Saraband and huddle there, alive and resting.

Only then can the chronic inattention
Of our lives drape itself around us, conciliatory
And with one eye on those long tan plush shadows
That speak so deeply into our unprepared knowledge
Of ourselves, the talking engines of our day.

DERRICK AUSTIN

We're Standing on the Sun

you say when I break the aloe leaf
and smear its sweet, clear gel over your body.

On the nude beach, you get hard
and stretch skyward like an unfurling touch-me-not.

You dive into froth, nearly impenetrable,
maybe the shadows

of a few darting fish. I mirror you above,
twin planets, untouched and indivisible,

borne along by our bodies toward a farther shore.

Let me be a lamb in a world that wants my lion

In the beginning, there was an angel with cloven feet who stood by me,
and the angel said, *My wings are an ocean*, and its shoulders split until
feathers fell around us. This is how you leave your country.

On the back of an ocean. Choked with feathers.

*

If someone gives you water, drink. And if they hand you a glass of blood,
tell yourself it's water. If they hand you a lamb and say *eat*, they will
see a lion. They will call you *lion* when you walk down the street.

When the towers come down. When blood is the water they drink.

*

When my belly sings with hunger, it's asking, *Will you die for an idea?*
I dreamt I walked the shore of my country and each wave cracked like
a bone. The sea of my childhood rattles with skulls, and their mouths—

agape with my name—drown its vowels, call me S, say it's the name
the sea spoke when I dragged my feet across an ocean and became
somewhere new. I call my dead *Beloved* but they have too much

time for me. If I close my eyes, I see my father on the beach,
his hands cupped for water. He says, *The dead are always thirsty,*

and I wake up in time to catch the L for work that hardly keeps me fed.

*

Heaven, leave your light on a little longer. I looked for you on earth
and found my daughters. I looked for you and saw your stars strung
electric as sorrow and they wound my current across their backs

and carried me here, the middle of a grocery store parking lot,
the whine of flood lights burrowing into my capped head
and the black night ahead, and I think, *My god, will I ever not be*

surprised by what I can survive? The long country of my loneliness
stretched out before me, my hands heavy with the food I can eat—
I'm so full of honey in a time of war, winter in a land

I'm learning to love, in a land that won't love me.

The Little Girl Is Busy Asking Questions about Desire

At school, they tell her that she can grow up to be anything, but what if she wants to tear a hole in the sky? Once, she climbed a tree & never came down. She wants to know if she is a tree. If she comes from a family of trees. She plants a petal inside her, waits for it to grow. She can't speak with a flower in her throat. Here is the answer. If a boy pins her to the ground, if he empties the air from her chest, he will call it a *game*. If she pins the boy, if she holds his shoulders in her hands, if she wants to fill him, all the boys who see will call her names, but never her own. She suspects this has something to do with pronouns, or the way she comes to school a rosebush & no one calls her a *faggot*. Either way, it's a distance made of language & no one will look a girl with questions in the eye. Look. There she is, still in the tree, watching the boys play across the street. Dandelion boys. Boys with hair rising from their necks like pollen. *Boy* blooming behind her teeth.

Inventory

Bridges and streets. The neon like candy.
Brake lights blooming in rain. Rain.
Concrete. Long live the concrete of cities.

Spoon. Chair. Bed, bread, and stitch.
This language of the house. Blond
light across the mirror. Soap. Salt shaker.

The ginger of you. The cream of you.
The eyes and bones. The scratch-and-sniff
of you. The back. The back of the hand.

Crickets and prairie. The trees standing
like husbands. The gold grass moving,
the pelt of earth. The fence-posts like souls.

Lunch at midnight, dinner at breakfast,
graveyard and swing. Machine that
is the father's pet. Machine that is days.

Breath, reed. Vowels, syllables. Strings.
The bluesman saying, I don't practice,
I throw some meat into the guitar case.

Moon that is the sun of statues. Cornice
pigeons, accordion storefront gates, trash
swirled into cowlick shapes. Box sleepers.

The wish, biding inside like a hive of bees.
The crow, a knuckle of the landscape.
The stone, which is tired of the discursive.

The Dyke with No Name Thinks about Landscape

I

At first it wasn't landscape at all.
Where you live is just where you live:

a place to walk about in,
drive your car through on the way to somewhere,

notice on a pretty day
when clouds are puffs and grasses blowing just so.

From a horse's back, tracking the skyline
grey sea became grey sky

and chalky paths down the escarpment
gashed the smooth flank of the downs.

Leaning over to unhook the chain
of a five-bar gate, she knew

just how fast to sidle the horse through
before the metal gate swung back with a clang

and the horse twitched an ear—
too familiar with the sound to make a fuss.

The windmills, Jack and Jill, spread their sails
and grew as organic as gorse bushes

or hares on the barren plough
but their spread sails remained unmoved

by the great wind which stirred up a great wave
in the grasses from Firle to Beachy Head.

Up there on her horse she too grew
organic as winter wheat

never naming the villages far below:
Poynings, Ditchling, Fulking, Steyning

distant clusters of roofs that revealed to her,
as if through a telescope,

a particular lytch gate, a brick well,
a post office serving cream teas.

2

When she left it became landscape—
a beloved green painting hauled around in her mind

while the next one (ochre and sage) unfolded
smelling of Mediterranean pine in the afternoon

and the one after that (sepia and umber)
threw open its chest and sang.

In these landscapes too, she wanted to grow organic—
spreading her limbs to the sky

on that almost-flat rock that jutted from the river
and held her between two swirling streams.

Pinpoints of spray pricked her skin
which dried and dried between the divided waters

while the river too—turbulence, rocks,
moss, trout, and human body—

pried open the hot thighs of the desert
with the persuasive pressure of wetness.

Was it then that it started—
then she began to feel the eyes watching?

In each landscape, people grew from the shadows.
In each landscape, people belonged.

But here on her rock,
head in the V of the parted waters

the dyke with no name sees herself
as if with eyes watching from the hill above,

sees the desert intersected by river,
sees ponderous rocks, shaggy falls, the cruising hawk,

and herself, a human figure growing from shadows,
herself in the frame, on the rock, not belonging.

3

The trouble is not nature, she thinks,
but the people who tell you there's always one of each—

starting with Noah
and his couple-filled floating zoo.

Pistils and stamens, winged seeds from trees,
insects waving their various appendages:

she remembers her smudgy drawings from biology;
she knows what they left out and why.

The trouble with pastoral scenes is the lovers—
the hand-in-hand, one-of-each, "lover and his lass."

She knows it's more than looking wrong in the picture.
But does she know it's a matter of life and death?

4

Whose life? Whose death?
All she wanted was to move again like the winter wheat

to live in her skin touching the earth's skin
to feel spray and rock and the finger of the sun.

Once, a long time ago, she made love
on a hilltop under copper beech trees:

leaves turned to mulch underneath her
as she breathed the sky through her lover's hair

and somewhere close by a pony snickered—
a friendly snicker; an acknowledgement.

She still remembers what it felt like to lie in those arms:
some of them beech roots, others human and female,

trusting the pony like a brother,
the sky looking down the same way she looked up.

That was before the two hikers were shot—
the two women, stalked for days by the man

who killed one and left the other for dead.
One each for life and death as it turned out.

5

There is nothing organic about cars.
They skim across surfaces, separated

from the landscape by hard, black tarmac:
no danger of putting down roots.

Even when a car disintegrates in the ground,
blackberries filling the bent frame of its windshield,

rusty chassis sinking into the earth
to blue up some passing hydrangea,

even then, its chrome and oil and plastic seats
spurn the comfort of ordinary rot.

The dyke with no name kept moving,
her rubber tires grabbing the blacktop with a squeal

as she pushed sideways through bends,
kept everything skidding.

Tall haystacks with poles poking out the top
dashed by her window. She noted their shape,

their resemblance to some señorita's hair
held up by a protruding pin.

She watched the show through glass
as if she had put in her penny on the pier,

watched herself from the hillside above
speeding through picture after picture

silk headscarf flying, arm on the door tanned
hands turning the small leather wheel.

Sometimes, when her head raged with pain
she parked the car in a field and slept,

all doors locked, all windows up
while the grasses tickled the hot skin of her tires.

6

Now she is lying on a blanket, the sand below
moulded to the shape of her body.

Sudden swells slap the shore beyond her feet:
a barge has passed by,

trudging down river with its load
like a good-natured shire horse

its throbbing lost now behind the breaking
of that great wave which seems to rise from the deeps.

The turbulence is quick: a lashing of the sand
followed by September's lazy calm

as the river moves unseen again,
cows from another world low on the far shore

and the seagull's body, a fragile handful,
dangles gently between its two tremendous wings.

The trouble is not nature, she thinks
but the people who say I'm not part of it.

They're trying to paint me out of the landscape
says the dyke with no name

but her thighs in hot sand remember a horse's warm back
as the wind makes a great wave from Oregon to Beachy Head.

SAMIYA BASHIR

Ground State

bend into my mouth
before frost ends us

this long year
I've lumbered—spin
devour spin—paced this crest

impatient for your nest
to tumble my nest for

the hum of your dulcet strum
and when I must bear you—maw

each strand still between my teeth
bend into my mouth

impatient for the tumble
I'll weave of you the dust
of a thousand more of us

lace the absence of your touch
into a clutch

Kissing after Illness

Our lips are so slow. They meet cell
by cell, as though they've traveled vast
distances like pilgrims, bent under
their tin pots and blankets. Our lips
arrive, but even when they touch,
they wait. The way a midwife enters
the room of a laboring woman and says
nothing, does nothing. Just watches, joining
the river of the woman's breath.
So our lips wait. But not exactly wait.
Nor exactly rest. But press, suspended
in a stillness that is the marrow
of kissing. The stem-cell of kissing.
A laden, blood-filled lull. Our lips
are not eager, not glad. They are almost
free of intention. There is only
a brush against inquisitive
nerves. Our lips mate like I once
watched the mindless bodies
of leopard slugs slide over and under,
infinitely slow in their voluptuous entwinement.
Strange. And strangely beautiful, how their long
shining translucent penises, fluted and frilled,
unfurl from their heads, swirling, knotting
around each other. Then blossom, swell
into a flower. It takes hours. Our lips
stunned into stupor, our tongues
still sleeping, hot, mute,
in no hurry to be born.

Prairie Dogs

for Khyber Oser
and in memory of Matthew Shepard (1976-1998)

They tenanted the far high school field,
the dispossessed *Lotaburger* lot, the dog run.
Shifty, sometimes rabid, they dared to stand

upright, almost human, and stare. I feared their deft
hands, the shrug of shoulders before they spiraled
underground. That day one hung panting on a twist

of barbed wire; front paws scored the dirt.
A ripped haunch, roiling and bloody, flashed,
and I turned away, yanking the dog behind me,

when my young cousin whispered *what's*
this, and groped for a stick to free the leg,
and when that didn't work, he knelt in the trashy

run, his face close to the scrabbler, fingers
plying the greasy, furred gash, the entrails
glazed with flies which might have deterred

someone else, but he sat, now cross-legged,
unwinding the wrecked limb the way the hands
that lifted the boy in Wyoming must have worked.

Poet Wrestling with Why the Heart Feels So Bad

In another life, I'm a plant given to a lonely woman
who keeps me alive with stories of her sadness.
She waters me a little too often. Rarely trims
my stems. There are splinters & stray hairs
& cobwebs in the wicker work I rest against.
Returning home every night, she stumbles
before the whiskey is in her hand.
Usually, my kind don't lose
track of time
& neither did I,
until I come to learn the story of her life.
From there, I grow
so tall & wide,
spreading across the walls & windows.
Along the ceiling I dance over
the dark spot
of a bath running over,
a ritual
that shakes me hard enough
for a few leaves to brown & shed.
This goes on,
with my vines
covering dusty bookshelves,
the cracked glass of photo collages,
last year's calendar & unwound clock.
This goes on & on
until the night
she finally takes
stock.
How a plant can't really share
time with anyone, or go anywhere.
With a heavy grunt, she lifts
my pot. I've only felt
the night air once,

when I first broke ground.
Never again will rain & thunder
terrify me when she leaves
& lightning breaks
me
from drenched
soil
& terra cotta
shell.
At sunrise,
not quite myself & unsure
what I am
doing,
I kick on her door.
In this other life I was a plant
who's just turned into a pink-maned horse,
sopping
wet & starving
when the door opens
with her gasps
& curses & stares as still
I stretch my entire
length,
basking
in the new sun.

It doesn't take as long as you'd think.
We fall in love.
We tear apart
that wreck
& paint over & spill
countless pastel
upon cream
& eggshell,

leaving little cracks
in this new
Plantae-Animalia
kingdom-making.
Lavender & mint blossoms grow in a sea
of pink waves off my head & along my spine
with a few too many vertebrae,
I think, because she'd watered me
a little too much.
It's a love as wild as you can imagine.
I bask in windows during heat waves
before she rides me,
rootless
& everywhere.
& when I'm ill & my buds wilt,
she plucks them from my ashen mane.
Holds me when I die
briefly,
each season,
going into a deep
sleep that lasts
weeks.
She keeps me warm in our double-king-sized bed,
my rambling, trailing
legs & tail
shriveled up against her
heaving chest.
How blessed
that I'm an annual
animal.
How blessed that my heart & my
memories
don't work quite
like hers. How it's not necessary

to say that even after she's gone,
I'll plant my hooves every night
at her grave & tell her
stories of my day,
the plant-horse who works
as a part-time display
in a flower shop. How I delight
children with the bright, muted
colors of my mane,
with my soft
green eyes. How they giggle
& sigh & even shed
a few tears, eventually letting
go of their mother's hands
& comforting thighs.
I'll go on dying,
every season
just to lean down
so they can believe
I'm real
when I drop
the last unwanted
bouquets
on my love's headstone,
those cut & bound,
& roots still
wet, as if they were never
so close
to death.

Outing, Iowa

If you've ever doubted that a body can transform completely, take the highway north from town, past the crowded diner with the neon sign for pork loin sandwiches, and go left at the arrow for the lake. Can I tell you? The land where I was born was born an ocean, and that ocean born of ice. Researchers and floodplains have undressed its chipped-up secret: plates shifted, glaciers melted into river, into rows of corn that flipbook past your car. Park anywhere and follow the trail back in time toward the effigy mounds, the sacred piles of earth we've managed to preserve, and all that's buried underneath. I still bleed, still weep: what we used to be matters. Here's a brachiopod, here's me twirling in a gauzy blue dress in the afternoon sun. Trace these fossils with your tongue and place them in my hands, which will never be any larger. Lay your ear against an iceberg while there's still time and sing to me its trickle. Lift a geode from the ground and crack me open. I'll sparkle so hard you'll forget you thought this land was flat, as though you'd never find the valley, bedrock, ancient sea.

Pastoral for Effective Teaching

We must head
to the hilltop—uncostume.
And I don't mean
in the swanlike way.
Raise a rocks around a sinking.
I mean: the night is so helplessly
white. Girl and Boy
cling together at the roadbottom—
a dangerous turn.
In the bushes hear one thing
eating another.
Glimmer goes the thinpan
moon. The decorative
hillside
where weeds lie waiting
spring sheep at the end of a season
at the tail end of a mountain
slapped like a whale.
The forest sons
a river's daughter.
You are still wearing
the narrow bridge, Lillian,
slicing up the coyote's paw.
Untake this business
of brilliant chill.

Creatures of Hurt and Heal

Let go, says the hawk. Let go,
says the dirt; let go, say the vines that wrap
tight to become protective skin.

Become another heart beating counter
rhythm, become an extra spleen
for mysterious functions

of filter. A month ago, light balanced
on the edge of dark in equal
distribution. We lifted our palms up.

Now, we move slowly toward
the solstice. Then, we will move
slowly away. The branches are thin, dark,

newly liberated from their leaves. The flash
in the morning fog might be a cardinal
or a siren in the distance—a marking

of this world where light is something
we calibrate closely. I have come into forty,
softer than at twenty, stronger than at thirty.

The world's injustice clashing
with my deepest convictions. Every day
I do the only work I know—small shifts

in the balance of power. Again
and again, hard and joyful, the only
way toward change. Every night

I kiss the woman
I can't get enough of. We move toward
the sun and away from the sun.

Toward light, away from light,
elliptical, steady,
bound and unbound.

Song for the Rainy Season

Hidden, oh hidden
in the high fog
the house we live in,
beneath the magnetic rock,
rain-, rainbow-ridden,
where blood-black
bromelias, lichens,
owls, and the lint
of the waterfalls cling,
familiar, unbidden.

In a dim age
of water
the brook sings loud
from a rib cage
of a giant fern; vapor
climbs up the thick growth
effortlessly, turns back,
holding them both,
house and rock,

in a private cloud.

At night, on the roof,
blind drops crawl
and the ordinary brown
owl gives us proof
he can count:
five times—always five—
he stamps and takes off
after the fat frogs that,
shrilling for love,
clamber and mount.

House, open house
to the white dew
and the milk-white sunrise
kind to the eyes,
to membership
of silver fish, mouse,
bookworms,
big moths; with a wall
for the mildew's
ignorant map;

darkened and tarnished
by the warm touch
of the warm breath,
maculate, cherished,
rejoice! For a later
era will differ.
(O difference that kills,
or intimidates, much
of all our small shadowy
life!) Without water

the great rock will stare
unmagnetized, bare,
no longer wearing
rainbows or rain,
the forgiving air
and the high fog gone;
the owls will move on
and the several
waterfalls shrivel
in the steady sun.

Break Me to Prove I Am Unbroken

You say you will come
Again; this time I wait through

The extra burning, the vicinity of your
Tongue making a slow way toward beginning and this

Then becomes the argument, the only one
In the collar of moonlight as finally I cause you

To answer your several names. It is all
About return, enough faith to live

On whatever remains. While your hand seeks
The broken glass of what has not

Happened yet, it breaks everything
Along the way. The old vines tighten

Around the untended kingdom while some still sleep
And the long approach

Of no footfall becomes the road I hurry home on
To a place where I learned to leave the body

Not so much in safety but with the best intentions,
And into the smallest space I crawl, a taste of mud,

An edge of light into the room so each morning the world
Can solve itself against the abandoned stones.

RICHARD BLANCO

Burning in the Rain

Someday compassion would demand
I set myself free of my desire to recreate
my father, indulge in my mother's losses,
strangle lovers with words, forcing them
to confess for me and take the blame.
Today was that day: I tossed them, sheet
by sheet on the patio and gathered them
into a pyre. I wanted to let them go
in a blaze, tiny white dwarfs imploding
beside the azaleas and ficus bushes,
let them crackle, burst like winged seeds,
let them smolder into gossamer embers—
a thousand gray butterflies in the wind.
Today was that day, but it rained, kept
raining. Instead of fire, water—drops
knocking on doors, wetting windows
into mirrors reflecting me in the oaks.
The garden walls and stones swelling
into ghostlier shades of themselves,
the wind chimes giggling in the storm,
a coffee cup left overflowing with rain.
Instead of burning, my pages turned
into water lilies floating over puddles,
then tiny white cliffs as the sun set,
finally drying all night under the moon
into papier-mâché souvenirs. Today
the rain would not let their lives burn.

Swimming Hole

Ruined when motor replaced oar
In steel-boned hull,
Lilting gasoline
Fills each breath as I come up for air.
I dive deep for a reminder of how this used to be,
Sea glass felt safe in my small hands.
I once held oxygen in my lungs for over a minute,
Now half.

Bottles pollute beach,
Hook-mouthed fish rise
And break surface,
Unbreathing.
Beneath, mussels
Slice bare feet.

Perhaps blood will become water
Or water blood
So I may reclaim this body

Regarding the Absent Heat of Your Skin on Letters I Receive While at Sea

Paper wing   Words smudged
in your hand's stroke   What
has been sealed   Torn mouth

Lung-must

And a shiver along
my lateral line, olfactory
lobe lit up

Breath on the paper
Wind on the water (& off it)
Breath from the water
And ill wind   Tear-salt

Fish near the surface, glinting
Plankton rising   forced

Scent of panic   (lung-must)
Petrels arrive because of
Patter and feed

Your eyes on the horizon
are greedy, could eat
leagues   Call my name

Breeze   Wind   Gale
Let the air clock around your mouth

It pushes, unturned,
against your mouth

If you stand on the shore and call
I'll know

Unruly

Hushed whispers in an undisclosed room

    Take it out of the girl

a child, boyish in nature   their smallness magnified.

Outcasted—the soft bodied animal you are

determined unruly animalia,

        what survives inflation & inertia?

The body is a set of complex feedback systems

nothing is as it appears

       the coexistence of a beard & breasts

       evidence of the body's willfully defiant nature.

The body's resilience amid the promise of perish:

      somehow the child survives their own hand

      the day's weary edge inverted toward grace

A child, boyish in their nature   & barrel shaped

    survives sedimented against the residue

    of dunes, soil, leaf litter,   & the bodies of a lesser

What couldn't be excised

    your boyish nature

    your untamed phylum,   your small heart pulsing loud

       notes against the night.

in the cut

for Cedar Sigo

"his being punished / for talking Indian."
——Cedar Sigo, "Prince Valiant"

person of clear salt water
warm clear deer

the mosquitoes I am
delicious to them
because of my fairy
or my indian blood

he is immune
to poison ivy
because indians dont
call it poison

utter unfaith in humanity
leaves dont turn right
the leaves so that
they dont know how to turn right

when the guy at the bodega
complained about white ppl & gentrifications
you said me and my friend are native
I'm Suquamish, look it up

I vaporize the weed
we had for breakfast when
I come home from the poetry reading
thinking how low & how lively
we know of the cut

droppd my parasol in a ditch
pretend it didnt happen

Fast

Since you've gone I've fasted having made the ṣoup
whose recipe I sent (the mail-
man came I wanted to
send something) cold curry thick with oranges
sweet clear onion underneath
the lid. The skin

of this truth's onion isn't
clear. Leathery obstinate I think
how boiled tongue peels simply how it is
the taste buds (cellular abused by heat) that give
way to a larger muscle: tongue truth the matter of
taste and lack thereof the matter of

desire. Hear
me love. I'd do
anything and have to keep this in and you too anything
and have to keep from hearing. Is it complicity
that breeds contempt? Hypoglycemic
fasting for this sense

of desperation forcing me
thin as a needle without compass to let go
of hope and pray for clarity of mind of sky the cold
polar luminary any
finally cold clear star. Solstice
equinox solstice equinox nine months

without desire every time a reason why (ill-
ness fatigue exposure trauma of old
love new love) all true
enough. Enough. I am not pushing
a friendship campaign like you said but love
intense unlimited perverse familial unpretentious.

love
is it possible
that it is not enough? Without desire
in a field of stars the cold moon rising hungry
cold lip of a moon the pounding of my hungry
blood the starved

brain screaming *sugar* trembling
at last with clarity transparent lying
in the grass palms joined at the heart in love
desireless in prayer.

Lion

I wish you tamed. I wish what you fear—
A night alone in the forest.

A father who leaves you there. I wish you
Were ten years old again. And in love

With Marvin Gaye. I wish you saw his daddy
Shoot him. I wish you asthma. An attack

In the field. A lump in your chest. A doctor
Who won't touch it. I wish you'd live forever

Afraid of dying. See the circus and be content.
Animals crawling like infants for the men

Who made them. I wish you would
Sniff a man. I wish his whip

Sharper than fangs. I wish you could know
How bite-less I feel, the mouth

I don't close, his head in my throat.

Self-Portrait as Land Snail

Don't get me wrong.
I'm a modest girl, couldn't even strip off
at one of those nudie hot springs out west,
the whole place a flotsam
of much-nursed areolas and buoyant
scrotums while I sat prim
as Gidget, legs crossed and awkwardly
smiling on the shore. It's just that the snail
is on to something—neither boy nor girl
but both, the critter is nearly mythic—a true
hermaphrodite that all alone
will go to its own kind of cyrobank and baste
itself, make a new batch of not-so-bouncies
in thin, flea-sized shells. Or better, with another
intersex other it will take
aim, flex back its bow, shoot a dart,
then wait to be impaled
in return. I couldn't make this shit up
if I tried—this is no metaphor
but scientific fact—a *telum amoris*—literally,
a *weapon of love*—a James-Bond-worthy arrow
equipped with four blades spiked
with all the dirty talk a snail could want.
Cupid's got nothing on this
mollusk congress, and because you know
how snails go, the foreplay is slow—
slow, slow, slow—my kind of sex—
going on and on until the hussy
who first received that dart has enough
then rises to fire back. Now, knowing this,
I can say I didn't *come out*
all those years ago, whatever that means. No,
when I finally made a home
for my body in the bed of another

woman, I simply became
a land snail. Tired of being
a leaking receptacle for a man's desire,
I needed to feel
an equal's push against my own,
a willingness to be wounded and to
wound, receiving and giving at the same
time. Plainly said, I needed the kind of love
that finally let me take
my time; I needed to fire
an arrow of my damn own.

Hurricane Lyric

The husband lands
as winds whip up
charcoal cloudbank
over Newark, Jersey
smokestacks thicken
the soup so away
we zip across Canal
to brick tenement flat
beside the brackish
Gowanus freshly
aroil in such gusts
we quickly walk
before apocalypse
begins, duct tape
x's pepper the panes
& we hold hands
as chainlink sings
then home just off
mandatory evac
to cling in blanket
cocoon wondering
what night brings,
whether water will
rise to the sill &
we'll swim for it.

Home

after moving from Virginia to New Mexico

And now I am here where I do not know the land.
During daily walks, thousands of tiny grasshoppers
jump and scatter, some into the space between
my foot and its sandal. I walk on, feel the sticky
smash and crunch between skin and cork.

At dawn I let out the dogs, and as they piss on strange,
stubby desert trees, families of prairie dogs panic.
Herds of them huddle on desert dust mounds, their barks
surprising, their fear of us on their once deserted land
stark and open-mouthed. I stumble forward. The leashes

pull me into the orange day. Sharp, high desert plants
and seeds stick to my skin, needles and thistles scratch
my toes. One of many habits I didn't know my body
adapted: the ease of East Coast flip flops for any
errand. Locals say wear boots, watch for rattlers.

I haven't seen one yet, so I pretend I'm not afraid. I do see
my first black widow, and a second, and know my girlfriend
played with tarantulas in her backyard like many kids here,
rode stubborn horses bareback before she could fix her own
meal. I sat on one of her mother's old beasts for a few short

trots around their fenced corral, and cried when she bucked—
how easy to forget which heel to dig, which rein to pull.
Who are we now? Who am I here? I followed my love
to her home. These mountains around us are not the Blue Ridge,
but from a distance, I sometimes can't tell the difference.

STEPHANIE BURT

Hermit Crab

That shell is pretty, but that shell is too small for me.

Each home is a hideout; each home is a secret; each home
is a getaway under the same hot lamp, a means
to a lateral move at low velocity.

I live in a room in the room
of a boy I barely see.

Sometimes the boy & his talkative friends raise
too-warm hands & try to set me free

and I retreat into myself, hoping they place
me back in my terrarium, and they
do, with disappointed alacrity.

Scatter patterns in sand, adnates, cancellates, gaping
whelk husks, a toy tractor-trailer, cracked
and dinged, beside the spine of a plastic tree,

the helmet-shaped shelter of a shadow cast
by a not-quite-buried wedge of pottery . . .

if I have a body that's wholly my own
then it isn't mine. For a while I was
protected by what I pretended to be.

For the Feral Splendor That Remains

for Kazim Ali

sometimes I strain
to hear one
natural
sound
when gender blurs in a
poem my world sets a
tooth in the gear
if god is in me
when will I ask for
my needs to be met
every god is qualified
it is not such a secret
when I was afraid of the
road I learned to drive
map says name of
your city in ocean
line drawn to it
towing behind
the big party
history of life on
earth might be
interesting to a
visitor one day
chewing parsley and
cilantro together is for
me where forest
meets meadow
in a future life
would we like to
fall in love with the
world as it is with
no recollection
of the beauty
we destroy
today

Who Holds the Stag's Head Gets to Speak

Dear God who lives inside the stag's head
even after the stag's shot and lies slumped and abashed
on the forest floor. Protect him.

Even after he's been heaved onto the car's dark roof.
Forest Green. Or Pacific Blue. Nowhere he can see.
His body stiffens like a trellis above the driver.
Help him. Hold him in your sight.

I know the age of prayer is over. I read it on my newsfeed.
Someone said someone said someone said, *Faith is a weapon
of the Man.*

When they take him down in the darkness
he looks like any body. Could you rest the muscle of your breath
against his neck so he won't sag? So the man thinks he's alive
and quakes in the awful company of the risen.

You are the Blue Lord I prayed for when I was hunted.
You came to me through the branches. I could hear you
in the upper room where I had hidden in the cupboard.

The moment the blade goes to gut him please make of his entrails
a phalanx of butterflies. And of his lungs a great bear
charging. My Lord. When I was the cowered beast
you turned me clear as water so the Hunter could not find me.

I beseech you. Abide.

What I Would Give

What I would like to give them for a change
is not the usual prescription with
its hubris of the power to restore,
to cure; what I would like to give them, ill
from not enough of lying in the sun
not caring what the onlookers might think
while feeding some banana to their dogs—
what I would like to offer them is this,
not reassurance that their lungs sound fine,
or that the mole they've noticed change is not
a melanoma, but instead of fear
transfigured by some doctorly advice
I'd like to give them my astonishment
as sudden rainfall like the whole world weeping,
and how ridiculously gentle it
slicked down my hair; I'd like to give them that,
the joy I felt while staring in your eyes
as you learned epidemiology
(the science of disease in populations),
the night around our bed like timelessness,
like comfort, like what I would give to them.

KAYLEB RAE CANDRILLI

On Harvesting Oneself

In rural America, bad
land is trans land.

And I have lived
in the fragile

space between drawn
property lines—

ownership is just
controlling both

the chisel
and the block.

What a thrill to cut
with such sure intention.

The Hummingbird

Bright whirligig that knows no grief,
sudden gem whose engine
is diligent and beatific,
in pure communion,
I've opened and taken you
deep into my being.

Scion to your quick colors,
your tiny hosannas, I poise
before my love's body
become a thousand thimbles of weeping
for dawn,
keen galaxy I'd test and savor
with a deft, regaling bill:
all this majesty is for me—

Now the hours are deities
of nectar and sweat.
Now the hours are flower-gorged,
filled with his breath—

Suddenly, I'm flying
backward,
fleet hovering in the moment,
breakneck marionette:
grit gone, God yes,
and panic's balcony:
the carnage in the eye burned away.

Drown

Yes, we drowned, then changed our minds,
        then drowned again,
         because we could,
    because no one would know the difference—

       a leaf to its trembling
when it is no longer a leaf
but just a trembling.

        We splashed against the current—
a zipper of palms opening and closing.

We were too busy to notice
        that everything we touched
      was a little bell that was a little famous.

The sun opened its curfew and song

        as I swam to shake the sounds
of your laughter off me.

Lesson of Bread

Our wool socks steaming
by the tiny stove, we poise
over tea, encountering the animal

smell of ourselves
in each other. The tea itself
incidental but necessary,

cooling in our mugs. We sip
and stare at our hands,
our drying pants legs, the stove

steeping in the room's
sourdough air. *How people
used to meet*, I think,

*yes, keeping yeast starter
alive in their clothes,
breaking isolation*

*like bread, a trail
going only so far. This is
my body, the least*

I would have you know.

Post Op

Looking down is necessary,
the tangle and tuft matting deep

in the berm. Our cuffs bristle
in seed and we make the shy

gestures of those who bruise
another's thoughts, pillow slip

apart down a muddy path. Blue
over the bluff, briefly an arc

of giant wings. Within her sleeve,
the scar rises still, its bumpy ridge

not really fading. Weeks of illness
scraped clear off the kitchen calendar.

Snow for a while, loud pellets,
on nylon jackets, softening at last

to blanket the black dog.
Roots snake across the path,

gleaming in ice. Her fingers now
may practice again their forgotten

stretch. Each night we trail
something rough, something

smooth, over hyper-sensitive skin.
We gaze down and we count

out loud, how far, how steep
the path and curving.

XXIV.

bieng tran is a unique kinde of organe / i am speeching

materialie / i am speeching abot hereditie / a tran

entres thru the hole / the hole gloms inn the linden / a

tran entres eather like a mothe / wile tran preseeds / esense

/ her forme is contingent on the feeld / the maner sits

cis with inn a feeld / wee speech inn 2 the eather / wile

the mothe bloomes / the mothe bloomes inn the yuca

Elegy to Be Exhaled at Dusk

I am an elegy to be exhaled at dusk. I am an elegy to be written on a late
October leaf. An elegy to be blown

from its tree by a late October wind. To be stomped on & through
by passersby old & young

& dead & unborn. To be crinkled & crushed into tiny brown-
orange pieces. & then

collected, painstakingly, no, pain*fully*, piece by piece, & assembled like
a puzzle or collage or

Egyptian god, but always incomplete, always a few bits & limbs
missing. An elegy to be

misplaced, stuffed away in the attic's memory, & only brought out again
once every occupant of the house has

ceased. Yes, I am an elegy properly architectured by ruin. An elegy that has
experienced crows & lake effect

snow, an elegy that has seen Ukrainian snow falling on the forehead
of Paul Celan, Paul Celan's mother,

the German tongue, the tangled tongues of all your literary
& literal ancestors—but more

than that, an elegy that has felt light, the early morning light falling
on your lovely someone's

loveable bare feet as he walks across the wood floor to sit by the window,
by the plants, with a cup of jasmine

& a book he will barely open but love to hold the weight of
in his lap. I am,

my friend, an elegy that has taken into account, into heart & October wind,
the weight of someone's soft

hair-covered head in someone else's warm, welcoming lap.

Dear O

I was born, they said, a boy
into a heritage of paper

If a fire is placed in a crumbling wall
it leads me to you, separated from the screen

I am not here often

The one who arrived, I lost him in the sea

I was born
so much missing your eyesight
blooming without birds

My body unfolds
and the sound it sings in line

I lost you in the sea.
An ideal neighbor a stone buried below my mother's whitegrain building

A blue vat dye, burning stones to throw

All my unborn reckless as a lamp
strung as a light
broke a path

There was a boy who was not me
because I was a bird singing double-
hearted in the floating line by the sea

soft-throated to face down.
the audience

Magnified

My brother got a microscope for his twelfth birthday,
hope of the family, excelling in all subjects, graced
with straight A's and a brain for chess, the gift
was an early enticement into the illustrious world
of medicine; but he was too busy playing football
to bother with it, so after it lay in its box
for months, I took it on as my own. Dinky, plastic
thing it was, but I felt like a scientist in a foreign
TV movie. I set the instrument up in our study room,
used the table lamp and shone its harsh bulb onto the reflective
mirror, redirecting the light through
the slide and into the magnifying eyepiece. The microscope
set came with ready-made slides: a tiny piece
of pink feather, a sliver of an unnamed insect's wing.
But I wanted to see what I wanted to see. I learned
how to prepare slides. I took a sewing needle
to the spore bags underneath fern fronds and scraped
spores onto slides. (I saw round black saucers.)
I stripped leaves and petals of their epidermis
by painting them with Cutex nail varnish and carefully
peeling that layer of hardened goop off. (I saw
brick walls of cells in perfect order to respire and
to photosynthesize.) I looked at onion skins. (I saw
exquisite paperthins.) I looked at droplets of swamp water.
(But I saw nothing.) I caught ants—the small black ones
and the ferocious Kerringa fire ants—and pinned them
under glass slides. Still alive, their segmented bodies
struggling, magnified to horror movie proportions.
The red ants snapped their pincers in despair and anger,
the black ones waved their six legs in tired resignation.
Once I turned the magnification too high and the lens
crunched into the slide, cracking the cover slip, squishing
the ant. Its grizzly death, full of juice and torn
segmented bits, magnified 200x. I looked at moths' wings

and butterflies' wings, mosquitoes' proboscises, beetles'
legs. I looked at hair, saliva, dead skin peeled off from a sunburn, dried
blood from scabs, toenails, a drop of blood.
Later, my dad let me use his microscope. An impressive
thing: heavy and metal, not the light plastic toy I had
been playing with. And the magnifications were much higher.
This was how adults saw things. And everything I had seen
magnified before, was remagnified into a grander scale.
Cells broke into smaller cells, colors broke into a myriad
of more color and detail, light into more light. Amazements
into marvels, marvels into epics. The droplets of swamp
water that revealed nothing before now teemed with wriggling
things and strange life. The drop of blood now took on
more red, and life's movement shivered within that smear
on the slide. I looked at my semen and saw sperm cells,
the little bits of me wiggling their tails, swishing away
to a futile ruin. Everything I had dared to cram under
the lens and everything I could scrape and mount onto glass
slides was made up of small things of such delicacy,
and smaller things even, that when assembled
together constructed a greater beauty. The dead bits
laying on those slides were to face up to the harsh
realities of the world's atmosphere, to give flight,
to fight, to hunt, to repair, to prettify, to live as much
as the fragments, the living crumbs, held together.
And everything that was examined and dead, peeled
off and amputated, separated from its larger life,
was renewed with as much, even more
glory than the day, and the day after that, imagined.

Wildlife

> "In the Canadian province of Alberta, a massive wildlife—uh, wild*fire*—
> exploded to ten times its previous size Thursday."
>
> —Amy Goodman, host of *Democracy Now*

They say the blast was triggered by a passenger pigeon's ghostly
coo, swifting over the oil fields—at which the grasses stiffened,
shot up a warning scent—which made the beetles shudder from
their beds—which spread a rumor among the earthworms, until,

so quietly at first that no one noticed, a thin hoof cracked
open a patch of earth: last spring's last-born caribou, the one
who'd gotten separated from the herd and gutted by flies, now back
and raising an orchestra of dust with its kicking, calling forth

hoof by hoof, the whole herd, stampeding from their graves,
flesh and fur remapping onto bones as they percussed out,
pulling with them the pine martens and black-footed ferrets,
who regathered their bones from the soil and darted up

to hop aboard the pine trees now rushing from the horizon,
stretching their newborn necks toward the sun's familiar laugh
as shrikes and warblers flocked giddy to their shoulders, *we're back,*
we're back, they giggled as firs and ferns yawned upright to marry

the sparrows and the softshell turtles, whose humble jaws birthed
ponds and marshes with each exhale, inviting the whooping cranes
to unfurl their bodies from the wind and gladly, gladly swoop
down to bless the fish, which in turn gave the whales the idea

to distill back into their old forms from the clouds overhead, until
the sky was clogged with blubbery gods—right whales, gray, beluga,
and even a rumor of a blue whale somewhere over Calgary, casting
a great gray shadow over the baseball fields, every parking lot

and highway cracking open as the earth remembered, rejoiced
with its remembering—and as some of the humans kept trying

to drag up the earth's black blood, to sell off their mothers'
old marrow, suddenly, then, each pump and spigot spouted forth bees,

butterflies, short-horned lizards, plovers and prickly pears, grizzlies,
snakes, owls of all feather and shape, shrews, sturgeon, each drop
of oil renouncing its war draft and returning to its oldest names:
muscle; stamen; tooth; hoof—the land and water laughing aloud,

a laugh that spread the way a fever spreads, like the opposite of death,
of drills—just the earth, with its thousand mouths, singing: *I will. I will.*

Desire as Blue Fog

in my arms coming through these tall trees of your land
your gift of time
My hands suck your breasts   our mouths know
my eyebrows singe curling
Your belly my horizon
sea where I catch myself glowing teal
Your pink nipples near my dark brown ones tell the roads
& differences between us   Times we've opened
our eyes together every morning
Deaths we've survived
Tears & laughter in my fingers which enter you always new
singing with memories of your wet rose rolling
the wet edge of my tongue a harvest moon of fat gold
Your green leaf eyes part the blue smoke of need
I feel your heart pounding in your rose
cantilevered over the cliff of pines rising
Thousands of kisses our tongues hold each one
I rise to meet your light   a leaf flames under water
haloing the silken web of your fingers
Beating in my throat a blue cry to have you   possess you
to be torn open by your sobbing pleasure
to ride you through silver fog
reaching for thousands of miles
rushing with speed of light to screams again & again
your muscles take me delirious inside of you
my whole body pulsing with your need   Gasping
nothing is left of us but a silver mist we swirl though
flaming the trees with a stillness that moans
our bodies heaving with rich heat
shimmer of water on roads illusory as song
I warm myself with our sounds the anchor of your tongue
that goes so deep
steaming with your juices
I roll pounding
with the blue spirit of you coiling my heart
into a gold rose

Twin Cities

This city park sign tells me
Land that once was the highest point
Is now the lowest,

Just as where there once were trees
There now are lakes,
And in a corresponding spot across the river,

Where there once were lakes,
There now are trees.
Curtainless windows at night

Show the clear-cut inscapes
Of once old buildings,
Now white angles and recessed lighting.

On the freeway I passed an old-fashioned RV,
The kind I wished for when I was young
So my family would be safe

Even on yellow-lit highways, with
The impersonal landscape fading
Into oily black mist.

In a trailer like that,
Parked in his mistress's driveway,
My father locked us one night

So that they could fuck in privacy
Inside her ranch-style house.
When I woke up, my mother

Had the county and her lawyer
Unlocking the door.
So why should I daydream now

About a life on the road?
Last week a solicitor rang the doorbell
Of the home I live in with my husband,

And I looked out the window
Instead of answering.
I saw from the back

An old man in a trench coat and hat
Who could have been my father.
He left a pamphlet damning homosexuals,

Which fell from the lintel
When I opened the door.
How can we live like this?

Maybe by knowing
I live in a city that is one half
Of a whole,

And by knowing the rule here is change—
Where something is removed,
It must also be returned,

Just as I know, with time,
Where I have once been empty
I will someday be full,

And in the places
where I once have received,
I may later give.

[this the forest]

monoglottal polylimbic slightly amorous
loose-lipped, spurned a grunt from flower
precambrain multiplicity in the densing
postapocalyptic forest wolf me down.

multivalent deluge in the nether regions
bi-polar supersonic vast visceral nets cast
this defunct etymology of tongue-tied
neanderthalithic croon tender & prone.

all diachronic many-petaled yes gentle
slipshod continent spinning a drift gifted
anticipatory polymorphic glee a bizarre
wild synapse in numerous crowned skin,

listen orchestral architecture listen neural
network, wire, branch, spark, pent-up multip
licitious postures, covalent hued sky, diaphanous
masculinity, low polyphonic human drone

rhizomic, lightly soiled, multigendered lily of
hypersexual ungraceful fluxuation, amassing in
mutagenic saprophytic bud all gown, strut o
lunge into this the forest where all nature's dethroned.

The Rock

It's nice to have a lake to love me,
which can see under all my disguises—
where there is only animal survival
and the brutality of the unconscious—
and still love me and give me focus
and intensity, like a robin listening
to dirt for worms (those birds have talents
I don't: flying around with one eye closed
and half their brain asleep).
                      Alone,
I like to swim (with no goggles, cap, or board)
out where I can see, high up, the white cedars,
and beyond that only the della Robbia blue.
On the other shore, a white pelican sits
on a rock, and, sometimes, feeding him—
beside the sign that says: DO NOT FEED THE PELICAN—
I think about all the dogmas and traditions
that are like well-made beds, with fitted sheets
and tucked-in hospital corners, to die in.
On my rock, it's as if everything is lit from below
or from within. There's no hierarchy
with pelican, water, rock, cedar, sky, and me.
A sense that all's right with the world prevails there—
and some kind of rock language,
with crude dents pressing my flesh,
and little fishes kissing my submerged feet.

Welcome to the Fall

There are things I still cannot tell you. Murmuring
I'm not the one who's so far away, another you touches me

In my dreams & I awake bereft, sweat along my neck.
Or your threadbare shirt ghosts my skin—article

Against clavicle—like baby's breath among the tiger
Lilies. I stir yesterday's coffee with a knife. No spoon

To be found. *Do you believe in god?* I rubbed the belladonna's
Psychotropic dust into my eyes trimming the hedges

Last Thursday, unbeknownst. Headache struck me
& I thought it was the light. Dizziness. Blurred vision.

One pinprick, one gaping pupil. Trees scurrying. I washed
A Valium down with Benadryl, flushed my eyes with cool water.

I meant to be rawer. The honey in the mystery. God's end
In godsend. The serpent you can tell by its spent skin.

In the uncanny valley—*whatever god believes in I believe
In that*—you circle, your shadow sweeps over me.

This was what I wanted wasn't it? Facedown & dumb-
Founded, as if frozen in avalanche, the yellow blooms

Stare at their thin reflection in the glass tabletop.

(An Orchid)

I've begun meditation, but don't know what it should be helping to clear.

An ordered array of expectations, a contiguous line outwards.

Today a rainforest canopy of rooftops. Impossible brown leaf of a drowning tree.

You bloom in my mind, an orchid. A glassed-in relic.

The machine in your ear I sometimes hear instead of you.

I'm writing in blue because words are not water.

I'm practicing desire.

Free radicals unspool the atmosphere.

To a Straight Man

All zodiac all
         radar your voice
                  I carried it
across the Atlantic
         to Barcelona
                  I photographed
cathedrals
         cacti mosaic
                  salamanders
I even photo-
         graphed my lust
                  always
your voice skimming
         a woman's skin
                  mattress springs
so noisy so birdlike
         you filled her room
                  with cages
camera bright
         in my pocket map
                  unfolding
in my mind
         I explored a park
                  leaves notched
& enormous
         graffitied boulders
                  then
three men

                  tall & clean
closed in
         they broke open
                  my body
with their fists

insufferable
                    your red wool cap
insufferable the way
          you walked
                    away from me
come back please
          the buttons
                    on your jacket
are finches
          I wanted to yell
                    as you vanished
into a hotel
          to drink with
                    your friends
there was nothing
          more
                    you could do
after my attackers left
          before I got up
                    I touched my face
almost tenderly

Voyages

I

Above the fresh ruffles of the surf
Bright striped urchins flay each other with sand.
They have contrived a conquest for shell shucks,
And their fingers crumble fragments of baked weed
Gaily digging and scattering.

And in answer to their treble interjections
The sun beats lightning on the waves,
The waves fold thunder on the sand;
And could they hear me I would tell them:

O brilliant kids, frisk with your dog,
Fondle your shells and sticks, bleached
By time and the elements; but there is a line
You must not cross nor ever trust beyond it
Spry cordage of your bodies to caresses
Too lichen-faithful from too wide a breast.
The bottom of the sea is cruel.

II

—And yet this great wink of eternity,
Of rimless floods, unfettered leewardings,
Samite sheeted and processioned where
Her undinal vast belly moonward bends,
Laughing the wrapt inflections of our love;

Take this Sea, whose diapason knells
On scrolls of silver snowy sentences,
The sceptred terror of whose sessions rends
As her demeanors motion well or ill,
All but the pieties of lovers' hands.

And onward, as bells off San Salvador
Salute the crocus lustres of the stars,

In these poinsettia meadows of her tides,—
Adagios of islands, O my Prodigal,
Complete the dark confessions her veins spell.

Mark how her turning shoulders wind the hours,
And hasten while her penniless rich palms
Pass superscription of bent foam and wave,—
Hasten, while they are true,—sleep, death, desire,
Close round one instant in one floating flower.

Bind us in time, O Seasons clear, and awe.
O minstrel galleons of Carib fire,
Bequeath us to no earthly shore until
Is answered in the vortex of our grave
The seal's wide spindrift gaze toward paradise.

III

Infinite consanguinity it bears—
This tendered theme of you that light
Retrieves from sea plains where the sky
Resigns a breast that every wave enthrones;
While ribboned water lanes I wind
Are laved and scattered with no stroke
Wide from your side, whereto this hour
The sea lifts, also, reliquary hands.

And so, admitted through black swollen gates
That must arrest all distance otherwise,—
Past whirling pillars and lithe pediments,
Light wrestling there incessantly with light,
Star kissing star through wave on wave unto
Your body rocking!
                and where death, if shed,
Presumes no carnage, but this single change,—

Upon the steep floor flung from dawn to dawn
The silken skilled transmemberment of song;

Permit me voyage, love, into your hands . . .

IV

Whose counted smile of hours and days, suppose
I know as spectrum of the sea and pledge
Vastly now parting gulf on gulf of wings
Whose circles bridge, I know, (from palms to the severe
Chilled albatross's white immutability)
No stream of greater love advancing now
Than, singing, this mortality alone
Through clay aflow immortally to you.

All fragrance irrefragably, and claim
Madly meeting logically in this hour
And region that is ours to wreathe again,
Portending eyes and lips and making told
The chancel port and portion of our June—

Shall they not stem and close in our own steps
Bright staves of flowers and quills today as I
Must first be lost in fatal tides to tell?

In signature of the incarnate word
The harbor shoulders to resign in mingling
Mutual blood, transpiring as foreknown
And widening noon within your breast for gathering
All bright insinuations that my years have caught
For islands where must lead inviolably
Blue latitudes and levels of your eyes,—

In this expectant, still exclaim receive
The secret oar and petals of all love.

V

Meticulous, past midnight in clear rime,
Infrangible and lonely, smooth as though cast
Together in one merciless white blade—
The bay estuaries fleck the hard sky limits.

—As if too brittle or too clear to touch!
The cables of our sleep so swiftly filed,
Already hang, shred ends from remembered stars.
One frozen trackless smile . . . What words
Can strangle this deaf moonlight? For we

Are overtaken. Now no cry, no sword
Can fasten or deflect this tidal wedge,
Slow tyranny of moonlight, moonlight loved
And changed . . . "There's

Nothing like this in the world," you say,
Knowing I cannot touch your hand and look
Too, into that godless cleft of sky
Where nothing turns but dead sands flashing.

"—And never to quite understand!" No,
In all the argosy of your bright hair I dreamed
Nothing so flagless as this piracy.

                    But now
Draw in your head, alone and too tall here.
Your eyes already in the slant of drifting foam;
Your breath sealed by the ghosts I do not know:
Draw in your head and sleep the long way home.

VI

Where icy and bright dungeons lift
Of swimmers their lost morning eyes,
And ocean rivers, churning, shift
Green borders under stranger skies,

Steadily as a shell secretes
Its beating leagues of monotone,
Or as many waters trough the sun's
Red kelson past the cape's wet stone;

O rivers mingling toward the sky
And harbor of the phoenix' breast—
My eyes pressed black against the prow,
—Thy derelict and blinded guest

Waiting, afire, what name, unspoke,
I cannot claim: let thy waves rear
More savage than the death of kings,
Some splintered garland for the seer.

Beyond siroccos harvesting
The solstice thunders, crept away,
Like a cliff swinging or a sail
Flung into April's inmost day—

Creation's blithe and petalled word
To the lounged goddess when she rose
Conceding dialogue with eyes
That smile unsearchable repose—

Still fervid covenant, Belle Isle,
—Unfolded floating dais before

Which rainbows twine continual hair—
Belle Isle, white echo of the oar!

The imaged Word, it is, that holds
Hushed willows anchored in its glow.
It is the unbetrayable reply
Whose accent no farewell can know.

First Date, Hawk Mountain

We sat together on the grassy mountain
where the sun shone clear and hard
in our faces, as we inched closer—
the stone beneath us soaking up our heat
and giving us back an ancient cold
that told of a love larger than the self.
I shivered when you took off my gloves
and kissed the hands that touched you
for the first time on top of that mountain
I knew we'd always carry within us—
muscle and bone of the place where birders
gather to trace the hawks' migration
as they cross overhead. I had this vision
of a thermal sweeping in and lifting us
into the same welcoming blue as soon as
our lips finally met. But when I came to,
we were still earthbound, of course,
seated on grass and leaves, eye to eye,
arm in arm, keeping each other warm.

Youth Sings a Song of Rosebud

Since men grow diffident at last,
And care no whit at all,
If spring be come, or the fall be past,
Or how the cool rains fall,

I come to no flower but I pluck,
I raise no cup but I sip,
For a mouth is the best of sweets to suck;
The oldest wine's on the lip.

If I grow old in a year or two,
And come to the querulous song
Of "Alack and aday" and "This was true,
And that, when I was young,"

I must have sweets to remember by,
Some blossom saved from the mire,
Some death-rebellious ember I
Can fan into a fire.

Once All the Hounds Had Been Called Home

When the grapevine had thinned
but not broken & the worst was yet to come
of winter snow, I tracked my treed heart
to the high boughs of a quaking
aspen & shot it down.
                              If love comes fast,
let her be a bullet & not a barking dog;
let my heart say, as that trigger's pulled,
Are all wonders small? Otherwise, let love
be a woman of gunpowder
                              & lead; let her
arrive a brass angel, a dark powdered comet
whose mercy is dense as the fishing sinker
that pulleys the moon, even when it is heavy
with milk. I shot my heart
                              & turned myself in
to wild kindness, left the road to my coffin
that seemed also to include my carrying it & walked
back along the trampled brush I remembered
only as a blur of hot breath & a howling in my chest.

The Art of Butterflying

lesbianism is an art form, one moment we are who we seem to be—a student, an anarchist, a housewife, a poet—and then we create that which seems to have nothing to do with who we are. we become mechanics, pagans, librarians, lesbians.

the transformations are more beautiful every time. we are but butterflied women.

art brings a dimension to its spectators that, before art, was not experienced by those who do not admire the world beyond black and white. what appears to be reality is broken: the coffin is a pleasure cove; the apple a bomb; the eyeball, a mandala.

the deconstruction of common meanings opens the paths to change. if the coffin is a pleasure cove, is death not welcome? if an apple is a bomb, should i have one for breakfast? if the eyeball is a mandala, does inner peace reside in the centers of our eyes?

change leads to evolution. the housewife becomes a radical lesbian separatist who becomes a pacifist, who becomes a mother, who becomes a housewife, who becomes an artist, who becomes an alcoholic, who becomes a truck driver, who becomes a father, who becomes a feminist, who becomes whatever else she wants to, until she decides, one day, to become a butterfly.

lesbian art requires no paint brushes on canvas. the rupture with identities that seemed forever real and true is sufficient for butterflying, by re-creating who we were and re-naming who we are, we let go of what would have been and become another invention of ourselves.

the transformations are more beautiful every time. we are butterflied women.

These Hands, If Not Gods

Haven't they moved like rivers—
like glory, like light—
over the seven days of your body?

And wasn't that good?
Them at your hips—

isn't this what God felt when he pressed together
the first Beloved: *Everything.*
Fever. Vapor. Atman. Pulsus.
Finally, a sin worth hurting for, a fervor,
a sweet—*You are mine.*

It is hard not to have faith in this:
from the blue-brown clay of night
these two potters crushed and smoothed you
into being—grind, then curve—built your form up—

atlas of bone, fields of muscle,
one breast a fig tree, the other a nightingale,
both morning and evening.

O, the beautiful making they do,
of trigger and carve, suffering and stars.

Aren't they, too, the carpenters
of your small church? Have they not burned
on the altar of your belly, eaten the bread
of your thighs, broke you to wine, to ichor,
to nectareous feast?

Haven't they riveted your wrists, haven't they
had you at your knees?

And when these hands touched your throat,
showed you how to take the apple *and* the rib,
how to slip a thumb into your mouth and taste it all,
didn't you sing out their ninety-nine names—

Zahir, Aleph, hands-time-seven,
Sphinx, Leonids, locomotura,
Rubidium, August, and September—
and when you cried out, *O, Prometheans,*
didn't they bring fire?

These hands, if not gods, then why
when you have come to me, and I have returned you
to that from which you came—white mud, mica, mineral, salt—
why then do you whisper *O, my Hecatonchire. My Centimani.*
My Hundred-Handed One?

Post-Therapy Room

Flatness is all. The sunfish lives in it,
and lichens spread in an insistent plane,
saving their strength. No time dimension.

Flat as a voice over the dictaphone.
Wires, Mama, they do the thing with wires,
as the sea-urchin spits his innards out.

To be the thinnest fillet of Dover sole
on the narrowest china plate, to be dead flat,
waiting for the steamroller's iron massage.

Mama, with wires. They hang my shadow out,
opaque as a Bible paper, and as thin.
I am a lampshade made of human skin.

They ironed my marrow to a pancaked cell,
and that was me. I was alive and well.
Only the sweetbreads of the past were gone,

the little bumps of glands, concreted bones,
rib cage and skull, they flattened and were gone.
Oh, I am superficial as the moon,

flat smirks of eyes. I gather and come down,
a single sheet of rain, a veil of shower
falling always in the same limited hour.

Flatness is all. The book has the one page,
and mirrors have undone the actual lakes.
I am too flat to inflate with lust or rage,

I am too large to be hurt, and spread too thin,
and kept too clean for action to engage,
or for relationship to enter in.

Could I but ride indefinite

Could I but ride indefinite,
  As doth the meadow-bee,
And visit only where I liked,
  And no man visit me,

And flirt all day with buttercups,
  And marry whom I may,
And dwell a little everywhere,
  Or better, run away

With no police to follow,
  Or chase me if I do,
Till I should jump peninsulas
  To get away from you,—

I said, but just to be a bee
  Upon a raft of air,
And row in nowhere all day long,
  And anchor off the bar,—
What liberty! So captives deem
  Who tight in dungeons are.

Wood and Rain

I am black man of woods
weeping
where old trees root
like men
hollering
in the wind
for lost children,
where folds of knotted skin
break off
and stab the ground, and fat
black fingers
sky-scratch a warning:

there is no hiding, there is no home
in wet woods or this soil.

Here a leaf
drops like a dead bird.
Listen, the woods weep.
My fingers grip the dirt where I fall.

LYNN DOMINA

The Basilisk

Diminutive offspring of a single elderly rooster,
the basilisk may be hatched only by another
cold-blooded creature, toad or serpent, mistaking the egg
for its own. In a first failed effort at language,
the basilisk explodes into hisses, its tongue
so caught within sibilants and fricatives
that neighboring lizards and adders and mute constrictors shudder
in horror. The basilisk is born
venomous, its glance adequate to overcome any creature,
beast or human, and dies, petrified,
the moment it spies its reflection
in a mirror or pool or pupil. The rooster lives on,
unafraid of the pressure in his abdomen, his desire
to expel life, monstrous offspring
of a single nearly dead and solitary father.

Deep Lane

Into Eden came the ticks,
princes of this world,
heat-seeking, tiny, multitudinous

—Lord, why have you given them
a heart, a nervous system, a lit microchip
of a—brain, is it?—if not to invite Manicheanism;

hard to believe the force that shaped the mild tortoise
traversing the undergrowth with smallest steps,
the sway-necked lily,

hard to countenance that same mind
dotting paradise with pinhead demons
wanting nothing but to gorge, to suck

beyond the dreams of their hell-brothers
the mosquitoes—implacable, without boundary,
pure appetite. I wouldn't know anything about that.

Going Home

> "Never forget
> America is our Hitler"
>
> —Chrystos

NEW ECHOTA, GEORGIA

We went back there
The air hot and thick as we
move across a field
that was once a street.

The city is a museum now.
Buildings burnt to the ground
by white farmers are reconstructed:
the court with its stanch protestant benches,
a council house with only four white walls,
the *Cherokee Phoenix*
where Sequoyah's syllabary
printed leaf upon leaf.

In the courthouse, a small bird
crashes violently against a window.
I open my palms and she lands in them.
I take her outside.
A *spirit* my mother and I say.

We photograph
a small garden of corn,
an old dark cabin,
a missionary's house,
one of the detention camps
we were forced into.

Marked with only a small plaque,
there's only grass and trees there, now,
and the soft sobs of grandmothers
that will never leave the earth.

HOPKINSVILLE, KENTUCKY

The Trail of Tears Commemorative Park
grieves next to the South Fork Little River.
On the edge of a vast parking lot
the graves of two chiefs moan.

On the other side of the river,
hundreds of ancestors unmarked.
Children and elders,
for the most part
my mother points out.

The center of the parking lot
displays flags of the states
the Trail was forced through.
I notice a small bird trapped
inside a lamp near the ground.

My father takes a screwdriver,
disassembles the lamp,
and lets her escape,
returning east.

SPRINGFIELD, MISSOURI

Trail of Tears? Never heard of such a thing.
Wouldn't you like to see a Civil War Monument?

TAHLEQUAH, OKLAHOMA

One thousand miles back home.

NEW ECHOTA, GEORGIA

We have no tobacco to feed our ancestors.
We move across fields and through woods.
My mother asks,
Do you feel like we're walking with ghosts?

We are, mama.

Conception Myth

First of all, there's no turkey baster,
just this needleless syringe and a plastic vial

with a salmon-colored frozen pellet
at the bottom, no bigger than the tip

of my pinky finger. The label promises
twenty-four-thousand swimmers

will emerge when the ice defrosts. We need
only one. And it seems easy, like that

carnival game where you shoot water
into the clown's open mouth and a balloon

blooms out of its head. Until we see
that movie where sperm weave like drunken

mole rats, bumping into fallopian walls
while the egg sits on her barstool, sipping

a last-call vodka, checking her watch.
Post-insemination, the bowl of my pelvis

warms like a room full of bodies, and I
wonder if one, which one will wander

down that hallway, hear her whispering
behind the closed door, and knock.

Sonnet

I had not thought of violets late,
The wild, shy kind that spring beneath your feet
In wistful April days, when lovers mate
And wander through the fields in raptures sweet.
The thought of violets meant florists' shops,
And bows and pins, and perfumed papers fine;
And garish lights, and mincing little fops
And cabarets and soaps, and deadening wines.
So far from sweet real things my thoughts had strayed,
I had forgot wide fields; and clear brown streams;
The perfect loveliness that God has made,—
Wild violets shy and Heaven-mounting dreams.
And now—unwittingly, you've made me dream
Of violets, and my soul's forgotten gleam.

Often I Am Permitted to Return to a Meadow

as if it were a scene made-up by the mind,
that is not mine, but is a made place,

that is mine, it is so near to the heart,
an eternal pasture folded in all thought
so that there is a hall therein

that is a made place, created by light
wherefrom the shadows that are forms fall.

Wherefrom fall all architectures I am
I say are likenesses of the First Beloved
whose flowers are flames lit to the Lady.

She is Queen Under The Hill
whose hosts are a disturbance of words within words
that is a field folded.

It is only a dream of the grass blowing
east against the source of the sun
in an hour before the sun's going down

whose secret we see in a children's game
of ring a round of roses told.

Often I am permitted to return to a meadow
as if it were a given property of the mind
that certain bounds hold against chaos,

that is a place of first permission,
everlasting omen of what is.

Pervert

The week before my mother died
I went to a feminist theory seminar,
and even though I can describe myself
as nothing other than happily married,
I wanted another woman.
An old school butch—
the kind of woman who exudes lesbian
through every pore of her being,
the kind of woman who sits comfortably
with her legs apart, who stands
forcefully, both feet firmly on the ground,
the kind of woman we describe
as ballsy and, on occasion, a ball-buster,
the kind of woman whose eyes
sear femmes's bodies,
making our nipples hard,
our clits erect,
our pussies wet—
the kind of woman I desire.
It was not just that I admired
her power, not just that I appreciated
her sexual being walking through the world,
glancing at me, giving me the benefit of lust.
No, I had to Indulge
in the full-frontal fantasy.
During two days of seminars,
I imagined her fist hungrily
inserted in my vagina,
her long fingers first stroking
my muscular walls, gathering
the rhythm of sex, opening me
to accommodate four fingers,
a thumb, squeezed into a fist;
I imagined how my body

would open for her, how my lips
would quiver when my body erupted
into orgasm. I imagined looking into her eyes
as the ripples of my orgasm
squeezed her tight fist more deeply
into my body. I imagined making
her core to my body, central in my life,
in the way that only sex and lust bring
two women together. I imagined sucking her nipples,
laughing with her in the afterglow.
I imagined how much she would want
me after I took her whole hand
inside me, and, though I do not
believe this, when my father called
to tell me about the bleed
in my mother's brain and how
I needed to come home to help him
with the work death entails,
to mourn with him,
to bury my mother,
though I do not believe this at all,
I could not help but think:
I caused my mother's death
with my lust. Her death was G-d's
punishment for being an avowed
homosexual, punishment for my desire
of someone outside marriage,
for my continual, unrelenting lust for women,
which my mother had condemned
since I was eighteen.
I could not help but see my mother
in death somehow justified
in her anger, in her continued disappointment
with my perversity. I could not help but

think: I am a pervert who caused
my mother's death.
I could not help but hear
her final, fatal words, crushing
the lust, the fantasy from the conference.
She knew all along I would kill her,
after death she hissed, *I told you,*
I told you so.

Settling In

How I loved
each bare floor, each
naked wall, the shadows on

newly empty halls.
By day, my head humming
to itself of dreams, I cleaned and

scrubbed
to make life
new; dislodging from the corner,

the old
moths and cicadas
pinned to the screen, the carcasses

of grasshoppers
dangling from beams,
and each windowsill's clutter of

dried beetles
and dead bees. But,
through each opening, each closing door,

the old life
returns on six legs, or
spins a musty web as it roosts over

a poison pot, or
descends from above
to drink blood in. This is how it

happens: the
settling in—the press
of wilderness returns to carved-out space, to skin.

Sex

after "Oh, what would you know about it anyway?"

How the room rained down
a mother's only blistering ash,
her words lifting then settling
clear and hot, then the branding
of me complete.

After she proclaimed,
to the rest of the family,
that whatever it is that I do
with another woman
could never even-steven
to what she does with Daddy.

As if my way to human pleasure was
too inefficient to be called the same.
As if we who do with a woman
should find a new name for the doing.

She believing that my body
coming together with another
woman's, a fake freak of nature,
not sex or love and could never be.

The sermon of her looks
always the same.

How my pot of woman
is not worth the salt,
because there is not the pepper
of a man there.

That in order for any woman
to cook up a thing worth
sensually serving,

a lid and seasoning
of a certain fit and taste
are required.

That what I offer to the diamond
and life of another woman, that
then streams up my two front
female spines, that branches off
into a desert orchid, that grows
into a family of complicated
spiraled things in the middle
of any hot springs geyser night,
is not worth its weight in sweat.

As if what I know about pleasure
and the microscopic fittings of love,
about the filling of an appetite
that lives somewhere between
cerebellum and thigh tissue,
that runs like a southern railroad
trestle to my heart bone emptying
next to my lung sacs, as if that
tenderness which douses all the gates
of my body clean and wet like all
the steamed water and wind that
ever were in this world, suddenly
let loose, as if what comes from
the zest and tongue of another
woman's capsule to my own,
that intricate complicated vessel
of how and what we shape our
loving into cannot be compared
to what she has felt between her
own gulf stream.

Mama, what appears shut sky
to you is heaven opened wide
to me.

once a marine biologist told me octopuses have three hearts

I wonder what I'd do
    with eight arms, two eyes
        & too many ways to give
            myself away

        see, I only have one heart
        & I know loving a woman can make you crawl
    out from under yourself, or forget
the kingdom that is your body

& what would you say, octopus?
    that you live knowing nobody
        can touch you more
           than you do already

        that you can't punch anything underwater
    so you might as well drape yourself
        around it, bring it right up to your mouth
    let each suction cup kiss what it finds

        that having this many hands
        means to hold everything
    at once & nothing
to hold you back

that when you split
    you turn your blood
        blue & pour
           out more ocean

        that you know heartbreak so well
    you remove all your bones
so nothing can kill you.

Ode to the Corpse Flower

In the language of flowers // I am the one who says // fuck you
I won't be anyone's nosegay // this Mary is her own // talking bouquet

never let a man speak for you or call you // what he wants // I learned that
the hard way // amorphophallus titanum // it sure sounds pretty in a dead tongue

except it's Latin for big ugly dick // I mean I am // but what an asshole scientist
I prefer to think of myself // & this may sound vain // as a goddess

cadaver dressed in drag // my stage name // Versace Medusa
part Lilith part calla lily // keep your heteronormative birds & bees // give me

the necrophiliacs // the freaks the meat-eating // beetle & flesh fly
there I go again allies / /getting all hot & bothered // being vulgar

vulgar meaning common // as when something is below you // like a girl
forbidden to say fuck // it makes a woman sound so common // oh come on

that's all you expect from a flower // to be likeable // but to keep it raw & 100
is to be abhorred // fine but even the haters will pay // to hold their nose

at a halftime show // they'll claim they are beyond Beyoncé // sick of Selena
yet they can't look away from the Live Cam // no one wants to miss // the showgirl

as she breaks through the cake // unhooks her lingerie // La Virgen de Guadalupe
with a twist of Santa Muerte // what in the hell is she wearing // glad you ask

death is the new Christian Dior // the latest Chanel is corpse smell // I am the week-old
ham hock whore of horticulture // I bring the hothouse haute couture // & I always come

in last place // dressed to the nines I get what I want // which is to be The Tenth Muse
Sor Juana Inés de la Cruz // little Evita de Buenos Aires // screwing & screwing over

los descamisados on my Rainbow Tour // fuck Whitman fuck Pound // give me Emily D
speaking of which have I ever told you daddy //only sun gods get me hard // you want it

I got it // let me show you how a chola really leans // mother nature may wear floral
but I ain't your mama // I thirst like Betty Boop at peek coquette // Marilyn Monroe

blowing in an air vent // say Malinche say Truvadawhore // give me more
I thrive in shade // my throat is my throne so // queen me bitch

In Transit

Sometimes? You're helpless as the black
snake in the middle of its dying: ground
open, driven over, whipping its sharp head across itself:

as though frenzy were a suture. The carcasses,
the cherished, the lost-and-never-missed: single

shoes on the berms and verges
of roadways and off-ramps: rusty
armature of a pram in a pasture

halfway to Tampa: candy-colored
doll house in the north-bound lane:

left wing of a heron adhered
to the macadam, catching
the shear of passing cars, waving

beside some cane field: hair bands,
receipts, thanks-for-shopping-come-
again! bags in rumble strips and ditches.

You stop the car. You have to. You hate yourself
for braking. Sometimes you have to see.

AEON GINSBERG

Poem in Which I Transition into Water

& you're everywhere to me / when I close my eyes /
it's you I see / & when while that's well and good
my body doesn't yet sprawl horizon across itself yet /
doesn't yet flow out from me in a way that holds itself /
but holds onto itself moreso than necessary / how hard /
it is to take a bath / when you are the bath / when I close
my eyes / I too see myself as I want / I am want to believe /
in the reality of my liquid self / how fluid I must be to fill /
the shape of containers placed around me

Sunflower Sutra

I walked on the banks of the tincan banana dock and sat down under the huge shade
of a Southern Pacific locomotive to look at the sunset over the box house hills and
cry.

Jack Kerouac sat beside me on a busted rusty iron pole, companion, we thought the
same thoughts of the soul, bleak and blue and sad-eyed, surrounded by the
gnarled steel roots of trees of machinery.

The oily water on the river mirrored the red sky, sun sank on top of final Frisco
peaks, no fish in that stream, no hermit in those mounts, just ourselves rheumy-
eyed and hung-over like old bums on the riverbank, tired and wily.

Look at the Sunflower, he said, there was a dead gray shadow against the sky, big as a
man, sitting dry on top of a pile of ancient sawdust—

—I rushed up enchanted—it was my first sunflower, memories of Blake—my
visions—Harlem

and Hells of the Eastern rivers, bridges clanking Joes Greasy Sandwiches, dead baby
carriages, black treadless tires forgotten and unretreaded, the poem of the
riverbank, condoms & pots, steel knives, nothing stainless, only the dank muck
and the razor-sharp artifacts passing into the past—

and the gray Sunflower poised against the sunset, crackly bleak and dusty with the
smut and smog and smoke of olden locomotives in its eye—

corolla of bleary spikes pushed down and broken like a battered crown, seeds fallen
out of its face, soon-to-be-toothless mouth of sunny air, sunrays obliterated on its
hairy head like a dried wire spiderweb,

leaves stuck out like arms out of the stem, gestures from the sawdust root, broke
pieces of plaster fallen out of the black twigs, a dead fly in its ear,

Unholy battered old thing you were, my sunflower O my soul, I loved you then!

The grime was no man's grime but death and human locomotives,

all that dress of dust, that veil of darkened railroad skin, that smog of cheek, that
eyelid of black mis'ry, that sooty hand or phallus or protuberance of artificial
worse-than-dirt—industrial—modern—all that civilization spotting your crazy
golden crown—

and those blear thoughts of death and dusty loveless eyes and ends and withered roots
below, in the home-pile of sand and sawdust, rubber dollar bills, skin of
machinery, the guts and innards of the weeping coughing car, the empty lonely
tincans with their rusty tongues alack, what more could I name, the smoked

ashes of some cock cigar, the cunts of wheelbarrows and the milky breasts of
    cars, wornout asses out of chairs & sphincters of dynamos—all these
entangled in your mummied roots—and you there standing before me in the
    sunset, all your glory in your form!
A perfect beauty of a sunflower! a perfect excellent lovely sunflower existence! a
    sweet natural eye to the new hip moon, woke up alive and excited grasping in
    the sunset shadow sunrise golden monthly breeze!
How many flies buzzed round you innocent of your grime, while you cursed the
    heavens of the railroad and your flower soul?
Poor dead flower? when did you forget you were a flower? when did you look at
    your skin and decide you were an impotent dirty old locomotive? the ghost of
    a locomotive? the specter and shade of a once powerful mad American
    locomotive?
You were never no locomotive, Sunflower, you were a sunflower!
And you Locomotive, you are a locomotive, forget me not!
So I grabbed up the skeleton thick sunflower and stuck it at my side like a scepter,
and deliver my sermon to my soul, and Jack's soul too, and anyone who'll listen,
—We're not our skin of grime, we're not dread bleak dusty imageless locomotives,
    we're golden sunflowers inside, blessed by our own seed & hairy naked
    accomplishment-bodies growing into mad black formal sunflowers in the
    sunset, spied on by our own eyes under the shadow of the mad locomotive
    riverbank sunset Frisco hilly tincan evening sitdown vision.

All at Sea

I am not blameless
living off of my mother's belly.
I know my thirst
and I know my crimes.
I know yours.

But do you remember—in your dreams—
our emergent bodies ghosting below the sea line?
Remember how we learned from the stinging flowers,
the viruses, the cetacean songs
that echoed below the ice-sheeted earth?
I miss those songs still,
how we thrilled in somatic reply
from body to body, to wave after wave.

Do you remember the coastlines
and their riches before we branched forth limbs
and stood ashore, our infant knees trembling forth?
And can you dream her up as she was then
before our fatal bloom across her giving breast?

They say the sea is a mirror.
Look, and there we are:
a fluke, a dying kind. And our mother now?
She is there, shrunken, sagging,
shocked by our overhandling
and the banquet we hold across the spine
of her back.

Like you, I am a monster of desire,
and when I drink her in, I taste my grave.
I have maimed her to the core.
But her logic of mercy is next:

when I thirst for the last time,
mother will be a yielding desert,
and I shall suck her bones dry.

pedicles, or this is where

every antler is an adolescence
that sheds its vascular skin—bloodied

velvet scraped like childhood against
a red maple's trunk. Call it ritual—

how you leave that tenderness on
the forest floor for these hardened,

honeycombed bones ephemerally
fastened to your skull. How your

flesh softens as your testosterone
begins to fade, and you remember

what it is to be more fawn than buck,
to feel that sharpness weigh on your

head and body like a shame that weakens
the blood. I am those heavy antlers;

this is where I leave you—between
eyes of burnt umber and soft salt-

&-pepper-furred ears. You'll learn
to seduce without a crown, to survive

without a weapon—hide soaked in
your will to grow and grow and

The Strangers Who Find Me in the Woods

after Thomas James

The strangers in the woods must mimic squirrels and crackle
with the undergrowth. They must not flinch at the cruelty
of breaking golden leaves with their feet, or of interring stones.
And like any of these deciduous trees in autumn they must be

stingy with shadow and move deceptively across the sludge.
I listen to these strangers stirring with the evenings. I invent paths
for them to the soft edge of the lake. Each descent is as graceful
as a sinking ship, but less tragic somehow because these strangers

don't possess a lung. I cannot hear them breathe, yet the air
is all whispers, all sighs—the same ethereal muscle that rubs
the color off the foliage. I lost my way out of the woods on the night
every bird went south or numb. A plump rat snatched the moon

and dragged it by the white rope of its tail. The strangers were
a cloak of silhouettes flattening against a trunk like bark.
I must have disappeared among them because the mouth I touched
was not my own and was cruelly closing in on someone's rib. I carried

such a bite on me, an arc of green and yellow on my side from the man
who said he loved me. In that darkness I knew as much about him
as I did of the amputee swimming his way up the hill with his
only arm. So this is the home of the unturned stone where

the fugitive keeps his kiss! Archeologists will discover a paradise
in the place no touch died of neglect. Is it any wonder all things
forgotten or abandoned find their way here? The winter is back, so too
the bloated body of a book I tossed over the bridge last week.

And there on the bench, is my old smoking habit, a cigarette
glowing on my mouth like a beacon. I'm patient, waiting for the fugitive
to claim me as his own. I'm as wise as any stranger here, alone but with
the knowledge that the grief of separation is always brief.

You Form

Before sex she is warming each finger in my navel
while telling me about an old myth of formation—
that oysters rise to the surface of the sea one hour each night
to inaugurate their pearls. There they unhinge to capture

drops of rain or dew before returning to the sea-bed, where
waters transform in years of darkness. Behind my lids
I see the flickering hyperbole of these creatures' prize dreams
like light splattered on their inner walls, their twitching

musculature burying the point of contact, effusing stunned
lumps of cold gunmetal, inky blue, orange in Burma,
golden in the Philippines, silver and rose off the Australian
coast, the mornings flushed with those beginnings.

The women in our families all married in pearls, their
rolling voices at the collarbone in the ceremony. My neck
still knows their exact weight, that sweet sixteen strand.
They came in a box that snapped when it opened, with a note

in ink on ivory. More unblinking and lunar than our eyes,
the loop rests by the mirror—mothers, and aunts and sisters
staring back from the constant round. Spheres that loosened
in the mollusk's soft tissues, without points of fixation

to mess a symmetry. No mark of fierce attachment, buried
molecule, gaping mouth to the interior. No nascent clue.
Pearls which contain no central nucleus, no sandy grain
or slip of wood. A white strand. It seemed best. Our eyes

trace each other, two across a small hard knot, color rising
in the nacre, the crystal thickening. Along my kneecap, ankle,
hipbone her lips suggest the asymmetrical semiround,
the irregularly shaped droplet, the gorgeously deformed

baroque, the ridged cerclée. Her tongue turns the pearls out
and they press each other insistently, a gothic form coming
just at the hinge of my feeling, as jagged and monstrous
as the emptiness of a ravine. Glowing a coppery brown

with something dark and liquid in its middle, its fogged face
conceals the slick of a fish once fixed in the shell's blue
walls, buried under the ripple of some possibility,
frozen into the face of its only hour of becoming.

A Migration

after James Wright's "A Blessing"

On the way to Baguio City
Mountain fog surrounds our parked car.
10,000 horses and their nostrils
Press upon a single gate
Breathing their animal sickness.
They've smelled the new grass as
We wipe the windows and look to the horizon
Where they too have set their eyes.
They nudge the gate, collect their weight on the fence.
With or without witness,
They huddle like cattle. Their love is theirs alone.
There is no ambivalence in animal attention.
On the other side, the oldest begin
To die. The yearlings guard the bones.
I would like to hold in my hand this image:
The closed gate opening,
My left hand lifting the latch—
Black, brown, gray, white, spotted,
Freed legs in the new wildness.
The charged air of their galloping,
Their skins rippled on ribs like a lake
First finding its shore.

There are no conclusions
Better than the ones that came before.

Heaven and Earth

                Heaven
and earth are made in the orchard

where a young man who hauls lumber
to jobsites in town since high school

puts down his tools, and a young man
with his breasts bound up inside

his shirt shakes a smoke with trembling
fingers from his pack, and the two eye

each other with a kind of affection
they can't disclose. Every measure

of time means something more. Hair
grows long, is shorn; laid end to end

one could knot together a tightrope
to the moon. Heckled for being

a dyke—*Learn your slurs!* he yells,
or wishes he could—he's ready to call

another place home. Cayenne colors the door-
ways here, dims to rust until the ants

again don't mind, begin to retrace their paths
in fading dust. What calendar

left on the sills in red pepper's
receding heat marks the years

some of us grew up, some left? The skin
hid beneath clothes—what wonder

it contains. Here, two who fear could turn
to enemies; instead they touch

each other with a tenderness men
might shy from. The pact neither needs

to make aloud: there comes
a last time for mending, for sharpening

a shovel's blade to dig through roots.
Every seed left unharvested breaks

open, sends out its small claim
on the soil. Look out over the hillside

stitched by bees. Dowsers pace the pastures
in search of unseen rivers the drought

can't shake. Kitchen counters teem again
with sugar ants. Someday they'll remember

a time in the orchard, will turn in their nest
of bedding to the person they've woken

beside for thirty years.   *My first time*
a carload of guys careened past, called

out Faggot! *at me? It was involuntary,*
the stitch of breath that rose in my bound chest:

familiarity.
The dark animal of my unconscious

warming to hear a sound
            that felt so much like home.

A Kingdom of Longing

Change curling against your thigh again,
a leaf at the base of a limb. Each vein
held to the iris of the sun. An amorous mouth

just beyond earth. How certain colors shift, thrusting
their calls within the mood of light. A finger, exhausted
from scratching and writing, curls into the palm

and tremors there a fracture. I am changing. Look
how I have become, as the sea.
My hands, in spasms, shudder from holding

words, scratching them from skin each night.
My mouth cups the seasons between our bodies. The sky
bursts with blushing. A horizon, arched like a woman's

neck, whose hollows catch both remorse and dawn.
I am changing. Look how I have become earth again.
I want between gulps and terrors. Without this ache

I can never be content.

Look how I have become, as a valley, shadowed
with clouds. My thighs, pulling and rocking
the last light from my center. I am changing,

thin between hungers. Each vein, blue before air, shields
dreams sunk under your eyelids. I want to see
how the light changes when you're opening

everything to me in a glare. Look how I have become
longing. A kingdom of longing
to force you.

El Beso

Twilight—and you
Quiet—the stars;
Snare of the shine of your teeth,
Your provocative laughter,
The gloom of your hair;
Lure of you, eye and lip;
Yearning, yearning,
Languor, surrender;
Your mouth,
And madness, madness,
Tremulous, breathless, flaming,
The space of a sigh;
Then awakening—remembrance,
Pain, regret—your sobbing;
And again, quiet—the stars,
Twilight—and you.

Not Children

I know. But let me describe how gently
I pulled apart the plastic, the cowl, how the plastic
split at its stapled seam, revealing wet, olive-
colored bark. I'm not exaggerating when I say
I've never seen anything more beautiful
in the human body, though it did most resemble
human skin. Let me talk about the winnowing
of fingers through barrows of the local clay
cut with composted horse manure, fingers, arms
up to the elbow, sifting, mixing, breaking up
clumps of the compost, feathering it over
heavy clay, aerating, leavening, darkening.
Let me describe the speckled brown:
how the mixed medium had richness, felt good
on the palms, soft on the soft parts of the body.
Now imagine yourself bending with me,
lifting a tree from the plastic, extricating a single
sapling from the bundle, how your fingers
relearn gentleness unlacing the hair of the roots
from other roots, how in the manner of a mother
washing a child, you touch the most vulnerable
parts of the tree, the places where it would be
frighteningly easy to choke off life. And now
let's stand together, lift it from the plastic
and wash it down again, the pressure of the hose
blocked by your palm, so water falls easily
on the young trunk. Its place in the world is prepared;
bring it over, rest it in, as if into human arms.
The earth will love the thing no more than we do.
And now imagine yourself with me
stepping back from the planted sapling. Feel
how you steep and rise, how your chest fills
and then the slow, steady release of air.

Words for Some Ash

Poor parched man, we had to squeeze
Dental sponge against your teeth,
So that moisture by degrees
Dribbled to the mouth beneath.

Christmas Day your pupils crossed,
Staring at your nose's tip.
Seeking there the air you lost
Yet still gaped for, dry of lip.

Now you are a bag of ash
Scattered on a coastal ridge,
Where you watched the distant crash,
Ocean on a broken edge.

Death has wiped away each sense;
Fire took muscle, bone, and brains;
Next may rain leach discontents
From your dust, wash what remains

Deeper into damper ground
Till the granules work their way
Down to unseen streams, and bound
Briskly in the water's play;

May you lastly reach the shore,
Joining tide without intent,
Only worried any more
By the currents' argument.

Queerodactyl

After they locate & excavate your wing fossils,
perseverance might be the trait you're known for.
How swiftly you sloped downward to pick up
the carcasses floating just above the bloodstained
surface of your old neighborhood. In the laboratory,
the paleontologists will use radiometric dating
to zoom into what bequeathed you that agency to fly.
This one might have outlasted all the others,
they'll say. *Might have even seen each one disappear*
behind a bolt of fire blasted from who knows where.
Or you might have been the first to vanish, directly in
the way of the asteroid's course. Who will, in the end,
exhume our myths conclusively? A young angel's bones,
shaped just like yours, were uncovered this morning.
A group of diggers hadn't found anything exciting
for months—in jeopardy of losing all their funding.
I, too, have buried myself under the heavy presence
of change, from a longing, perhaps, to find my remnants,
or their profiles, in places where curious strangers
might prize them. Church is anything with a pair
of wandering hands & a bucket. I, too, have questioned
the usefulness of finding a body stuck in a perpetual
position of near flight—arms extended like the incandescence
from a lamppost at night—& wished it be mine.

Sheltered Garden

I have had enough.
I gasp for breath.

Every way ends, every road,
every foot-path leads at last
to the hill-crest—
then you retrace your steps,
or find the same slope on the other side,
precipitate.

I have had enough—
border-pinks, clove-pinks, wax-lilies,
herbs, sweet-cress.

O for some sharp swish of a branch—
there is no scent of resin
in this place,
no taste of bark, of coarse weeds,
aromatic, astringent—
only border on border of scented pinks.

Have you seen fruit under cover
that wanted light—
pears wadded in cloth,
protected from the frost,
melons, almost ripe,
smothered in straw?

Why not let the pears cling
to the empty branch?
All your coaxing will only make
a bitter fruit—
let them cling, ripen of themselves,
test their own worth,

nipped, shrivelled by the frost,
to fall at last but fair
with a russet coat.

Or the melon—
let it bleach yellow
in the winter light,
even tart to the taste—
it is better to taste of frost—
the exquisite frost—
than of wadding and of dead grass.

For this beauty,
beauty without strength,
chokes out life.
I want wind to break,
scatter these pink-stalks,
snap off their spiced heads,
fling them about with dead leaves—
spread the paths with twigs,
limbs broken off,
trail great pine branches,
hurled from some far wood
right across the melon-patch,
break pear and quince—
leave half-trees, torn, twisted
but showing the fight was valiant.

O to blot out this garden
to forget, to find a new beauty
in some terrible
wind-tortured place.

Nearly a Valediction

You happened to me. I was happened to
like an abandoned building by a bull-
dozer, like the van that missed my skull
happened a two-inch gash across my chin.
You were as deep down as I've ever been.
You were inside me like my pulse. A new-
born flailing toward maternal heartbeat through
the shock of cold and glare: when you were gone,
swaddled in strange air I was that alone
again, inventing life left after you.

I don't want to remember you as that
four o'clock in the morning eight months long
after you happened to me like a wrong
number at midnight that blew up the phone
bill to an astronomical unknown
quantity in a foreign currency.
The dollar dived since you happened to me.
You've grown into your skin since then; you've grown
into the space you measure with someone
you can love back without a caveat.

While I love somebody I learn to live
with through the downpulled winter days' routine
wakings and sleepings, half-and-half caffeine-
assisted mornings, laundry, stock-pots, dust-
balls in the hallway, lists instead of longing, trust
that what comes next comes after what came first.
She'll never be a story I make up.
You were the one I didn't know where to stop.
If I had blamed you, now I could forgive
you, but what made my cold hand, back in prox-

imity to your hair, your mouth, your mind,
want where it no way ought to be, defined
by where it was, and was and was until
the whole globed swelling liquefied and spilled
through one cheek's nap, a syllable, a tear,
was never blame, whatever I wished it were.
You were the weather in my neighborhood.
You were the epic in the episode.
You were the year poised on the equinox.

The Valley of the Amazons

She went to the grocery store with me
in North Hollywood wearing a black tank top
and no bra. We stood together in line.
Everybody was looking at her breasts,
her aviator glasses, her hair slicked back
and one strand falling over her eyes.
I felt like we were in a clearing
ready to mount the horses.
The men stood at a distance.
Our nakedness was nonchalant, connected
to horses and skin warmth. We would ride off
when the checker tallied our purchases
and the clearing would smell like horses
the rest of the day.

The Kiss

Of course I feared them.
Who wouldn't? Honeycomb
like a cortex of coral,
the black-ribbed cap on sick

whitish stalks poking obscenely
from the dirt. Their cousins
can kill: a genetic blood bond,
code enough for me.

Even when mother fried them,
the little brains dancing
on skates of melting butter,
they looked more animal than plant

—soft flesh, an organ of edible rot.
Father, you called them 'miracles',
would inhale the scent. *Like a rain-
wet fawn slept here,* you once said.

*Remember, the dying elms
make morels thrive*—a whisper,
as you held my girlish wrist
and dragged me shivering

through the dark trails of long-
forgotten orchards, past
the wood's mossy trunks
of ash and yellow poplar.

That they ate death, their wetness
a curse, I could forgive. But you
plucked one from its dead
sleep and ate it on the spot.

You made me watch you swallow
the soft cap whole, and I knew you
saw I wouldn't have my own, that I
feared its kiss as much as I missed yours.

Bottle Gentian

Because you come in late summer
to wither in an August frost
or wilt with October's late fever,

your cobalt body
pleated like a fine sleeve,
a fluted tube,
a blue-faced flame,

blister beetles
gnaw your flowers.

Because you never fully open,
only the largest bees
are strong enough
to climb inside

to suck the last feast
of the season.

Closed petals clustered,
a handful of lanterns
above a strong stem.

Color of twilight
after the sun has dropped,
before the moonblack hours,
before the rustle of the coverlet,
the hand beneath the dress of night.

Because you come back
every year on winged seeds
to the rich low prairie,
to the mouth of the meadow,

your heavy yellow root
reaching deep underground
releasing your juice
to poultice our pains.

Endless bud,
you are always beginning,
sweet within
and bitter at the root.

Because you closed
your mouth,

Because you let no one else
come inside,

Those who do not know you
would call you blind.

JANE HILBERRY

Shadows, Saddle Canyon

The sand's loose. The river, careless.

After the last of the shifting fire,
they show sudden on the cliff, pitched
by the moon's illumination,
each a bud-sheath, hood and stem:
a procession of humped gods
ancient as breathing.

I'm altered by these shapes.
The current moves, taking, embracing.
For once, I'm unafraid.

The shadows, great and still, still unfold, I swell
toward spirit, then fall to what I am, less
than a minnow in the river's tail.

Grafted

Two parallel saplings grow to the side of a path :

         on the right a flaking gray pole : to the left

scarred white bark. Three feet up they lean in

         grapple graft in a bulbous striped cyst so

meaty it could burst with a prick a unified thing

         the cross piece in the letter H androgynous

yet able to disentangle into two selves with one

         difference : white continues in a direct line

above gray's roots while gray persists unfazed

         above white's lower trunk. Intolerable?

Bizarre? If you dare dispute biological truth plot

         the parabolic equation leave two Us co-

joined : one upright one upside down axes flipped

         leaves mixed in the sap's slippery switch.

RICHIE HOFMANN

Idyll

Cicadas bury themselves in small mouths
of the tree's hollow, lie against the bark-tongues like amulets,

though it is I who pray I might shake off this skin and be raised
from the ground again. I have nothing

to confess. I don't yet know that I possess
a body built for love. When the wind grazes

its way toward something colder,
you too will be changed. One life abrades

another, rough cloth, expostulation.
When I open my mouth, I am like an insect undressing itself.

Demand

Listen!
Dear dream of utter aliveness—
Touching my body of utter death—
Tell me, O quickly! dream of aliveness,
The flaming source of your bright breath.
Tell me, O dream of utter aliveness—
Knowing so well the wind and the sun—
    Where is this light
    Your eyes see forever?
    And what is this wind
    You touch when you run?

Tenor

after Jean-Michel Basquiat

Crows
   and more crows.
One crow
   with a rat
      hanging
   from its beak,
sloppy
   and beautiful.
Another crow
   with its wings
      plucked
   empty.
I wanted
   so much of today
      to be peaceful
   but the empty crow
untethers
   something in me: a feral
      yearning for love
   or a love that is so full
of power,
   of tenderness,
      the words
   fall to their knees
begging for mercy
   like tulips
      in wind.
I don't wear the crown
   for the times power
      has tainted
   my body,
but I can tell the difference
   between giving up
      and giving in.

If you can't, ask the crow
            that watches me
                    through the window,
            laughing as I drink
my third bottle of wine.
Ask the sound
            the tree makes
                    when the crow has grown
            disgusted
with my whining.
After years of repression,
            I can come clean.
                    I was a boy
            with a hole
other boys
            stuffed themselves into.
I have wanted
            nothing to do with blackness
                    or laughter
            or my life.
But about love,
            who owns the right,
                    really? Who owns
            the crow
who loves fresh meat
            or the crow who loves
                    the vibration
            of its own throat?
Everything around me
            is black for its own good,
                    I suppose.
            The widow,
the picture of the boy
            crying on the wall,

                    the mirror
            with its taunting,
the crows
            that belong
                    to their scripture.
Can you imagine
            being so tied to blackness
                    that even your wings
            cannot help you escape?
About my life,
            every needle,
                    a small prayer.
            Every pill, a funeral
hymn.
I wanted the end
            several times
                    but thought,
            Who owns this body, really?
God?
            Dirt?
                    The silly insects
            that will feast
on my decay?
Is it the boy
            who entered first
                    or the boy
            who wanted everything
to last?

Elementary Departures

A river blooms and revises the world.
This rendering precedes and inherits me,
a threshold of atomistic thistles and bees.

Each thistle blooms a thirteen-spiked morning
star, rolled round on the chain of wind.
Each bee's drone minutely stabs the day.

Time is pitted—my bare legs, pierced once,
scar. Ice cubes pop from the tray.
Moved by what preceded us, we will be

inherited whole, pointed in every direction.
A lover's fingers bloom in me. Hunger blooms
in a sub-Saharan belly. Angers bloom.

The first taste of rock salt shatters the deer's
previous body. Sunlight spigots forth.

Primer

A Florida child knows the safest part
of a lake is the middle. That gators
and moccasins shade in the lilies, hunker
shoreline in the muck just past
the trucked-in sand. Knows a snake egg
means a mother's nearby, angry.
That to kill her, you must bring a shovel
down right behind her skull—leave too much
neck and the headed half will keep
coming at you. To run zigzag if a gator
gives chase, their squat digger legs built
for speed, not for turning. Has a friend
who has a friend who lost a thumb
to a snapping turtle, has worn live lizards
as earrings, watched lake-caught minnows
devour a store-bought birthday
goldfish. Has been dragged on a field trip
to a sinkhole wide as a city block, though
that measurement was not yet known:
a red truck lay at the bottom, wheels up;
along with half a house and a wreck
of toys and books. Has been told it happened
on a day like any other. Has gone home
to tread water at the lake's calming
center; cool streamers of springs fluttering
her thighs, the sun a constant; the sucking
sound of a bathplug pulled, her imagination.

A Stranger Asks Where I Am From

1. *Biographical*

A forest atop a moraine;
a town inside the forest;
in the town, a house made of bricks;
a room from which I could not escape.

2. *Mythological*

A beast without a name,
a woman who wandered too far from home.

3. *Genealogical*

A tree of broken branches,
a trunk of stone,
a season without birds.

4. *Phenomenological*

I suppose I am from somewhere
because I am not from nowhere
but I am not from here,
so I am from there, another there,
which is not the here we know
but a former here. It still exists,
because I still exist.

5. *Quantum Mechanical*

Because no one opened the box,
I am still there, and also here.

Mesquites

In a field a plethora of mesquites grew.
Rampantly, and some of them unruly. Wildness
and fending off shames. Shames? you may ask.
For being bent, for shaping in unnatural ways.
It was said. And so it was——.
But magic, for none of these were trees
in the sense that trees should take root
and not tremble or growl or know Love
for one other. Water and wind. Earth,
Light. Saplings, thus groves. And some spread
their seedpods for the sole sake of giving them
up or taking another's seed. And pleasure
and wildness——. Earth and Light.
And this was the world.

Then. Something emerged
among the mesquites. And overcome,
unprepped, how the mesquites suffered——.
Over time, the seedpods grew strange, dire.
The field soon became a field.
People witnessed. The mesquites began
gradually, forthwith, to die off——.
So many of them. No one
could halt that suffering, though so many tried.
And distance and Grief——.
And heavy murk where once fullness
and Joy, and Wonder. A sad hymn
of sinews: dappled shadows, emptiness——.
For years the hymn hummed.
Harrowed, the field knew somberness
as if it were wind and Light,
the field knew erosion and understood
what loss uttered to its bones: the spirits
of every bird and the tall yellow grasses,

the souls of all the mosses
and the armadillos
digging grubs from the most tender soils,
the little deer
who relied on the mesquites
for shade, the coyotes who satisfied hungers
with the pods—. For many years, then: loss
and affliction, tribulation, woe.

      In time, in time, the mesquites
would return to the field. Newer ones,
and yes, some of the original ones, too,
older, unbroken. Often forgotten,
the surviving mesquites stood tall,
while the new ones easily fed on the field,
the nourishment of those mesquites
who had come before and given of themselves
to the soils on which we all stand.
And this newness was newness, too brash
and swaggering—. Sometimes, solipsism
and disregard—. But I can tell you
there are minutes, whole afternoons, full
seasons where a mesquite will feel unpresence—
the knot in its deepest wood or a hiccup in the root
span, and how it knows, for how can its body
not know that someone was once there?
An emptiness of spirit—a little voice
carried on the soft back of wind.
I tell you it happens, the mesquite
compelled to feel an aloneness only known
by mesquites of this field, for someone
should be here beside him, but isn't—.
And you might call this outlandish,
or you might comprehend this suffering,

the idea of all mesquites carrying this epoch—
and why? and how? and who? and does it ever
go away?

In a field a plethora of mesquites grows.
Rampantly, and some of them unruly. Wildness
and fending off shames. Shames? you may ask.
For being bent, for shaping in unnatural ways,
it was said. But magic. But water and wind.
Earth, Light. Saplings and seedpods,
whole groves.

Late Bloom

The name of the spotted apple
on the leafy floor in the woods

outside the white-walled bedroom
where the FM stereo was always

tuned to the same country
station my girl crush loved

was gall, name for an outgrowth,
a shell withering under leaf rot

near a spot where the surprise lilies
might remember, might

forget to bloom. Touch a weevil
and it will fall, legs and antennae tucked.

Blink and the arctic fox becomes snow.
The gecko, toes spread wide

on a tree trunk, passes for lichen.
Of all the ways a creature can conceal itself,

I must have relied on denial.
There were the Confederate bumper stickers,

pressures from seniors to tail gate,
the spindly legs of a freshman

scissoring out of a trash can,
how just the smell of Old Spice

could make my muscles contract
like a moth, wings folded,

the color of a dead leaf in October.
So that she might hear her favorite song

my voice would drop, and if the DJ answered
I would be Tim, Charlie, Luke, Jason

every name but my own.
Truer than gold.

Wasn't I the stripe in a tiger's eye?
The dapple in the flanks of an Appaloosa?

In daylight, how could I possibly explain:
A heart hunting after a body?

To a Strayed Cat

5 months you were destitute
Destitute
   and w/o that traffic of loves
who now pursue U
I took you in
yr verses I taught
    my acute footwork
yr sentences to perculate
the flute and woodnotes wild
    to pipe and trill
instructed you the skill
    of the metric
     well turn'd
    the unalterable line
to refine
Ah, but that was, as you'd say,
"the past" and anyhow now
    in the 'big city' you have
attracted numerous critics of whom
one has recently
    anthologized you
"doom of Atreus"
But the bed you slept in
    does not lie vacant
new fauns have come to my crags
    to try my tender fern shoots
Let there be deep woods between us
and a briar thicket impasse
    in the beyond.

Golden Egg

I packed a nature documentary for my nature retreat
     in a bundle of wool socks. I watch

emperor penguins skid like ellipses on their deflated bellies, each
     dragging a species on its heels, a single
          golden egg between its legs.

In the bathroom the splatter of a woman's dead eggs stains the wall,
     her cotton tampon soaked in blood,
          another golden month.

In the cranky refrigerator hollow sounds of a glacier recede
     into hallows distant as the dry cough of a goose
          pinned neatly into the story's pattern

while outside
the forest flings prayer beads into my throat's empty plume—
     19, 20, 21 prayers—& the last raven
          is a whooping monk between day & night.

A coyote mutters with spit jowl; human hunting
     season & deer are ripe with wild thyme
          sprouting in clusters.

Sometimes my eyelids seize under poetry's cleaving whenever a god
     stirs the pot or when a raven
          cracks a nut in its throat.

What was the origin of confession? When did the river stop translating
     the stars? I look to the forest for myth & the
          sleek bone of beak,

the skin of the sea gesturing for the white-flagged boat to set the
     planet free. I once imagined a golden deer
          resting its head on my shoulder, but

what I meant

        was that it saved me the way a story clings

            so closely to life that you walk into it

& wish hard that it may teach us how to live.

Drag

The dress is an oil slick. The dress
ruins everything. In a hotel room
by the water, I put it on when
he says, I want to watch you take it off.
Zipping me up, he kisses the mile
markers of my spine. I can't afford
this view. From here, I see a city
that doesn't know it's already
drowning. My neck shivers from
the trail of his tongue. I keep my
eyes on the window, just past
his bald spot. He's short. I can see
the rain that has owned us for weeks
already. The dress will survive us.
The dress will be here when men
come in boats to survey the damage.
He makes me another drink, puts
on some jazz, and the dress begins
to move without me. Slow like some-
thing that knows it cannot be stopped,
the dress seeps. The dress slides
with my body floating inside,
an animal caught in the sludge.
If he wraps his arms around me,
it will be the rest of his life.
I don't even know what I am
in this dress; I just sway with
my arms open and wait.

Letter to the Local Police

Dear Sirs:

I have been enjoying the law and order of our
community throughout the past three months since
my wife and I, our two cats, and miscellaneous
photographs of the six grandchildren belonging to
our previous neighbors (with whom we were very
close) arrived in Saratoga Springs which is clearly
prospering under your custody

Indeed, until yesterday afternoon and despite my
vigilant casting about, I have been unable to discover
a single instance of reasons for public-spirited concern,
much less complaint

You may easily appreciate, then, how it is that
I write to your office, at this date, with utmost
regret for the lamentable circumstances that force
my hand

Speaking directly to the issue of the moment:

I have encountered a regular profusion of certain
unidentified roses, growing to no discernible purpose,
and according to no perceptible control, approximately
one quarter mile west of the Northway, on the southern
side

To be specific, there are practically thousands of
the aforementioned abiding in perpetual near riot
of wild behavior, indiscriminate coloring, and only
the Good Lord Himself can say what diverse soliciting
of promiscuous cross-fertilization

As I say, these roses, no matter what the apparent
background, training, tropistic tendencies, age,
or color, do not demonstrate the least inclination
toward categorization, specified allegiance, resolute
preference, consideration of the needs of others, or
any other minimal traits of decency

May I point out that I did not assiduously seek out
this colony, as it were, and that these certain
unidentified roses remain open to viewing even by
children, with or without suitable supervision

(My wife asks me to append a note as regards the
seasonal but nevertheless seriously licentious
phenomenon of honeysuckle under the moon that one may
apprehend at the corner of Nelson and Main

However, I have recommended that she undertake direct
correspondence with you, as regards this: yet
another civic disturbance in our midst)

I am confident that you will devise and pursue
appropriate legal response to the roses in question
If I may aid your efforts in this respect, please
do not hesitate to call me into consultation

                    Respectfully yours,

purple

> "i don't care if you're Black, white, green, or purple"
> —ancient white proverb

i find it strange how these beings came to my planet
expecting to find themselves. as if the only thing i could
have been was a mirror. these bags of veins and alabaster
roughness, they sun don't even respect them. they won't
look me in my eye. won't shake my vines. won't learn
what's customary here. they expect i should know what
was never taught to me. they keep trying to convince me
they don't care what i look like. but i hear them, hear
them tell their friends i am lavender instead of raisin.
praise the lilac and periwinkle children they forced into
me. i see it, the slow erasure of my fig, my mulberry. i hear
them say *plum plague, plum magic, plum list, plum mail*
and i know that is not an accident. they offer me bleach
and name it peace. they teach my children to hate me in a
tongue i don't know. they tell me to never look back while
calling their history law. separate our families and call it a
statistic.

i miss watching the wild of my children spread without
fear. i miss the monuments dedicated to my darkness. i
miss facing my sun and saying good morning.

Love Poem: Chimera

I thought myself lion and serpent. Thought
myself body enough for two, for we.
Found comfort in never being lonely.

What burst from my back, from my bones, what lived
along the ridge from crown to crown, from mane
to forked tongue beneath the skin. What clamor

we made in the birthing. What hiss and rumble
at the splitting, at the horns and beard,
at the glottal bleat. What bridges our back.

What strong neck, what bright eye. What menagerie
are we. What we've made of ourselves.

Young Male

You sat quietly across the subway aisle . . .
raucous thunder howling in your throat,
thunder which would gag the breeze in mine.
Your tight fists are caked with sludge of cement;
hands which would slaughter six million buffalo
on the range if there were six million buffalo.
Instead, you build nuclear reactors.

Your hair is soft and loose, sports a blonde sheen;
hazel eyes send out suspicious messages,
afraid I'll scalp those flowing locks
tearing the bloody membrane from your head.
You squat on the subway seat like a mountainman
of the old as-yet-unconquered West, a green blade
ready to skin beaver or any cuss you don't much like
the crook of his jaw. Your thighs bulge, your heavy arms
are thick with electrical power of whips.
I wonder if there is a smile in your soul.
Can you bend to sniff a violet?
I doubt you'd scent anything but a double
whiskey, a hooker on the curb, your hunting boots,
your own rawness.
                    Your face is not ugly
nor does it appear particularly mean, even
those hazel eyes don't seem too cruel, but when I look
at those hands knotted in a crisp clench
I know you would crush me on a whim
for you are, America . . .
not the land, the rivers, mountains, desert or sky,
not hawk or wolf. You are the superhighways,
skyscrapers, acid streams clogged with dead rainbows and
you are Gary, Indiana; downtown L.A., Burger King,
"adult bookstores," Ronald Reagan, New Jersey
that stole the Giants and now teases the American Exchange.

Your prowess rumbles as the subway slides through
the harbor tunnel to Bowling Green Station;
when the doors open, you stand. I'm amazed to see
how short you are, shorter than me by an inch or two,
but bulky in rump and flank. We ascend the escalator;
you tramp off towards Broad Street; I amble to the Post
Office in the old Cunard Building to send letters home.
I know you are here to stay
and that you are scouting buffalo.

Conservation & Rehabilitation

Because we want to take pictures of bears and moose
without actually coming near them—though
already I have called to you, unloading groceries
from the car, when a cow and her calf clopped down
our street, taller than I thought, and faster, too—because
we want to look like *real Alaskans* to those East Coast
city slickers, those smog-breathers, those subway-riders,
our friends back home, we drive down the only highway
to the Center where, every five minutes for the duration
of our visit, we hear the eerie shrieks of the elk, calling
for one another in urgent lust, which at first I decide is
the angry scream of a small girl throwing a tantrum
in five-minute intervals but which Wikipedia
informs me is "one of the most distinctive sounds
in nature, akin to the howl of the gray wolf." And later,
when we learn from a colorful sign that females are attracted
to the elk that bugle the loudest and most often, I sympathize
more with the elk and with the caribou, too, locking
their antlers into one another because everyone in this Center
is in love, including me, because when I stare at you staring
at a muddy bison sleeping pressed flush against the wire
of her fence, and when I see your mouth move, and then
later, before I put my mouth on you, when I ask what you talked
with the bison about, you say *We understood each other*, which
I take to mean:

      Bison: *There is nowhere for me to be safe*
      Woman I love: *I have been your kind*
          [an elk shrieks]

Love, let's be the black bears that refuse our sirloin
steaks, turning our noses up to the Lead Naturalist,
or the intern—whoever is feeding us that day—waiting
patiently for a handful of frozen berries flung into
our yard. Let's be those bears who come when called,
eat our fill of this land, then pad back together into
the thick brush, trying to be as wild as we still can.

Sweet Briar

Today, my cusp. I have hit full bloom. Already you can feel me close, on my way back to you. You cannot see what rose is at my lips or where its tender arbors in my hair, white, soft as banana. Today, I am glutted with gloss. Today, anything I don't like I call postmodern. *Go inside a stone*, that would be your way. I am wandering the woodlots of childhood. No one knew then what to call the hatched vines snaking up these trunks like a hair shirt. But the pauses I remember, when the country lane gladdened the shed summer light or when the brown water disappeared under oak. Oak large as mountains. It is a wonder any one of us survived. I hid in the lilacs, their voluptuous violet shade, the cool dirt underneath I would dig my hands in. My people, or "kind grandparents of the corn and sun" have all but disappeared from the fields. We had a pact, much like the one I think I've made with you. Hey, day-dream, though the boys were harsh and cornered us. Though our mothers didn't protect the girls. We love those girls, would fill our lives with them.

A Little Bit of Ocean

Children squat on a float in the middle of the water.
The half-grown deer disappears

into a stand of juniper and bulrush. We know shells
were once alive, but it's hard to imagine

what stones once lived. Hard to be a creature of earth
in a world covered with water. I'm not worried

about being happy. I wanted to feel:
Mission accomplished.

I wanted to recognize the shadow I cast,
to cast more light than shadow. My daughter and I

reach the buoys that hold the rope afloat. Beneath us,
darkness, pushing up.

Perianth

By far the best farmers

lovers are

whose bodies glisten in the light they make

and throw so carelessly around them in molten afternoons.

Husbandry

is what it takes to make the world splash in our heads

exploding water light

so nothing's unhinged,

the far-fetched pleasure.

By fostering

the greenness comes again,

new arising,

flower world,

sweetness suck,

of naked verity.

Afternoons are molten because melting is consequence
of whatever passionate perception: without fusing them, the
Flower-of-Mind makes all things capable of extremity, not adjectival,

concentering,

as that toy lovers like us melt

reform

in solar innovation,

our substances now justified anew,

made accurate by bliss,

a balance,

a tempering,

a style.

Perianth is the word I wrote

meaning the sepals and the petals

to remind me of the floral unity of love

and also how we double on ourselves the world

when our bodies shoot

and the heavens open:

how we suffice each other in ourselves.

Breathing You In

The scent you say is no scent
rises from warm ports
between neck and shoulder.
Scent that isn't witch hazel, vetiver, camphor, lemon,
but is just your skin,
raises a breeze on mine, unpredicted
as freshness I found in woods
where a few blond leaves hung from twigs.
Sweet sharpness,
scent of something still to come,
something soaked in—
chlorine on the cedar deck your thigh presses,
foot drifting in water,
eyes yellow amber behind closed lids.
Soaked in like sun
in the river whose cold silk
wrapped your body in August,
opened dark folds around you.
Closed, opened, around you.

Self-Portrait with Scoliosis (II)

Warping
    fallow
   form
     encroaching
       upon what is
           meant to
             be vivid

a snarl
  gnarling at
    the root of
       things
      a mute
      engendering

   because arguments
   avail him
     nothing but

porous   conditions
      yawning
     between vertebrae
    longing for
      more than
        this body

selfish by
    design or
       like the climbing ivy
        too ambitious
        for its own
        good

can a jut then be
   lovely for what it
      longs to be

A Southern Wind

Quiet as a seed, and as guarded,
our walking took the shape of two people
uneasy together. I had the feeling
that on the anxious incline of that hill we gave the hill
one reason for being. What loneliness, what
privacy was in that? *Hey*, I said. *Race me to the top?*
Then is when I nearly tripped on the sly earth,
an earth shaping to itself again. A stone?
But, no, picking it up, bringing the wormed-through
black flesh of it to my height, I knew it for
an apple and gnashed and let the juices freak and down
my face. Don't ask me why I did it. I know.
I know there are poisons like these we have
to feed each other, promises we try to hold—though
how can they be contained? I wanted to give you
what I could of me. To be personal, without
confession. I wanted to believe in the constancy of that hill.
Daylight was tiring. The air, secret, alone.
I won, you said. *You did*, I said. So we stood there.

Amphibians

In Greek, *amphibian* means
"on both sides of life."

As in: amphibians live
on land and in water.

As in: immigrants leave
lands and cross waters.

While amphibians lay
shell-less eggs,

immigrants give birth
to Americans.

In water, gilled tadpoles
sprout limbs. On land

amphibians develop lungs.
Immigrants develop lungs.

Breathe in pine, fuel
and cold atmosphere.

Amphibians' damp
skin oxygenates.

Immigrants toil
and slumber deathly.

Their colors brighten.
They camouflage.

They've been known to fall
out of the sky.

Completely at home
in the rain.

Love Two Times

There are lovers and then there are thorns and thorny lovers

Who put their fists through walls Who goblin out when dinner is left cold

Lovers tall as moon beams Some with ribs full of spite My lover

Who wears houses on her head My lover who kisses ringworms

My chinny-chin-chin itches with her rancor and ways of barter

Good instead and Not good enough Pennies in my mouth

Yes Yes in my bed until the fright runs out No I will not

Ghost I will not leave when morning comes I have known lovers

Who waste my poor bloat with tinny sounds They come and go

What I want is the green ponder of The door left open but love stays

Love makes red patterns in my scalp Love remembers blood like flower

Thunder Cake

In the jar without air holes
Alabama
bayou stale

Auntie who is kin to me and
Auntie who is kin to you
are preserved like peaches
together
in their own sweetness

raindrops drizzle

Auntie who is kin to me
opens windows
Auntie who is kin to you
turns the dial with one finger until it clicks
to hush the whispering radio

dark clouds seep through their kitchen
moistening the sack of sugar
humid sugar clings together

Auntie is glistening with Crisco
Auntie is doused in flour

the cake
is cooling

rain comes down in silky gray patches
Auntie who is kin to me and
Auntie who is kin to you
step outside
screen doors swing behind them

smacking door frames
applauding thunder

red clay becomes smooth between toes
loosening their aprons
they step out of their light summer dresses

fragile faces lifted to the wet warmth
droplets roll from dreary rumbling tongues
like sincere compliments

rain saturates their thin slips
flowing over shoulders

pooling in clavicles

puddles splash and splatter their calves
with crimson clay
Auntie who is kin to me and
Auntie who is kin to you
return to their kitchen

to put the icing on the Thunder Cake

I Came

in your mouth and felt the season's first frost
spreading fast across every windshield in town,
each leaf surrendering its voice to a chorus
that swelled beneath the ground. Or was it death
asking you to kneel before the fountain of my groin
and drink in all of our days with parted lips
to the end of your desire? There were no words
in your mouth, only a river swiftly taking us down.

poem to my boyfriend's human immunodeficiency virus

you are not related to the bowerbird
nor crow nor any bird noted for magnificent plumage
you are not paradisaea apoda, not paradise minor
the king you are not
you are not a place where you can hear live jazz
seven days a week
you are not an island native

you are a shy bloomer
with neither petal nor sepal
not tough, not easily grown
not tolerant of his soil

you are not a family resort
dedicated to making a truly pleasurable vacation
not prized for dramatic display
you are not a charming villa
located on the hillside of bordeaux
you are not a small bird very near the beach

you are not a must
you are not fast growing
you are not a boat

you are forgotten, sterile
not licensed or insured
to cater our parties
you are not more of a bush not even a seed
you are not wild and free
you are not the cinematic equivalent
of one of those island falls

you are closed until further notice
you are not poised to soar

to heights in joyful praise
you are not easily seen from a treetop
you are not reliably evergreen

Coal

I
Is the total black, being spoken
From the earth's inside.
There are many kinds of open.
How a diamond comes into a knot of flame
How a sound comes into a word, coloured
By who pays what for speaking.

Some words are open
Like a diamond on glass windows
Singing out within the crash of passing sun
Then there are words like stapled wagers
In a perforated book—buy and sign and tear apart—
And come whatever wills all chances
The stub remains
An ill-pulled tooth with a ragged edge.
Some words live in my throat
Breeding like adders. Others know sun
Seeking like gypsies over my tongue
To explode through my lips
Like young sparrows bursting from shell.
Some words
Bedevil me.

Love is a word another kind of open—
As a diamond comes into a knot of flame
I am black because I come from the earth's inside
Take my word for jewel in your open light.

Falling, Falling, Then Rain, Then Snow

Time's sharpened her, me
Edged to a precipice, edged over, edged in,
Falling, falling, then rain, then snow.

I wake in disequilibrium untethered
By left, no north nor theory.
The double helix of her and me unravels,

Years of coils, unruly coils of years.
Some greater genetics codes
The helical arrangement of our souls

Then easily unzips us.
We understand this arrangement
To be physical. Now I am a single strand

Not even I myself can read. I am alerted,
But falter, to replicate a twinning
String of sense but my signals

Will not tune in, elemental
Letters won't hook up, won't
Mean. Nothing means.

Grotesque

Why do the lilies goggle their tongues at me
When I pluck them;
And write, and twist,
And strangle themselves against my fingers,
So that I can hardly weave the garland
For your hair?
Why do they shriek your name
And spit at me
When I would cluster them?
Must I kill them
To make them lie still,
And send you a wreath of lolling corpses
To turn putrid and soft
On your forehead
While you dance?

Viscous

You find it after summer rains, amoebic sores
of yellow and orange on rolled bales of hay,
slime molds climbing the mounds of dead pasture.

Being a boy, being eight or ten, you call it
monkey vomit. Being a boy, and older than him,
you dare your brother to touch the stuff: *touch it.*

It doesn't quiver; you think it should. It glistens
and spreads, it waits. It palms the hay, caresses
the moist rot. *Why are you afraid?*

It will dry to a crust, fade to stain, disintegrate
in a dust of dry spore, like the semen
on your lover's body, viscous, glistening, briefly

alive——is it 1988? and if he were positive?
It's 1998. He is not your brother. You touch
the crust on slope of belly, thin crust like sugar,

taste like salt. Scrape it off, wonder is it yours, or his.

Dove Season

September, Mississippi: the breeze was like convection,
insects went on wailing in the trees,
        a crescendo as consistent as the sun.
My father had his gun, and I had mine propped at my side.

Years later we would nearly come to blows:
        he must have felt he failed to raise a son.
It wasn't even anger in his eyes.

Back then, I sat beside him on the edge of that corn field,
waiting for a single dove
            to interrupt the blue.
And when at last it came, the bird dipped down and landed
        on a mound of dirt, twenty feet from us.

My father leaned my way and whispered:
                Be a man and pull the trigger.
      So I brought the gun up quickly, clicked the safety, fired
        into the ground.
Once the dust and smoke had cleared away,
           there was nothing left but a glaring hole
           neither one of us could name.

[Dear one, the sea . . .]

Dear one, the sea smells of nostalgia. We're beached and bloated, lie
on shell sand, oil rigs nowhere seen. It's Long Island, and the weather
is fine. What to disturb in the heart of a man?

A boy is not a body. A boy is a walk.

Shed the machine.
Must be entirely flesh to fight.
Must be strategy instead of filling.

What to disrobe, there, centrifugal logic, as in here is a slice of my
finger. Tell me the circumstance of your dick extension. When we
slip into imprecision, we lose control, windowless walls close in.
Awareness of being in a female body is a tinge of regret. "The human
frame to adapt itself to convention though she herself was a woman."
To receive, to be entered, to fret around upon entry. It's grand. I'm a
system. Plants tall as wheat to hide in.

The Way the World Comes Back

When did you notice it was no longer winter?
Skin sloughing away after the dry cold?
Or the moment you shed
the heavy coat you wear against the world?

This paring down is no small matter.
The urge to crack and cast away
the shell the body forged from years of grief.
The way the knife can't help but slip
and so much of the work must be done at twilight.

But what if the world came back?
Even in miniature or scarred.
Lush green or bruised yellow.
Wind strong enough to lift feather or leaf,
unravel the long scarf from your throat,

to sweep the dust from stone,
uncover bone or story.
What if your stone heart turned to salt?
What if it turned to water
and roared through your body like an ocean?

My Sideshow

Summers during the Eisenhower years, a carnival
Came to town. From my father's pair of bleacher seats,
The safety net under the Big Top's star attractions,
The drugged tiger, the stilted clowns, the farting scooters
All seemed as little death-defying as those routines
The high-wire trio staged with their jerky parasols.

With that singular lack of shame only a kid commands,
I'd sneak over instead to the sawdusted sideshow tent.
Every year *they* were back: the fire-breathing women,
The men who swallowed scimitars or hammered nails
Up their noses and fishhooks through their tongues,
The dwarf in his rayon jockstrap and sequined sweatband,

A buck got you into the blow-off where a tapered grind
Spieled the World of Wonders while a blanket rose
On seven clear ten-gallon jars that held
Pickled fetuses—real or rubber?—their limbs
Like ampersands, each with something deliriously wrong,
Too little of this in front or too much of that behind.

Four-legged chickens, a two-headed raccoon,
The Mule-Faced Girl, the Man with Four Pupils
In His Eyes, coffined devil babies, the Penguin Boy,
The Living Skeleton, an avuncular thousand-pound
Sort who swilled cans of soda and belched at us . . .
What I think of the Word Made Flesh developed in this darkroom.

Back then I couldn't wait for hair to appear on my face
And down below, where my flashlight scrutinized at bedtime.
I'd rise and fall by chance, at the table, on buses, in class.
My voice cracked. I was shooting up and all thumbs.
Oh, the restless embarrassments of late childhood!
My first pimple—huge and lurid—had found its place.

I kept staring at one jar. The thing inside seemed to float
Up from a fishtail that was either leg or penis—or both.
(I could hear my father now, outside the tent, calling me.)
From its mouth, a pair of delicate legs emerged,
As if it had swallowed a perfect twin. I gulped. Something
Unspoken, then and since, rose like acid in my throat.

ANNE HAVEN McDONNELL

Coming Out in the Ozarks

The truck beds lined
with dead squirrels parked
along the one-room post office—

The yawn and teeth of that
long silence, creaking floorboards,
a rocking chair adjusts.

All eyes stay down—
the men in overalls stare at their feet,
the woman fidgets behind the counter.

A tiny bloom spread through
my chest, the whine and creak
of my footsteps across that room.

Outside, you wait in the car
like a sunrise, thickening
my voice at the counter,

My freshly shaved head,
a new animal in your hands.
I don't know what I said—

Back at our farm, you pour
candlewax, cover each tiny bite
the raccoon left in every winter squash.

That year we ripened
with seeds we spread to dry
on clean white paper in the barn.

All that knowing condensed
in hard tiny bodies—
we blew away the rest.

I Know My Soul

I plucked my soul out of its secret place,
And held it to the mirror of my eye,
To see it like a star against the sky,
A twitching body quivering in space,
A spark of passion shining on my face.
And I explored it to determine why
This awful key to my infinity
Conspires to rob me of sweet joy and grace.
And if the sign may not be fully read,
If I can comprehend but not control,
I need not gloom my days with futile dread,
Because I see a part and not the whole.
Contemplating the strange, I'm comforted
By this narcotic thought: I know my soul.

Dear Canaries

Thank you for sending the sparrow
emissary

        to remind me of space
and to encourage light.

          I miss your singing
voices and consequently mornings.

             Routine
is now too much about myself. The cage

sits there.   Insists that I'm an animal.
That I need to travel.

América

The river was deep & wide.

Wild girls grew along

the riverbanks. Wild strawberries grew

among the wet grass. A girl tramped barefoot.

Her tips arrowed. The tracks wept

in the distance. She scavenged

wild strawberries. The river water stung her mouth.

The water turned her skin sky. Alone

the girl knelt to sift water

through her fingers. There was once a dock

with a wooden boat. Once a general.

Once a sister. Once a mother who hid

behind the general. Once a machete.

Once a girl who swallowed the salt.

She held the resonance of chromatic

harmony. The quiet of faded mist.

The lines of riverbank made everything still.

The girl understood the river's undying blue.

The river of uncut red flowers. The river

                flooded &

          drowned. Once a sodden hummingbird.

Once a lone foal. The girl was not allowed

             to speak Spanish. The girl wore a garland

of speech. She found she was only half

             of everything. Half of her mother.

The general took her downriver.

                  Scavenging.

             The wild strawberries. It was spring.

           The strawberries were held below ice.

It was winter. The general commanded

          her to lie down. The pain

was a thud of a knife & boot blade

             deep in the hull of her hips.

The girl left her body. Her spirit rose.

She herself became the crumpled shape

of a saturated bow. The river

created a halo of sound.

She still held a strawberry in her hand.

She looked like a perfect crumpled bow.

She was lying on the ground.

She thought she was lying on the sky.

The quiet of the faded mist.

The lines of riverbank made everything kill.

The girl wanted to escape the undying blue.

The girl was only half of her mother. The girl was

strong against tide. The girl learned

to forget. The girl was nothing but water.

She lay on the sky.

For Two Lovers in the Year 2075 in the Canadian Woods

If you have lips and forests,
you creatures years from now,
here are some lines to tell you
that we were among your trees
in extraordinary flesh
and ecstasy now gone,
and our tongues looked for each other
and after that for words.

If you have August moonrise
and bodies to undress,
here are some words we've left you
when we had had our say.
Put them beside your cummings,
if you still carry books,
not as sweet as Landor,
not as quick as Donne,
wrap them in still-warm clothing
beside your sleeping bag
for when you want to speak.

These trees are stirred by ghosting,
not only ours but others'.
Enjoy the feathery presences,
no sadder than our own,
they gather from the past—
last August's moan and whisper,
the leaves renew the weavings
and lacings of the flesh.
Here is the sound of ours.

The Lovers

They met in loving like the hands of one
Who having worked six days with creature and plant
Washes his hands before the evening meal.
Reflected in a basin out-of-doors
The golden sky receives his hands beneath
Its coldly wishing surface, washes them

Of all perhaps but what of one another
Each with its five felt perceptions holds:
A limber warmth, fitness of palm and nail
So long articulate in his mind before
Plunged into happening, that all the while
Water laps and loves the stirring hands

His eye has leisure for the young fruit-trees
And lowing beasts secure, since night is near,
Pasture, lights of a distant town, and sky
Molten, atilt, strewn on new water, sky
In which for a last fact he dips his face
And lifts it glistening: what dark distinct

Reflections of his features upon gold!
—Except for when each slow slight water-drop
He sensed on chin and nose accumulate,
Each tiny world of sky reversed and branches,
Fell with its pure wealth to mar the image:
World after world fallen into the sky

And still so much world left when, by the fire
With fingers clasped, he set in revolution
Certitude and chance like strong slow thumbs;
Or read from an illuminated page
Of harvest, flood, motherhood, mystery:
These waited, and would issue from his hands.

Sonnet XI

I shall forget you presently, my dear,
So make the most of this, your little day,
Your little month, your little half a year,
Ere I forget, or die, or move away,
And we are done forever; by and by
I shall forget you, as I said, but now,
If you entreat me with your loveliest lie
I will protest you with my favorite vow.
I would indeed that love were longer-lived,
And vows were not so brittle as they are,
But so it is, and nature has contrived
To struggle on without a break thus far—
Whether or not we find what we are seeking
Is idle, biologically speaking.

Eating a Mountain

You stand in the kitchen, cut
up a buck that a friend
shot for us. I watch you trim,
slice, decide: this is stir fry,
this is steak, this is stew.
These are treats for long-suffering
dogs on the porch, panting. Oh,

we are rich! I rinse, pack,
mark the cuts, this beautiful
deep red velvety offering.
Eating this deer means
eating this mountain:
acorns, ash, beech, dogwood,
maple, oak, willow, autumn olive;

means devouring witch hazel, pine,
lichens, mushrooms, wild grape,
fiddleheads, honeysuckle,
poison ivy, crown vetch,
clover; means nibbling wild onion,
ragweed, beggar's lice, Junegrass,
raspberry cane, paw-paws,

crispy green chickweed,
and so you give the meat
your most honest attention,
dedicate your sharpest blade—
carve up that deer with gratitude,
artistry, prayer, render a wild, sacred animal
into wild, sacred sustenance.

How we eat this deer is a debt
that comes due on the day
we let this mountain
eat us.

SUSANNA J. MISHLER

Hemispheres

His half is smaller,
his yellow wing
darker on its leading edge.

Her wing splays large,
also yellow,
a small triangular tear

in its trialing rim.
Both wings veined
like a river delta,

both misted with
black ovals as if someone
flicked ink on them

as they flapped by.
Their brown is the brown
of an overripe banana—

camouflage for fall leaves.
His antenna fans,
eyebrow-like,

hers a smooth, penciled arch.
Say the letter
p into your palm and that

whisper is how their body
feels, perched
on your hand.

Their fleeced head, thorax,
abdomen fuse
them together:

male on left, female on right.
Two sovereign hemispheres
operate a moth body.

This never happens
to us, our hormones
make other

mistakes. Even if it could,
we're cross-wired:
female brain would flex

male thigh, male brain
would extend female bicep.
The man with mincing

walk, the woman with
cocky shoulders would then
somehow negotiate

to walk themselves
as a single person,
to the store, at first, for oranges

that they take home,
peel at the kitchen table
and feed to each other,

sticky juice
dripping
down their chin.

The Complete Tracker

Bent-kneed, interpreting signs
  I trek the wreckage of myths:
toadstools on a felled tree, or

the crescent-shaped impression
  from a hart's escape to his denning
ground. His hoof print is a split heart.

As a phantasm you wander
  a remote path. Lost, I open
the guidebook, its spine rolls.

It reads, *Examine closely the leaf-strewn*
  forest floor on the way to low-
lying shorelines. Every creature

that moves on earth leaves
  a mark of its passing,
though the trails are seldom linear.

I may never find my way back—
  Your prints canter northward
where in a blue jumper and wild hair you said,

After the rut, bucks lose interest.
  Trailing anyone proves a gamble on wet clay.
You folded your route scribbled on

a diner's placemat and left.
  Now your voice is placeless,
a coyote howl in velvet.

Your footprints are covered over
  by leaves and other men's heavy soles.

Shared Plight

Bound to whims,
bred solely for
circuses of desire.
To hell with savannahs,
towns like Rosewood.

Domestics or domesticated,
one name or surnamed, creatures
the dominant ones can't live without
would truly flourish
without such devious love,
golden corrals.

Harnessed. Muzzled.
Stocks & bonds. Chains
& whips held by hand.
Ota Benga in a Bronx cage,
Saartjie Baartman on display—
funds sent to her village
didn't make it okay. Harambe,
Tamir, Cecil, Freddie—names
of the hunted, captives
bleed together. The captors
beasts to all but themselves
& their own.

Two endangered beings in a moat
stare into each other's eyes.

Slower than light, mercy
must not survive entry
into our atmosphere, never
reaching those who lose
unbridled lives

long before they die
in this world of zoos
& conquerors who treat
earthlings like aliens.

Real Curvature

Your sense arose in me before it arose in landscape

I felt a variance inside

As if you could shine light on a field and illuminate

rain darkening the redwoods

My downward window with trees an aura nearer

than you were in the past

Before I knew my own sense of dissipation,

landscape was a line of rain and moving branches

As if the whole depth together was my own motion

rising inside the hollow bark of the tree

One motion only, a line is a wave of feeling

Who measures what's outside before she leaves

Hawk like a Steeple

Sitting at the crest of Waterworks Hill
we decided we'd never get married.
I spread my arms to say *just this.*
You'd already left every home for me.

It was the most Quaker wedding,
simple, you and me in our coats
looking south over a new April
stranger town. Held a branch
behind your back like a bone,
ate strands of each other's hair—
no ring or witness. Rainless sky.

Our mothers want us to be mothers
and your father, who has been so dead,
is not dead to me. I tell him quietly
that I won't have you be anyone's wife.
Silence can't help but sing the coal trains
in their couplings through the valley.

He Says, Oyster

Tongue's
pleasure like the torture artist's
cleft in two: at Tricks

he says he won't eat
seafood that reminds him
of a woman's *down-there*. Her *what?*

Who saying *oyster*
grimaces? As if he weren't
tasting his final

fulsome morsel. As if he
weren't one of us
cowering with delight

remembering the ceremony
when we liked *how*
we were loved. As one

taking the other's
enemy skin in. Enjoying
the tonguing, fingering & being

himself the oyster
sucked clean of
salt & warm lemon,

entered
& stolen from
& used. Another man's

rough mouth at these tinged wet
edges, vulnerable & wrinkled
lying in succulent

mignonette. Labial
& tough ribbon. Heat's
black-gummed house—

A plate of mouths
& the imagined accusation of so
many heated, pulsing silences . . .

His self-loathing
loathes me. *Try,*
I said. *Say, oyster. Pocket of Oil. Heart's*

Carafe. The wine
spilled with laughter
& shame, but I'm serious—

Enjoy it with your eyes
closed. It's homesick,
but say, *Mother—*

Muscle of Love, Little Moist & Plosive
Purple, Morbid Mouth . . . Vampiric
Lyric, Lingering . . .

For aren't these silken
oysters also
dying like him?

It can't hurt
to say it, for your own sake.
Now, here. *Taste.*

EILEEN MYLES

[I always put my pussy]

I always put my pussy
in the middle of trees
like a waterfall
like a doorway to God
like a flock of birds
I always put my lover's cunt
on the crest
of a wave
like a flag
that I can
pledge my
allegiance
to. This is my
country. Here,
when we're alone
in public.
My lover's pussy
is a badge
is a night stick
is a helmet
is a deer's face
is a handful
of flowers
is a waterfall
is a river
of blood
is a bible
is a hurricane
is a soothsayer.
My lover's pussy
is a battle cry
is a prayer
is lunch
is wealthy

is happy
is on teevee
has a sense of humor
has a career
has a cup of coffee
goes to work
meditates
is always alone
knows my face
knows my tongue
knows my hands
is an alarmist
has lousy manners
knows her mind

I always put
my pussy in the middle
of trees
like a waterfall
a piece of jewelry
that I wear
on my chest
like a badge
in America
so my lover & I
can be safe.

For the Era of Extraordinary Weather

You and I choose the worlds we want, devour novels
about utopias, super-heroes, space colonization, cyborgs,

evolutionary leaps and hijinks within the quantum fabric.
Outside, the downspouts can hardly contain the rain, which

falls like a beneficence after months of drought. We step
across new urban rivers, quotidian flotsam afloat in the

burlesque of the gutter, and wonder what we'd do if the air
fell so far from its rhythms that we had to start over, retreat

to some skeletal shack in the desert while distant skylines
went black against orange conflagration. We've seen too many

movies about how that last bang or whimper could befall us,
too many epics where lovers, outcasts and all the left-behinds

pull each other through the end times. Yesterday we watched
startling news about a weird thunderhead over Costa Rica, how

it gleamed with a luminous, iridescent crown, like a rainbow
inside of a bubble, an anomaly beautiful but foreboding,

under which the locals crossed themselves and said a prayer
in the hope of preserving the world. We want to save it too,

even if the next day dawns with mutants popping up like
grotesque Darwinian jack-in-the-boxes, sudden alien eyes

regarding us under the old sun. In all of our favorite cinema fables
a once reliable law goes haywire, jumps out of the natural order:

a gargantuan reptile ravages cities; planets careen toward
collision; *The Incredible Shrinking Man* fends off threats from

inside a house that's become a huge cabinet of menace;
the populace flees the *Fifty-Foot Woman*'s car-hefting fury.

We smile at the outlandish and you say, *I don't think gigantism
works that way*, as we move through another day in a world

where enough real monsters manage to rise. We try to keep faith
that the state of affairs will still hold entropy at bay, and I

remember how I stood, a child among my congregation, fervent
in the prayer that we raised toward the ceiling, our chant and

our hope going up to what might be a waiting God,
world without end, Amen.

Changeling

Standing in front of a mirror, my mother tells me she is ugly
says the medication is making her fat. I laugh & walk her
back to the bed. My mother tells me she is ugly in the same voice
she used to say *no woman could love you* & I watch her
pull at her body & it is mine. My heavy breast.
My disappointing shape. She asks for a bowl of plain broth
& it becomes the cup of vinegar she would pour down my throat.
Everyday after school, I would kneel before her.
I would remove my clothes & ask her to mark the progress.
It's important that I mention, I truly wanted to be beautiful
for her. In my dreams I am thin & if not thin, something better.
I tell my mother she is still beautiful & she laughs. The room fills
with flies. They gather in the shape of a small boy. They lead her
back to the mirror, but my reflection is still there.

On Trans

The process of through is ongoing.

The earth doesn't seem to move, but sometimes we fall
down against it and seem to briefly alight on its turning.

We were just going. I was just leaving,
            which is to say, coming
elsewhere. Transient. I was going as I came, the words
            move through my limbs, lungs,   mouth, as I appear to sit

peacefully at your hearth   transubstantiating some wine.
            It was a rough red,   it was one of those nights we were not
forced by circumstances   to drink wine out of mugs.
Circumstances being, in those cases, no one had been

transfixed at the kitchen sink long enough   to wash dishes.
            I brought armfuls of wood   from the splitting stump.
Many of them, because it was cold,   went right on top
            of their recent ancestors.   It was an ice night.

They transpired visibly,   resin to spark,
            bark to smoke, wood to ash.   I was
transgendering and drinking   the rough red at roughly
            the same rate   and everyone who looked, saw.

The translucence of flames   beat against the air
            against our skins.   This can be done with
or without clothes on.   This can be done with
            or without wine or whiskey   but never without water:

evaporation is also ongoing.   Most visibly in this case
            in the form of wisps of steam   rising from the just washed hair
of a form at the fire whose beauty was   in the earth's
            turning, that night and many nights,   transcendent.

I felt heat changing me.   The word for this is

          transdesire, but in extreme cases   we call it *transdire*

or when this heat becomes your maker we say

          transire, or when it happens   in front of a hearth:

transfire.

To You

What is more beautiful than night
and someone in your arms
that's what we love about art
it seems to prefer us and stays

if the moon or a gasping candle
sheds a little light or even dark
you become a landscape in a landscape
with rocks and craggy mountains

and valleys full of sweaty ferns
breathing and lifting into the clouds
which have actually come low
as a blanket of aspirations' blue

for once not a melancholy color
because it is looking back at us
there's no need for vistas we are one
in the complicated foreground of space

the architects are most courageous
because it stands for all to see
and for a long time just as
the words "I'll always love you"

impulsively appear in the dark sky
and we are happy and stick by them
like a couple of painters in neon allowing
the light to glow there over the river

Wild Geese

You do not have to be good.
You do not have to walk on your knees
for a hundred miles through the desert repenting.
You only have to let the soft animal of your body
    love what it loves.
Tell me about despair, yours, and I will tell you mine.
Meanwhile the world goes on.
Meanwhile the sun and the clear pebbles of the rain
are moving across the landscapes,
over the prairies and the deep trees,
the mountains and the rivers.
Meanwhile the wild geese, high in the clean blue air,
are heading home again.
Whoever you are, no matter how lonely,
the world offers itself to your imagination,
calls to you like the wild geese, harsh and exciting—
over and over announcing your place
in the family of things.

Three times on the trail, I looked back for you

At the corner where the pines beam
with Christmas bulbs,
it began snowing,

and the next turn, the sky went blue.
I had almost forgotten
the darkness, how it smolders

with depth. Say weight. Say raven. It vanished
just as quickly—gray an incantation
over the brush

and hillside, snow gray, lung gray, ice terse
across the rink, ice plating the inlet.
Say it another way.

The water pooling thin lakes above
your collarbone, steam rising into
the towels, soft

scrape of your skis laying track
along the path behind me.

Toward

Toward a flower-
ing I came

lowly lupine raised
wrist

a loop of memory and its variable
eye

the deer coming closer—

Out of she
to you

how many sights
circle absence

the hollow and lake

how many transfigure
positioned against

the ear of my ear and the ghost
of the ear

Thrush

The Central Park Rambles
rush with bird songs
trickling through pines,
a kind of uncovering, a lifting off of stones.

Last year Jay was harassed here,
for cruising, by an officer of the law:
"What's the matter, pretty boy—AIDS got your tongue?"

Jay held his ground in silence,
projecting himself into the unexpected music
of a distant hermit thrush,
a rare bird rarely heard to sing.

This year, Jay is in St. Luke's
with a case of thrush that makes it
hard for him to speak.
The yellow fungus on his lips
makes him look like a fledgling,
open-mouthed, awaiting the arrival
of a saving grace poised in the air
between talons of light.

Propped up in bed, between sips of soda
from a straw, he rambles about "apocalypse ecology,"
gesturing at the evidence, a nest
of Newsday clippings: dogs
leaping from high rises, disappearing frogs,
and the drastic decline of song birds in America.

Throat swelled with sphagnum,
legs cracked to the texture of red birch,
head increasingly in the clouds—
so he is becoming the tree of his own falling life,

a favorite of the minor gods:
north side moss,
south side hardened bark,
sensation unpeeling from his limbs like leaves.

Radiance versus Ordinary Light

Meanwhile the sea moves uneasily, like a man who
suspects what the room reels with as he rises into it
is violation—his own: he touches the bruises at each
shoulder and, on his chest,

                  the larger bruise, star-shaped,
a flawed star, or hand, though he remembers no hands,
has tried—can't remember . . .

                    That kind of rhythm to it,
even to the roughest surf there's a rhythm findable,
which is why we keep coming here, to find it, or that's
what we say. We dive in and, as usual,

                    the swimming
feels like that swimming the mind does in the wake
of transgression, how the instinct to panic at first
slackens that much more quickly, if you don't
look back. Regret,

             like pity, changes nothing really, we
say to ourselves and, less often, to each other, each time
swimming a bit farther,

                leaving the shore the way
the water—in its own watered, of course, version
of semaphore—keeps leaving the subject out, flashing
Why should it matter now and *Why,*

                  why shouldn't it,
as the waves beat harder, hard against us, until that's
how we like it, I'll break your heart, break mine.

Nature Poem with a Compulsive Attraction to the Shark

the hive swells outside
as its residents itch to lick our inner walls

for moisture and respite

from January's cold appendages
                    nature   having thrummed
on its own
blood and grace for millennia

until ours—a short tailored tenure
a blip in comparison to the shark

more ancient than flora
killing only to feed

moving so it will not die
it wants only what the sea has brined

the shark does not know
                    implication

violence fades to nimbus
depletes blue to red the tides

where pleas parch the lips of tempest
the terror in the land the terror at sea

on the eve of our industrial revolution
made weapon of hungry thing

I've heard this slave
song before

boats from across the ocean escorting
these mature predators in swarms

mouths that hungered about

                    the taste of slaves

men and the sharks parting at shore
shaking with a taste for each other

turning the word with every tide
the currents lap at my latent limb

every volta America wrote
                    for me had teeth

                    won't you allow me now
to lift my lip and show you mine

[This white guy asks do I feel more connected to nature]

This white guy asks do I feel more connected to nature
bc I'm NDN
asks did I live *like in a regular house*
growing up on the rez
or something more salt
of the earth, something reedy
says it's hot do I have any rain
ceremonies

When I express frustration, he says *what?* He says *I'm just asking* as if
being earnest somehow absolves him from being fucked up.

It does not.

He says *I can't win with you*
because he already did
because he always will
because he could write a nature
poem, or anything he wants, he doesn't understand

why I can't write a fucking nature
poem.

Later when he is fucking
me I bite him on the cheek draw
blood I reify savage lust

Migration

Last night when you lowered your body down
on top of me, I thought of the monarchs
at the tops of pine trees in Mexico.
It was high in the mountains.
I'd been gone from home for a long time.
I stood in the pine forest and listened
to the thick body of those butterflies.
Heavy in the trees. The limbs
clotted as with snow. Monarch on top of
monarch and the outer wings shifting
to keep position. Some sort of pulse in the trees.
As if breath itself had taken on a body.

Landscape with Lymphatic System, System of Rivulets, System of Rivers

My body, when did you amble down
   from the levee, begin to wade

with no bead head midgefly or green glitter jig
to flick, quick winglet, at the end of translucent line

nor noontime college bake party
   along the weed-slumped banks

     nor the tiretube, tame-water floating.

   Nor encounter with same vivid weekday man
previously unknown to you, and unknown still.
Stepped down to you, into the water with you,
parted you, transfigured you said leave me alone
said punish me I am an unrepentant boy.

    You are not that body now.

Wherever you were headed was not this stream.

Your asscheeks sag. Your abdomen distends.
   Nothing has a tight hold on your guts.
Guts spill at times when they're not tucked away.

Winded, white-haired body. Splotchy skin.
   A face uneven as a river jag
and asperous as the mullein's flannel leaves.

My undesirable body, you're all I have to fiddle with.
The fiddle's wood has cracked but it still plays.
The music, rival falls into the eddy, into brisk cascade
   and latterly to rest on strand exhausted.
You are the form of my exhaustion as you break.

Tenderness in the testes, tenderness of mind.
     I have come to admire you in the water.
You are the yellow crown of some narcissus afterward:
          the fizzled salvo. The burst of yolk
that has begun to dry on the stoneware plate.
The mess. A young Picasso's stab at fingerpaints
hung and fading on his mom's refrigerator door.
     But not without a certain coruscating charm.

     You are run-off from the melting foothills,
with your specks of gold. Mostly pyrite,
          though that captivates as well.
We need those flecks to break the river's surface,
     its decided syntax. I need you to come down
from the sunflowered shore. Unexpected oxbow.
Unexpected age. You are an engineering failure.
     I'm your systemic glitch.

Here, where the shallows pool up into habitus,
     I behold the imperfection of you, my mass,
my faulted body. Despite the plunging falls
          with you, I swim.

Burning Water

In the YouTube video a man flips a lighter, flare,
holds it to a belching faucet, the water catches fire,
not a miracle, the companies hydro-fracking the earth
for gas, the movement of capital in ground water—

And there's that unpoetic word again, so overt,
admittedly abstract, some even say clichéd, a word
I'd never even heard when me and the cousins sat
in the shrimp boat stern, grownups on vacation
playing penny poker all night in the front, as we
watched the dark horizon line between deep sea
and deeper sky fall behind us and never change.

We hung our legs into strange bioluminescent foam
flung up by our wake, if we'd scooped the water
up with a glass jar as we did the air for fireflies,
we'd have caught eighty species, galactic diatoms
invisible to our eye, to us just some murky water
from the Gulf, which is licked over today with oil
from the blown-out rig, all for lack of a cut-off
trigger, costs half a million, comes out of the foul
profit now crawling on sand—or the drill was too fast,
after all time is money, that is, less for the workers,
more for the company, yes, theory again—or pooled
experience, since there is a connection from abstract
to specific, the translucent organisms that work
to filter water are this morning drinking in oil,
when they float to the surface, when the sun stares
down on them long enough, they will begin to burn
from inside out, microscopic dying stars in the Gulf.
But not the result of a natural, inevitable process.

What I mean is once I saw a flock of little sting-rays,
each no bigger than my palm, arrowing like tiny geese

where water met sand in the shallows of Tampa Bay,
I stood in the Gulf and they winged between my feet,
going somewhere I didn't know. Now what will they eat?

The connection between there and now not inevitable,
matter striking our minds, us trying to catch the spark,
consciousness.

Lost Season

winter didn't come
the lake remained open and moving
the robins never left

we waited for the muffling
for snow to fall through the hours
absorb all the hum and clang

crows failed to gather
high in the bare trees
and something happened

to our sleep to our ground
all that couldn't go dormant
strained in the growing light

the pull from freeze to thaw
went slack and the sap
held back in the maple

we needed one another less
no bitter wind to recoil from
nothing to crack or loosen

so we said what would
have been left to silence
and felt our old lives forget us

Livestock

When they come to pluck me, I am
neither girl nor boy, clam nor cock.

I have neither hooves nor snout.
But I do have claws—I can grunt and growl

and show my teeth. I do not need wings
to create a windstorm, I do not need talons

to break skin. I can snarl and scrape.
I can unhinge my jaw, to fit a head twice

the size of mine inside. I can be razor-backed
and spike-edged when he tries to skin me,

unscale my silvery back, debone my brazen
hen-hide. I will be foul-mouthed and crooked-necked.

I will be the chicken-head they know me to be,
if it will save my life. When he comes for me,

I will remember the coop, how they gathered the fowl
girl up by the feet with warm hands and cooing.

How her brown hung low when they entered her
into the guillotine and severed her head. How they

plucked her body until she was bare. I will remember
the blood and what happens when they want you as food.

Backyard Rock

That year I learned to float by filling my body
with questions. Swimming at night with my father
was the first time
                            since the fog of childhood I'd seen
a man naked. The lake thickened with bloodsuckers,
the moon a sliver in the sky—
                                        uncut, tucked within
a hood of skin, unlike mine, his tip the backyard rock
split in three. Think of Ham
                            who too saw the nakedness
of his father. Think of God enlarging Japheth. It was both
what I did
                and did not want. How I understood myself
uneasily as my own dim reflection, uselessly as my shadow
cast at night.

                *

It happened, I'm told, because water trickled down
a crack and froze,
                            expanded and split apart this rock
or boulder, whenever a rock becomes a boulder,
in millimeters, then inches,
                            then feet. I walk this path
through the rock, and where one side indents,
the other extends, so that one could put it back
together again
                if one were God. On the northern cut,
my fire glows and the ice on the trees around me rears up
like a question, like a knife.

                *

I have summoned the hair I know exists inside to sprout
across my chest like his, I've culled the same slate rocks
and still my body, newly unbuilt and barren.
My father and I share our name

                    yet he goes by *Jack*.
I want to believe we're tied to the same chicken wire
but here I am—here we are—

                    the earth undigging its graves,
the clouds wringing out their water. The day I convinced
a squirrel to eat from my hand, its tiny nail-feet sticky
with sap, I could have

              if I was that kind of person
snapped its leg simply by closing my fist. Could have
even if I was not.

      *

Walking at night in winter, I'm headed away
from an encounter with a man I've met on the internet.
When he asks for a name,

              I give him *Jack*. My father,
drunk and lolling in a hammock, once told me
his first time was with an older woman
and three other boys. I mull this over by way of ice.
Bed, breed, burrow:

             two mammals leap in
and out an old fishing hole. I step closer;
the frozen lake protests.

          Too small to be beavers,
too large to be muskrats, they leap in and out.
I step closer; the frozen lake, a dark marble,
clouded and cracked,

          protests. It's not a fishing hole,
I realize, but the edge of ice—beyond them

black open water—and for once in my life I can measure
how closely I stand

                        to the periphery of danger.

                    *

I believe in the father and the ease he raised
fire with, using only

                        the leaves around him, an act
I couldn't do with gasoline. I believe in the glory
of the day birds at midnight,

                                the egret that follows
the swallow, the sand crabs that corkscrew up
the salt marshes. I believe I first learned lust
by watching

                the men in my family swim,
and even now that boyhood water still feels like silk.
I believe the day will come

                        when this too feels ordinary.

                    *

Out on the frozen lake stripped pale as a face,
out where the ice heaves

                        beneath me, a groan
or a snap, and at five inches deep I know it will hold
I know it will

                even if my knees—the sweat pilling
my fleece—does not,

                        out in the sun-lock, the ice-blister
of the day, out where I watch the trap I've set
sit and stay,

                drawn low below me while trout
tangle under the ice in a diamond of a dance,

out where my father had stood, his boot-prints glazed
by snow and rain,
                              out where his traps snapped up
at once, a fish's frenzy to yank down the cords,
to impale their flap-cheeks on the barbs
and feel that sting,
                              that pull into air, their blood
patterning the snow in scales, I understand
I am not my father,
                              not earlier today by the woodshed,
by his fell, sailing an axe over my shoulder
and into the block of wood
                                        where it plants, shakes loose,
the log still standing solid, unsplit, and whole:
I try to understand how
                              if I hack and hack, the log
will come apart in pieces, strips, first bark and slivers,
but eventually, as it must, it will halve
                                        and halve again.

Gerard Manley Hopkins Drafts the Light

"... I am writing a popular account of Light and the Ether ...
and my hope is to explain things thoroughly and make the matter,
as far as I go in it, perfectly intelligible."

—Gerard Manley Hopkins

Empedocles taught fire behind the eye: the eye's diaphanous membrane lets loose leaves of light, which congregate to the perceived body. Plato, to a degree, agrees: fire, fawn-fire, leaps from forests in the deep eye, mingles with sunlight, erects a <u>Body of Vision</u>: a sill, swelling and shriveling, ruled by swivels of soul, where things touched with ghost—body, body of a boy, the beauty of him—"enter seer through the eyes." ~~But the eye is a limb of the mind, and the mind is eyes of Christ. Channels to teeming charnel: whiskers on barleystalks and river's skin two million brushstrokes, boys lanky as barleystalks; sea flashing silver, coiled tiger; boys with striped socks and damp lips, Malebranche in laps, under an ash; and a blot on the long ash, and blond-down burls of thigh, and its rushes, and its moles, and the fruit on the ash, the hitch and plait of the shirt taut in the teeth, the slip of hip, and it's a thrush on the ash when the eye is a hand of flesh and the hand fills the hand fills~~ To Aristotle, light is satiation (<u>Actuality</u>) of a medium blindly wishing (<u>Potentiality</u>) transparency; objects with potentiality to color, when in light, attain actuality to color. Color, via air, enters the glassy nave of the eye, and therein rides blood down to heart, the gatherer-of-senses, the <u>Sensus communis</u>. Vision, says Aristotle, is the soul of the eye, the <u>Final Cause</u>, breathing purpose into animal.

~~But the eye is a branch of mind~~ The ancients were wrong: soul witnesses light, mote among mote, but does not forge it. Light performs out of doors. How, then, the sojourn in the eye? Look—boys dive into the Liffey; they float there, ~~skin~~ The tiger ocean reels in river and with it a garland of ripening boys. Space intervening the eye and ~~burl~~ what it sees is not empty, being infused with such riparian fluid, the <u>Ether</u>, which bears light just as water bears boys to the sea. ~~Vision happens in a kind of estuary: the eye is limb of the~~ The ethereal medium, posits Newton, is far more rarefied than air, more elastic, and upon contact vibrates more minutely: the vibrations of air "made by a man's ordinary voice succeeding at more than half a foot or a foot distance, but those of ether at a less distance than the hundredth-thousandth part of an inch." Ether palpitates, expanding and compressing: when crumbs of light take compressed ether-parts, the denseness brought about by compression <u>Reflects</u> light; when ether expands, light sluices into interstice between two vibrations (as the drop of the foot through an imagined step), and is <u>Refracted</u>. Vision, then, is a happening in mingles of ether and sparked flesh. In the eye's proscenium, the <u>Retina</u>, is the sheer meshing (like pithwork under an orange rind) of the ends, or <u>Capillamenta</u>, of the <u>Optic Nerve</u>. Light sets these pulsing, and the nerve carries vibration into the sensorium of the brain, which translates movement to color, to vision, vision of the beauty of a boy, vision of the beauty of this vision of a boy.   .

But ether is so rarefied as to be invisible, and still ether folds light. One sees light but not ether. Where, then, ends ether; where begins light? Put another way: ether is self, say, and light desire. Is desire self? Certainly not, yet each acts upon the other. ~~Lord, why does my desire make me in your eyes?~~ When one is desirous, what is meant is "I am alight in desire, light with desire, heavy with it," inside all that yearning, self and desire intertwined. Carrying this through, then: ether is a thing forever alight with desire; take light away, and there is no need for ether. Yet, light propagates. So, something shall bear it.

Head of the Gorgon

As the reedy sonata of squelch and blade-spun air cinched its
climax like a drawstring sack around us, I did not dodge behind

the broken pediments monolithing men who always meant
to unbuckle burdens here then look away into some certain

softer land than this. How precisely as a sting had thingness
warped me into horror: the very wrong span of my lifetime,

the rigor sitting below my collarbones, my being not the great
work but the body at the end of which it could find itself great.

Strange to them, a gaze fatal and not theirs. Stranger still to be
beheld and collectible and them. What they think I used to be

was, if in possession of eyes as well as agency, preposterous.
I didn't move. I knew he would tell them, because he must,

that I had murder-thirst, hid needles on my spine, my hips a thrift
of diamonds. He could have it that way, but here was the stillest

minute slipped between me and the myth of myself: mirrored
in the shield: the secant angles of his skull: the wide eye within it:

the iris's loose grip on the pit that held my face, which was
stunning   coal-hard in all that it had borne, a monstrous feat

of weathering this world—that it would not be changed by me
had been for the longest the tyranny of its terrain, but look

at my garden   And the black field blown alive around me,
the hair-raised woodlands, the hills at their backs, bluff shore

beyond that somehow in earshot: the stone churn overturned
the green sea. Cradled in the valley, I became a fault in him.

No stitch of briefer things ever had been so undone.

uncoil

wait   said the   grass
and the girl
lay down   wait   and the girl raised
her arms   above her head   willing green
she breathed
                wait   the sky
pressed down   wait   pressed down
                                wait
said the girl
                and the grass cried out

Horses in Snow

Fading dusk turns the snow into stars,
the sky and the horizon line into
a black dome. The only world I know
exists in the twin beams of my headlights.
I'd forgotten what it's like, driving
a country road in a blizzard, the way
the wind swirls the snow across the road
in eddies, like water on a troubled lake.
I'd forgotten the hypnotic effect
of the flakes flying at the windshield,
how my eyes try to focus on each flake,
lose sight of the road itself.
I've never been afraid of night
in the city, but night in the country,
the storm enveloping everything,
makes all of the folktales
true, all of the cautionary monsters
stalk the forest that fences in
the freeway. I become a child
behind the wheel, a boy sent on
a man's errand because there is no one else.
I drive slowly from village to village,
seeking out the safety that will not
be found. When the tires hit a patch
of ice, I'm pulled back into myself,
back into the doubled view of
the headlamps, and as the car reaches
the top of a rise, its lights shine
into a bend in the road, a pasture beyond.
There, for a moment, stand dozens
of horses. Some are unmoving under
blankets of snow. Some are feeding
from hay-filled troughs. And one
is galloping, moving fast as me,
head down, trying to outrun the storm.

Memory as Missionary Position

Inside the dress, there is a creature, she
                    careful

is a cliff in a girl's body.
And the cliff was a lizard once *still*   turned
to rock she gazed too much like she

              careful

      had a kingdom *inside.*

Inside the dress, holes are cut
      so the cliff can breathe and
            any girl watching
            any girl waiting
            any glint of a girl's

mother's metal scissors can *still* find her—

    careful
there are still pins inside.

To fit a lizard, the jaw of this dress unlocks.
      Fitting sounds like eating and mothers
          tell their daughter to shut their eyes
pins inside the unmarried
pins to decorate
      the insides of a church.
      Girls wear dresses that mothers sew for them.

              this dress // shroud // napkin // flag

In the 1800s my greatgreatgreatgreatgreat grand
mothers swam to ships

to trade sex for cloth, iron, and mirrors.
     A body for a body.

Did you see yourself in their glass, mother?

Did you cut the shape of your body
     and send it whistling through the ocean?

                         when a cliff becomes altar
and the Pacific
in the name of civilization
is properly dressed

    daughters *inside*
        pine away

the altitude of faith.

heart of the bell

Prague, 2018

if the heart of the bell breaks
catastrophe will strike: that is the legend

last time, a flood;
next, who can know but the bell, its cloven meat
quiet crack of bronze anticipating its own demise
drowned in the clang-like fist & metal murmur

what other creature keeps its heart inside its head full
of the hour's secrets & tender prayers?

I do not doubt the stories—
how bells say & say even after
they have been lost
in the rubble or at sea

say & say how they paced
into hiding, or grieved their knell siblings
melted for war's hungry rounds,
how they stilled their blood
in the chill of state restraint,
that longest & most silent hour
of the body's yearning, say:
a silver bell is really a thumbscrew, no
heart at all, say: touch me,
I am no longer a bell if I do not ring

how bells say & say
perfectly tuned by centuries, their
hammered & quarreling overtures
haunting ringent ears
calling the forgotten, calling me, I'm called

to pray in the clamor, holy brazen speech
carapaced in its stony tower, devout lick of metal
to the ferrous brim, its chime sway waking my deadest earth

to pray which is to taste you ring you
loud to greet you a thousand times
offer my heart to your mouth & bellow the walls—
anything that reminds me how small we are:

to be swallowed by the boom of fullest sound,
the agony & wonder of wanting the Beloved's more
crisp break of a mere day off the year's chanted yearnings,
intonations that we will never last
longer than a breath in the face of the infinite

to want to be pealed by the hour, to say & say
to invite the lightning by this thunderlust,
lure the cry of livening a shatter
near to feel the crack of the ampersand
organ in the vesper's dusky light

to know the catastrophe to come
but nonetheless
ring & ring & ring & ring

Diving into the Wreck

First having read the book of myths,
and loaded the camera,
and checked the edge of the knife-blade,
I put on
the body-armor of black rubber
the absurd flippers
the grave and awkward mask.
I am having to do this
not like Cousteau with his
assiduous team
aboard the sun-flooded schooner
but here alone.

There is a ladder.
The ladder is always there
hanging innocently
close to the side of the schooner.
We know what it is for,
we who have used it.
Otherwise
it's a piece of maritime floss
some sundry equipment.

I go down.
Rung after rung and still
the oxygen immerses me
the blue light
the clear atoms
of our human air.
I go down.
My flippers cripple me,
I crawl like an insect down the ladder
and there is no one
to tell me when the ocean
will begin.

First the air is blue and then
it is bluer and then green and then
black I am blacking out and yet
my mask is powerful
it pumps my blood with power
the sea is another story
the sea is not a question of power
I have to learn alone
to turn my body without force
in the deep element.

And now: it is easy to forget
what I came for
among so many who have always
lived here
swaying their crenellated fans
between the reefs
and besides
you breathe differently down here.

I came to explore the wreck.
The words are purposes.
The words are maps.
I came to see the damage that was done
and the treasures that prevail.
I stroke the beam of my lamp
slowly along the flank
of something more permanent
than fish or weed

the thing I came for:
the wreck and not the story of the wreck
the thing itself and not the myth
the drowned face always staring
toward the sun

the evidence of damage
worn by salt and sway into this threadbare beauty
the ribs of the disaster
curving their assertion
among the tentative haunters.

This is the place.
And I am here, the mermaid whose dark hair
streams black, the merman in his armored body.
We circle silently
about the wreck
we dive into the hold.
I am she: I am he

whose drowned face sleeps with open eyes
whose breasts still bear the stress
whose silver, copper, vermeil cargo lies
obscurely inside barrels
half-wedged and left to rot
we are the half-destroyed instruments
that once held to a course
the water-eaten log
the fouled compass

We are, I am, you are
by cowardice or courage
the one who find our way
back to this scene
carrying a knife, a camera
a book of myths
in which
our names do not appear.

Backflash: Hinge

"Oysters will change sex once or more during their lifetime."

—*National Geographic*

If I could turn
            back—not girlhood, but before—
                        I'd be an oyster's

spit-sheen, drift first as a spat.
                  Smaller than a pinkie
                              nail polished

for junior prom. I'd pick
                  my own debut,
                              starting here, at the hinge.

In saline, where the first
                  attachments form, but before
                              the complications

of buckling
            down in bed. Before calcium
                        spit into rings

of protection, before the need
                  to count back to the rock.
                              I'd choose blood

without color, pre-
                  scarlet drawn by needles.
                              I won't be marked
O or X. I settle now
                  for water, the easy
                              plain of cells.

The gray sea umbrella

        lets some light

                in, refuses the rest. Below

we know to filter

      slime, slung mud,

             to quarantine—

myth or not—our irritants with nacre.

          Before the snare

              of sex—*Cross your legs*

or *It's not personal*—I'll learn a self-

              reliance. I'll fashion

two hard lips

      to house my feeler

           and lacy mantle.

Landing, we block out

         euphemism: no "naughty pearl,"

"no-no button," or

        "little man in a boat."

              There's not a language

where we latch. Just *laissez-faire*

         anatomy, and watered sounds

                we don't decode.

Hero Worship

Two boys wrestle over bedsheets, past
statues of godheads, offered fruit,
hands interlocking with ankles and edges
of lips. They learn to fight—
one white, one dark-skinned, old story.

I love a boy who doesn't love me back.
His skin is incense
dissolving, already gone from the nose.
Dusty palms. Thin fingers tapping out
Bollywood songs on the side table.
Lithe in stickball sunlight,
always the hint of a scowl. Stink bombs

erupt from our palms onto church steps.
Chocolate candies expire on our tongues.
Our bike tires make lazy circles, spelling out *gratitude*
over and over. A memory. I pray for extended
hands to brush my cheek,
make of my earlobe an apricot.
Restful tangling of body and body,
consumed. My desire to be the girl he wants,
burst forth from my skin like a citrus tree blossoming—

this is my latest delusion. I need
eight new arms:
two to embrace him, four to destroy
our separate bodies. A purpose,
surely, for the two at rest—to catch
myself tumbling swiftly
dirtward, wipe smudges of earth
from my face. See him stand over me.
Gestures doubled by dizziness, the victor
in darkness. Setting sun halo,
his black hair a crown.

How a Thought Thinks

A thought is dumb,
without eyes, ears,
opposable thumb,
or a tongue.
A thought lives
underground, not
wholly mole-ish
but with some
of the same
disinterests.
The amazing thing
is that it isn't helpless.
Of all creatures
it is the most
random eater.
Caring only for travel
it eats whatever
roots, ants, or gravel
it meets. It occupies
no more space
than moles. We know it
only by some holes
and the way
apparently healthy notions
topple in the garden.

Fairy Tale

a boy's kicked out of his house
so he moves into the baths
+ becomes the steam
men breathe in + out again
+ this is a kind of homecoming,
tendrilled in these strange lung
gutters, aqueduct full & emptying
of mucous & curses. *god*
as he passes through a hand
clamped over a drooling mouth.
god as he's sucked back up
inside a body. can you believe
there's freedom in being so out
of control you can pass through
a man unseen, lay dormant
as an idea or disease until
you reemerge years later
through his speech or semen?
in this way the men bring him
into their homes, kiss him
onto their wives' + children's
sleeping foreheads. in this way,
the boy is everywhere + everywhere
is the boy. sort of how matter
can never be created or destroyed,
that same idea, just much
much sadder.

Await

The scars upon the day
are harsh marks of
tranquility. I scarcely
know where you are:
awake? After lunch, a
Sunday snooze? Is
the ivy weeded yet?
Let the frost do
it its way. Smile, my
dear my dandy, when
you see this. That's
not much to ask, though
no smile on order
is quite the spontaneous
real thing. The day
grinds to a halt all
dusk and yellow rose.
What's a hundred some
miles or so? Or—let's
see—fifty hours?
Time of all things
is most variable, a
seed you plant to see
what in the world
it is a seed of: time,
hours compressed into
a kiss, a lick, or
stretched out by a
train into an endless
rubber band. All we
know is that for such
as us it is not end-
less: is time too to
be found of an atomic

structure? I
would be the last to
know, busily waiting
to see and smile
as you smile and bend
to kiss. Why soon it
will be only forty
nine hours, cubed in-
visibly like the sec-
tions of a creek.
A record spins,
these keys go clack
why soon I'll see
you and soon you'll
see me. I can enjoy
the here and now
but, wind shivering
clear day, I live
and love to anticipate
my hands on you and
yours on me, the
hours flow by and
a white gull is
black against
November evening
light, expressed,
it seems, from
late yellow grapes.

Many Things Are True

Thirst and the animal
slaking of thirst, and how the
snow-drunk wind sometimes
caresses, in its teasing, tender way,
the chimes,
while also lashing them to music,
devastating, inescapable,
so hard it seems they could break
with the making of it—

and how we drink each other darker
than the crisscrossed bodies
of the winter trees,
trunks opaque as scars
on the mute gray sky.
Darker than the torn-down fields,
the stubbled rows.
While in some other place, I swear,
we're climbing up the stairs

of a new planet.
Climbing toward the sun as legend,
the sun as itself—
burning and sinking in the cold sky.
Woodpeckers drilling their one nail
into the heart of every tree:
they are not our gods.
All these husks and gnawed-down cobs:
they are not our lives.

Woman Circling Lake

Oh transcendent, this aqua blue and all these health nuts
running back and forth hold nothing—no sea gnome,
no salt to scour your bones clean—only placidity
and motionlessness, no dark fugues or phosphorescence.
It's your turn to stir the waters. Don't
back away from brittle plains and dry wheat saying
you're too far above us for encumbrances. This
is your place, your time: Chicago, gate of a millennium.
Your fainthearted sallies fall deep into space, closer
to no one who knows you. See, cloudling, how the collie pup
chases the gray squirrel up bare sleeping trees. How
old snow banks the blue-green line of Michigan.
The collie is so happy and powerful. The squirrel
steals from ash to oak as if possessed by abandon,
rising higher into sky than any jubilant unchained creature.
You are the end of winter, sea light. Little star eater,
come back, it's not your turn to die.

Unbearable White

Undertone—
Cradling.

I did not know
I'd been running from it.

Unnamed
It was there, waiting

For me to see
And say,

Of course, you—
My "*my.*"

—And so

For thirty years
An outline

Of a body
Traced into white sand

Stood firm, waving,
Calling others

To join,
Reappearing each time

The saltwater came
To wash.

I'm Over the Moon

I don't like what the moon is supposed to do.
Confuse me, ovulate me,

spoon-feed me longing. A kind of ancient
date-rape drug. So I'll howl at you, moon,

I'm angry. I'll take back the night. Using me to
swoon at your questionable light,

you had me chasing you,
the world's worst lover, over and over

hoping for a mirror, a whisper, insight.
But you disappear for nights on end

with all my erotic mysteries
and my entire unconscious mind.

How long do I try to get water from a stone?
It's like having a bad boyfriend in a good band.

Better off alone. I'm going to write hard
and fast into you, moon, face-fucking.

Something you wouldn't understand.
You with no swampy sexual

promise but what we glue onto you.
That's not real. You have no begging

cunt. No panties ripped off and the crotch
sucked. No lacerating spasms

sending electrical sparks through the toes.
Stars have those.

What do you have? You're a tool, moon.
Now, noon. There's a hero.

The obvious sun, no bullshit, the enemy
of poets and lovers, sleepers and creatures.

But my lovers have never been able to read
my mind. I've had to learn to be direct.

It's hard to learn that, hard to do.
The sun is worth ten of you.

You don't hold a candle
to that complexity, that solid craze.

Like an animal carcass on the road at night,
picked at by crows,

taunting walkers and drivers. Your face
regularly sliced up by the moving

frames of car windows. Your light is drawn,
quartered, your dreams are stolen.

You change shape and turn away,
letting night solve all night's problems alone.

Geology of Water

for Maureen Seaton

"The sea grows old in it."
—Marianne Moore

1

Striated tides draw their lines
in the sand, leave them behind
in retreat. Warm layers on the colder
to blind indigo, strata of temperature
and color down to bedrock
settling, plates shifting in their cobalt sleep
to nudge the continents apart.
The sea grew old in me, the blood
as salt and turbulent, as unpacific.

2

There's someone who foundered there
and lost his way: he's in above his head,
out of his depth, he's been concealed
beneath his representability or gulf
stream. If I bend closer I can hear him
drown, a man made out of water
whose words arise like bubbles
to the surface: something survives
in every carbonaceous molecule, every

3

intermittent spindrift's punctuation.
Fossils compacted in the bluff's rush hour
say things change, but never for the better:
they've stairstepped four geologic eras just stay
in place. Their smashed catastrophe theory confirms
some things aren't worth surviving. Evolution
croons its single song, *come out of the sea,*
my love, to me, and never adds, *and drown*
knee-deep in air.

4

The trilobites are tired of epochs
of being pushed around, steadily
heaped-up resentments: they're writing home
I don't love you, don't come back. Their deaths
are sedimented in long memories
like scars, the rings a fallen tree keeps to
itself, erosion's clear cut through the palisades:
sun and steel, moon and slate, nothing
worth lasting for. What the end says

5

is *wait*, but they've been waiting
long enough. Water is a memento
they've thrown back. From the Cambrian
to the Silurian, the Carboniferous
to shale oil exploration on the continental
shelf (whichever million years distilled
to burnoff from offshore drilling rigs), crinoids
nurse their sessile grudge against dry land
and those who came too late to be remains.

6

It's true: the sea grew old here, and here
it left its will to live, a testament
to what it couldn't take back, couldn't help
but keep. It drank itself and sank for good.
Wash that sea in me and wring it clean,
ocean to ocean till there's no water left.

Boy with Flowers

My aunt loved me, asked me:
will you be the flower
girl at my wedding? But I'm not
a girl, I argued, and she persuaded me:
you'll get to throw rose petals

onto the aisle, walk before me, both of us
crushing them beneath our feet, my gown
dragging over them. I agreed. I wanted
nothing but chivalry.

At the church, my mother and I
waited in the small room. She brushed
my aunt's hair until the dress arrived.
Isn't it beautiful? And I agreed until they tried
to put me in it. I'd seen my father

and uncle earlier, standing in a circle
of other men, smoke hovering over their heads, a halo
and their voices kind, quiet, and deep. I told my aunt—
I want to wear a suit like them! She promised

if I wore the dress I could wear anything
I wanted after: army pants, a sheriff
badge, cowboy hat, and pistols. My mother shot her
a look in the mirror where we posed, both of them
angelic in white, and me, not yet

dressed. Today I wake from another dream
in which I have a beard, no breasts
and am about to go skinny-dipping
on a foreign beach with four other men.

I'm afraid to undress, won't take off my shorts,
so they grab me, one at each ankle, the other two
by each wrist. I am a starfish hardening.
The sun hovers above, a hot
mirror where I search for my reflection.

I close my eyes. It's too intense. The light
where my lover is tracing fingertips
around two long incisions in my chest. Each sewn tight
with stitches, each a naked stem, flaring with thorns.

November 19, 2016

for Joanne Kyger

(1)

Poetry is the part

    that no one sees

clip the flower

    burn the brush

        watch rain stream

                down
        the moon viewing

      window
six drops fold together

           then glimmer

burn a stick of Autumn Leaves

           crack the screen door
write longer

        have beams shooting

out and over

        the blessed
bountiful body

Do not revisit

        poems the next day

they have already rejoined the actual

        matter
        daily music fallen
back into the fabric

to acknowledge mastery

would violate her

flexibility

even further terms (the heat

and shape of the mountain)

(2)

Bring

the outside in . . .

the gray continuous

tangle of moss

posing as a mandala

burning the

sudden white

tiny

cracks

in between

outside

Lovesong of the Square Root of Negative One

I am the wind and the wind is invisible, all the leaves
tremble but I am invisible, bloom without flower, knot
without rope, song without throat in wingless flight, dark
boat in the dark night, pure velocity. As the hammer is
a hammer when it hits the nail, and the nail is a nail when
it meets the wood, and the invisible table begins to appear
out of mind, pure mind, out of nothing, pure thinking.
Through darkness, through silence, a vector, a violence,
I labor, I lumber, I fumble forward through the valley as
winter, as water. I mist and frost, flexible and elastic to
the task. I am the hand that lifts the rock, I am the mind
that strings the worm and throws the line and feels the tug,
the flex in the pole, and foot by foot I find the groove,
the trace in the thicket, the key in the look, as root breaks
rock, from seed to flower to fruit to rot, a holy pilgrim
moving through the stations of the yardstick. I track,
I follow, I hinge and turn, frictionless and efficient as an
equals sign. I flip and fold, I superimpose. I become
location and you veer toward me, the eye to which you
are relative, magnetized for your revelation. Hook and bait,
polestar and checkmate, I am your arrival, there is no
refusal, we are here, you see, together, we are already here.

Love Letter to a Dead Body

on our backs in burr and sage
                         bottles jangle us awake
              cirrhosis moon for eye

fists coughed up
              we set ourselves on fire

copy our cousins
                    did up in black smoke
              pillar dark in June

Drunktown rakes up the letters in their names
              lost to bone
                         horses graze where their remains are found

and you kiss me to shut me up
                    my breath bruise dark in the deep

leaves replace themselves with meadowlarks
                         cockshut in larkspur

ghosts rattle bottle dark and white-eyed
              horses still hungry
                    there in the weeds

What's Required

Hunting taught me early to walk at least three paces
behind my father to stop vines and branches from
smacking me. We looked like an animal with its young:
the big one, the little one, the same. My father taking
long, quick strides, leaving me behind in brush, fighting
to free myself from thorns. When we came home
he had me strip so he could search
my body for ticks that hid like secrets I learned
to keep from him, the boys on the bus calling me *sissy!*
In gym class I was *faggot! pussy!* I killed
a deer, arrow cutting clean through its heart
and lungs, a quick flinch, a few steps back,
then a glazed blackness in the eyes. I'll never forget
my father's face that day: chapped smile,
brown eyes soft as soil. He pulled
me close, half hugging as men do. For men
this is what's required, some sort
of bloodshed, a tearing down.

alternate names for black boys

1. smoke above the burning bush
2. archnemesis of summer night
3. first son of soil
4. coal awaiting spark & wind
5. guilty until proven dead
6. oil heavy starlight
7. monster until proven ghost
8. gone
9. phoenix who forgets to un-ash
10. going, going, gone
11. gods of shovels & black veils
12. what once passed for kindling
13. fireworks at dawn
14. brilliant, shadow hued coral
15. (I thought to leave this blank
    but who am I to name us nothing?)
16. prayer who learned to bite & sprint
17. a mother's joy & clutched breath

Closing the Gay Bar outside Gas City

As if I'd dreamed it up, the front door
still swings, and the dance bell rings
before it dies amid alfalfa, stalks of corn.
On the floor: a faded pair of jeans,
buttons from a shirt. Two condoms
coil like sleepy salamanders
in the back. In Indiana nothing lasts
for long, though here the bathroom lock
still sticks, nourished each winter
by ice and snow. Outside: bones
of rabbits, possum-blur, some ghost's
half-eye through the window screen
where now the only seed that spills is thorny
vine and thistle taking back what's theirs.
Even the magpies, locked in some
blood-sleep, stir in the eaves as if
to speak of patience and regret. Stains
from tossed eggs mar the sides, dents
from stones pitched through windows
boarded where *FAG* and *AIDS*
are sprayed in flaking paint along
the front. In fifty years, only birds
will couple here. Deer will pause
where a door once opened out to starlight,
locust thorns tearing like some last testament
to beer and lust. Even now, a raccoon
stirs near the window, looks in at me
as it moves past, like some stranger
no longer interested, some boy
who left his lip print on the glass.

Queer Earth

> "Sexual expression is permitted only within marriage, between man and woman,
> male and female. Anything else is an abnormality and is against nature."
> —Pope Shenouda III

You speak of nature as if you
invented it. Or gutted it & used
its bones to fashion a white castle,

to keep you safe from all the animals
you refuse to see.

Tonight, each grain of soil, each blade
of grass, each droplet of blood
is a time machine. Each cell

rewinds you four & a half billion
years back in history. We were once
genderless cells splitting our own bodies—

in two—now growing gills,
fins and feet. 65,000 queer
& trans species.

It's always mating season
on planet Earth: look
at the way leopard slugs

make love: upside down
from trees—two penises coiling
into orchids. A penetration

so mutual—it is worthy
of *bioluminescence.*

Look at the way bonobo monkeys
resolve conflict: queer polyamorous sex
in the morning, evening and afternoon.

Look at the penguins mating for life,
warming the egg of another mother
with the heat between their bellies.

When an oyster produces a perfect pearl:
they transition from male to female.
For crustaceans, gender is a border

that does not exist. Do you hear
the orchestra of dolphins? Masturbating
against the seabed, penetrating

each other's blow holes, as if this human
history never began. If our love defies
the logic of your biology,

then what is queer pleasure if not
heavenly? Is this queer ocean
not the tidal waves roaring

within your bloodstream?
Is this queer Earth not the same
carbon that birthed your flesh?

To be queer, Earth, and alive
is to be hunted & marked *wild*.
A beast banished from heaven,

a bleached coral reef, a jungle clear-cut,
a planet domesticated like cattle, and butchered
in the hands of machines.

Yet, our queerness is an ancient
persistence. So tell me:
we be against nature.

& our bones will remember—
we've been queer
for 3.6 billion springs,   ·

summers, falls & winters.
& even after
your infant empire

collapses into dust,
we will still be queer.

The Joshua Tree // Submits Her Name Change

She stepped across our chest
      Dragging her shadow & fraying // All the edges
            Our nipples bloomed // Into cacti // Fruit & flower
                  She ate // Then we did // A needle pricked her

We've seldom seen this woman cry // Squeezed like a raincloud
            She cried because // Two men // Two men
                  Built a detention center // From bone & clay

The first bone— Our clavicle   The second— Her spine
She howled // As the fence // Surrounded her
               She coughed & combed the floor // Our chest shiv
               Shivering

Inside the detention center // She was renamed // *Ill-eagle*
            She forgot 15 pounds & mental health & her feet were
                Cracked tiles // Dirty dishes

This border // Isn't a stitch // Where nations meet
            This border's a wound // Where nations part

For Mac

A dead starfish on a beach
He has five branches
Representing the five senses
Representing the jokes we did not tell each other
Call the earth flat
Call other people human
But let this creature lie
Flat upon our senses
Like a love
Prefigured in the sea
That died.
And went to water
All the oceans
Of emotion. All the oceans of emotion
Are full of such fish
Why
Is this dead one of such importance?
Died
With blue of heart's blood, the brown
of unknowing
The purple of unimportance
It lies upon our beach to be crowned.
Purple
Starfish are
And love. And love
Is like nothing I can imagine.

Lifting Belly (II)

Kiss my lips. She did.

Kiss my lips again she did.

Kiss my lips over and over and over again she did.

I have feathers.

Gentle fishes.

Do you think about apricots. We find them very beautiful. It is not alone their
colour it is their seeds that charm us. We find it a change.

Lifting belly is so strange.

I came to speak about it.

Selected raisins well their grapes grapes are good.

Change your name.

Question and garden.

It's raining. Don't speak about it.

My baby is a dumpling. I want to tell her something.

Wax candles. We have bought a great many wax candles. Some are decorated.
They have not been lighted.

I do not mention roses.

Exactly.

Actually.

Question and butter.

I find the butter very good.

Lifting belly is so kind.

Lifting belly fattily.

Doesn't that astonish you.

You did want me.

Say it again.

Strawberry.

Lifting beside belly.

Lifting kindly belly.

Sing to me I say.

Tonawanda Swamps

As it would for a prow, the basin parts with your foot.
Never a marsh, of heron blue
                              but the single red feather
from the wing of some black bird, somewhere
a planked path winds above water,
the line of sky above this aching space.

Movement against the surface
is the page that accepts no ink.
A line running even
over the alternating depths, organisms, algae,
a rotting leaf.

Walk naked before me
carrying a sheaf of sticks.
It's the most honest thing a man can do.

As water would to accept you,
I part
a mouth, a marsh, or margin
is of containment,
the inside circuitous edge.

No line to follow out to ocean,
no river against an envelope
                              of trembling white ships.
Here I am landlock.
Give me your hand.

Visiting the Natural History Museum with the Son I Don't Yet Have

How do I explain
to the boy beside me
that the bones before us
are not dead?

That they were born on Christ's birthday
and roamed the forest as wild things
for over a hundred million years?
That we burn them as oil,
those forests as coal?

That Jesus is fewer than five seconds old,
and one second ago Columbus
landed in San Salvador,
formerly Guanahani,
and boasted of his ability
to massacre like an asteroid?

How do I explain resurrection,
when he reaches to touch
what says *No Touching?*

How do I explain that he is not nine years old,
but one-sixty-fourth of a second;
his mother and me, untouched natives,
one-sixteenth of a second?

Or translate stories from Social Services
into the literature of selection,
the contingency of *I chose you?*

How do I explain
that in less than one second
we have seen science and revolutions,

world wars and moon landings?
Not the passing away of the previous,
but the life of writing?

When he strains to sound
the Latin names of species,
how do I explain that what he does with his life
still counts,
      every split second?

The Exchange

Now my body flat,
the ground breathes,
I'll be the grass.

Populous and mixed is mind.
Earth take thought,
my mouth be moss.

Field go walking,
I a disk
will look down with seeming eye,

I will be time
and study to be evening.
You world, be clock.

I will stand,
a tree here,
never to know another spot.

Wind be motion,
birds be passion,
water invite me to your bed.

Estuary

Something like love found me. I did not tell anyone. Or I did, but the words turned to birdsong on my tongue. (Her name? When the body cannot contain the heart.) An estuary carries letters. Lovely script, trailing, sinuous. Backlit in blue pulse.

The feathered word that hums about us, between us, is *unmoored*. What we share. Roots of the air. (My name? The flower.) Half this, half that. The great sea has set me in motion, set me adrift, moving me like a weed in the brine river. I have the letters.

(Our names? Both exchanged, for the sake of our grandmothers. We could not take up their tongues because their song is part of what we lost.)

Weeping bloom. With/out. Here's what the letters contain: boats, oceans, currents, moons, flowers, nests. Unnamed shades of love. We are soil-less, too. (Tai tano.) She reached across the map, set a bloom adrift in the surf to wish my healing. In the bed for weeks, my snapped knee a misshapen breadfruit, I lolled in a lightless chasm. All the while willing a string of petals to unfurl from my chest—the longest lei seeking her across oceans. Did it find her. She says my name is everywhere she looks. Little red flowers, rarer yellow. Both/and. Blossoms, street signs. The stars, the ocean, the green, green trees, winged things, flowers, earth, sky, rain. Her name is everywhere I close my eyes. The upward welling, when the heart persists.

How can you miss what you have never held? I have seen her pictures. Something about her eyes. My last love, her mouth. In dreams I construct a lover of parts. She sees, she sings. But one cannot chance the bird.

In dreams I have everything. In my palms. The bird, the pinfeather dust. The havenot breathing as one.

In dreams I am the flower me—all flush and nectar—the bees' humming in my cheeks.

Little Errand

I gather the rain

in both noun
& verb. The way

the river banks
its flood, floods
its banks, quiver's

grammar I carry

noiseless, easy
over my shoulder.

To aim is—I think
of his mouth.
Wet ripe apple's

scent : sugar,

leather. To aim
is a shaft tipped

with adamant. Angle,
grasp, aim is a way
to hope to take

what's struck in hand,

mouth. At the river
flood so lately laid

down damage by,
geese sleep, heads
turned under wings

wind tests tremor
in like archery's
physics shifts

energy, potential
to kinetic : flight—

but not yet :

this grammar's time
to string a bow, draw
taut the air, send rain

from.quiver to verb
to aim to pierce

the scent of such red

flesh. Hope's arrow's
anatomy : thin,
feather's fletching

trembling, it
crests to end.

in brightness.

Field Song

Running through the field
is what damages. The trail circles
itself: an infinity of my making.

I fall in waist-high weeds.
When I lie flat, I vanish, become part
of its look: undisturbed, even.
Many have gotten lost in this grass.

I stretch my hands
into velvet reeds, small multitudes
rush across my palms. Dull bells
of seed hide within husk.

In the low places wind wheezes:
the sound of a feather, singular,
separate from its body, and held
beside the ear. To dusk

I announce nothing, not this trampling,
or the beat of sun that bleaches
some strands—
like unwanted touching, this won't vanish

easily. Behind me are winged spaces,
a whole stream of wild wheat
kicked and clawed over.

The War with the Dandelions

They sound like a slur for what we are. Dandies
and, at times, when it's called for, lions. Chris and I
are in the backyard after a week of heavy spring
rains have called out prides of them. After weeks
of the news channels talking of disappearances,
a plane cut from the sky, two hundred Nigerian girls
swallowed by the night's voracious hunger, blooms
have upturned toward the sun like children or mystics
who read some dispatch in the fat, wetted clouds.
Chris has recently taken up a complaint. Our neighbor's
yard being spotless and coveted, uniform as military
garb our neighbor wore in another time that landed him
a Korean wife and a bullet in his hip. Chris wants
to know his secret, life without weed, without
the serrated edges of those leaves slicing up the soil.
Chris pumps poisons into canisters, this now being
a world where death is engineered with the finest
precision, tinctures so refined they can stifle
what we hate while sustaining our green joys.
I always loved them, as I often do anything slated
for abuse. I see them pushing their way into the early
season, roughly shouldering through the crowds.
Picture them preparing themselves in the night, arranging
their skirts, the quiet gossip as they wait. After it's done,
I will watch them wilt. Lithe, pink stems twisted
earthward, writhing. Maybe they're too much like us
to win our affections, like the progeny who carries
all our flaws—a disarming exuberance, vanity
they don't even bother to conceal. I often fail at empathy.
What will I be without the later hush of them
letting go, the skirt's billowing, even as their heads,
heavy now, lean toward the support of their arms
like children exhausted by figures, by genders
of language, the general questions?

Garden

Then let's plant a garden
with the memories that keep
 me awake. They'll grow

together, you and what
I didn't tell you
about my backyard,

like Sundays saved
for weeding the wings
of dill, first clumsy

handfuls through work
gloves then held like
quills between my farthest

fingers. I was allergic
to everything green and still
I keep flowers in vases

outside my door, even
the bouquet you worried
never made it

to me, days anxious
if a neighbor got my roses.
Maybe I wrote this poem

to say I'm sorry
if loving me was stressful
or when I tell people

I love them now
your name's the antecedent
so every bud or reliable

fig tree I prune before
the hurricane is proof
you're still alive

to me. Or I'm sorry,
I blur the borders
between tribute and denial.

Or love isn't just stress
all the time. Here:
a corner of the garden,

where at ten I planted
corn—corn!—in our desert
soil, yards from any sprinkler

but still it grew, without fear
of joy or shame and faster
than I could eat

but mostly it was a thing
to witness, to marvel, so much
growing out of almost nothing.

the aftermath of what

I

is it raining ash there?
it's raining ash here.
bits of mountainside catch
in the window mesh
sap holds ash to oak leaves
all light red
shadows, red
red holes in shadows
ash so pale in all that ::
the whole street lit as if by ::
the volcanoes :: south
hold quiet
in the aftermath of what
exactly

II

who knew mountains could burn
a range ablaze
my lover sweats out
a fever in the living room
the wind coughs through window screens
soot collects the sill grey
the grass sleeps yellow
   overhued and oblivious

III

ash films spider webs
when you mourn
where   does it go

Beast Meridian

THE ANIMALS   CROSS.

girl   never

forget this night sky   torn into in your center—

the widening line that splits   your body into halves

was always a star map   to home. In grief,

body and breast to earth,   let your middle open

toward that old strange   hurt & this is your

deep memory: dream its starry dark

and long trees   vined with heavy flowers

the afterland where   you find your dead

gaze always upward   at each animal constellated

in your inner knowing   forming its language

mictlan   *nepantla*

that which separates   you from home

you from history   you from your mothers

every star pattern   is a watchful grace

find their names &   the split will heal & return the land

to that lineless open   join hands with   the invisible

the disappeared   the forgotten   river flooding

the land nourished   the blooming mourning

                             the return of the beasts

IRENE VILLASEÑOR

Instructions for Opening up the Heart

My heart is like a
murder of crows

If I want to scare you
it will be clear
where I deposited
the carcasses

My heart is like an
unkindness of ravens

With tails and wings
and everything else
straight to the point
not evil in disguise

My heart is like a
clamour of rooks

I want a lot of space
but don't always need it
and what once was silence
is now known for noise

My heart is like
the tidings of magpies

Walking free, finding
someone to nest with,
and full of good news

Torso of Air

Suppose you do change your life.
& the body is more than

a portion of night—sealed
with bruises. Suppose you woke

& found your shadow replaced
by a black wolf. The boy, beautiful

& gone. So you take the knife to the wall
instead. You carve & carve

until a coin of light appears
& you get to look in, at last,

on happiness. The eye
staring back from the other side—

waiting.

Butch Geography

"The desert is butch"
—Robin Becker

It's true some places are butch—
some locations, no matter how solid,
a quicksand of subversion. Cathedrals,
the mouths of sailors, the shedding
of pine trees in the yard, butch.
Where phones are ringing, where
suspension bridges rise up, butch.
Train stations, orchids, oak wood,
butch. The river with unbearable
currents, butch. Fires clearing
out the mountains, butch—
the maps, the trails themselves,
butch. Entire cities: Pittsburgh,
Tulsa, Los Angeles, Lincoln,
also butch. Infrastructure,
circus tents. Any place there is
wind, any place there are
sandstorms. Deserts, yes.
Playgrounds, yes. Beach dunes,
under the backs of bike tires,
yes. Wherever there is
cavernous depth, wherever
there are tapped-out wallets,
or strapped-on sex,
or pat-down checks
from cops on chests.
Wherever there is grit
dressed up as a gentleman.
Wherever there are
ladders and lips,
or shutters and bricks,
or man-things to fix.
Wherever there is factory-

made bravado, or a purely
chivalrous motto.
Indeed, in the desert—
barren, hot, and silent—
lizards and ring-tailed cats,
no water, cold nights,
the possibility of snake bites,
and yet—survival, the anthem
of those places we've always been.

A Natural History of Gay Love

Knowing our land used to rest
deep down, south of Florida, long before

Google street view, I think of how we, too,
have drifted. Once upon a time, my love,

we were flow awaiting eventual form: microbes,
schools of barracuda, sharks. These bodies

we've given marriage vows contain a history
of great white teeth, tentacles and scales

but, this time around, our skin is perfect.
If we swam backwards in time, we could meet

our queer protocells splitting and merging,
drift and seafoam. Glowing like coral

in the shelf, we might've first met
on our land long before these lives.

After so long, we've been drawn back
to our beginning, this garden the sea became.

The Third Measure Paused & Set to Your Breathing

How might it feel to be a vessel
of light? Like a moon held in the throat

of the sky—a cold pressing the lips
enough to shatter the tongue

of any open mouth. Somewhere
at the distance of centuries

your body could penetrate the skin
of my eyelid like this

until the ceiling of the house
burned away. Leaving me

& you on the bedspread—side-
by-side—our bones never once touching

lost in orbit around *tonight*. I swallow
what remains of the failing air

like a casket dissolving
over a god's awful taste

buds. So how might it feel, Lord—
to live only behind

the teeth. Death pointing inward.
The spine reaching

in both directions. The stars
unraveling from inside

the head. How might it feel
to be so vanished

that any movement is
but a brief torch lighting

your scented ankles now
gone—a smear of

fire ignited in some-
body's lost history. Lord

press your fingertips
into me. Let me treasure

your touch enough to cave
my ribs in. To crush me

so gentle now that I am made
to be the very last light

gravity remembers.

Iowa

Many will have you believe
this flatland has nothing to hide.
Her curses are one of many
elements she conceals.

Geodes, the state rock, require damage
to reveal their glisten.

My name rings long across the loess hills,
but no one knows how to call it.

My insteps are the bends of the rivers,
the natural borders between this beautiful
land and the next.
Blooming prairie grass is the hair
falling over my temples.

Lay your cheek against the earth.
Let your hip bones press into the dirt.
Feel the hillock, its slight rise
as if moving to meet you.
Stay in the tall grass until the moon reappears.
Remember this soil carved so long ago
by glaciers. Where I was born,
in the driftless zone of steep
hills and valleys, you'd almost think
you were among mountains.

No one who sees me now knows
the land where my heart was born.

Tail

There are little words
that can fit in little places
if you say them small enough.

To fit a song into a pore
you have to be prepared
for the day it will sweat.

If words could stick to people,
they would become different
creatures when spoken.

Blindfolded and turned
five times around, nothing
in you knows what it knew.

This is the fun part:
Prick the girls you like best
while pinning the donkey's tail.

Skin Movers

How still we are in sleep
as though morning holds its breath.
Our bodies rinsed with light
like soaked birch.

Half awake I travel down you again.
Crow, dark crow, we smell of burnt leaves and wine,
the night before taking crystals bitter as Jesuit Root.
Now we turn slowly in the weight of love,
the way ships move heavily between moon and sun, not lost
but like a well-piloted dream.

You speak of a river near home named Dancer's Run,
almost dust in summer that tells the story of the village.
I know your body so and kiss the star mole on your back.
Wanting more, you say yes in that miraculous way.

In this joyous season I know my heart won't die
as you and the milk pods open their centers
like a first snow in its perfection of light.

Good love is like this.
Even the smell of baked bread won't make it better,
this being out of myself for awhile.

Parable

He shaved his head to plant
   the hair in his garden, said

     I'll make something
grow. Held his hands, his curved fingers

    as if to cup light. For weeks he didn't
     eat, for weeks we never

spoke, never touched. I dreamed
   he grew so thin all his clothes

     fell off, I dreamed
his mouth full of suns,

    I dreamed he called my name
     to the room's farthest corners.

Heart with a hole in it.
   Hand that drops the stone

     it holds. He shaved his arms
because he liked the way

   they moved through the air,
     smooth and mechanical.

Once, he told me about
   hunting with his father,

     its strange beauty.
How the word *dress* means

   to adorn oneself, but also
     to be hung on a hook

by the foot, for everything
   to be stripped away.

This Compost

1

Something startles me where I thought I was safest,
I withdraw from the still woods I loved,
I will not go now on the pastures to walk,
I will not strip the clothes from my body to meet my lover the sea,
I will not touch my flesh to the earth as to other flesh to renew me.

O how can it be that the ground itself does not sicken?
How can you be alive you growths of spring?
How can you furnish health you blood of herbs, roots, orchards, grain?
Are they not continually putting distemper'd corpses within you?
Is not every continent work'd over and over with sour dead?

Where have you disposed of their carcasses?
Those drunkards and gluttons of so many generations?
Where have you drawn off all the foul liquid and meat?
I do not see any of it upon you to-day, or perhaps I am deceiv'd,
I will run a furrow with my plough, I will press my spade through the sod and turn it
    up underneath,
I am sure I shall expose some of the foul meat.

2

Behold this compost! behold it well!
Perhaps every mite has once form'd part of a sick person—yet behold!
The grass of spring covers the prairies,
The bean bursts noiselessly through the mould in the garden,
The delicate spear of the onion pierces upward,
The apple-buds cluster together on the apple-branches,
The resurrection of the wheat appears with pale visage out of its graves,
The tinge awakes over the willow-tree and the mulberry-tree,
The he-birds carol mornings and evenings while the she-birds sit on their nests,
The young of poultry break through the hatch'd eggs,
The new-born of animals appear, the calf is dropt from the cow, the colt from the mare,

Out of its little hill faithfully rise the potato's dark green leaves,
Out of its hill rises the yellow maize-stalk, the lilacs bloom in the dooryards,
The summer growth is innocent and disdainful above all those strata of sour dead.

What chemistry!
That the winds are really not infectious,
That this is no cheat, this transparent green-wash of the sea which is so amorous
    after me,
That it is safe to allow it to lick my naked body all over with its tongues,
That it will not endanger me with the fevers that have deposited themselves in it,
That all is clean forever and forever,
That the cool drink from the well tastes so good,
That blackberries are so flavorous and juicy,
That the fruits of the apple-orchard and the orange-orchard, that melons, grapes,
    peaches, plums, will none of them poison me,
That when I recline on the grass I do not catch any disease,
Though probably every spear of grass rises out of what was once a catching
    disease.

Now I am terrified at the Earth, it is that calm and patient,
It grows such sweet things out of such corruptions,
It turns harmless and stainless on its axis, with such endless successions of diseas'd
    corpses,
It distills such exquisite winds out of such infused fetor,
It renews with such unwitting looks its prodigal, annual, sumptuous crops,
It gives such divine materials to men, and accepts such leavings from them at last.

Juneberry

Though others name you shadbush, shadblow,
saskatoon, and sugarplum, you're always June to me.
Your bruise-hued fruits fuse blueberry and apple, cherry and pear.

I planted you. Watered you, watched your orange flames
flicker in autumn, your snowy blossoms flash in spring.
You torch, fan-dancer, branches smooth as sanded glass.

On each rare visit I note your growth—I've grown, too, with less show.
You can't see new leaves sprouting on my ribs, the dangerous
flower poised beneath. I call it Hookbow.

Once you fit in my car. Now you're the size of it.
I haven't planted in years. You, the lilac, the buddleia—last
root balls I opened and bedded. If the new tenants don't praise you,

call out to me, shadbush, shadblow, sugarplum,
your blooms white and fragile as fish bones. I will prune you
to a shape like fire, name you until each leaf brightens like a kiss.

A Poem for Trapped Things

This morning with a blue flame burning
this thing wings its way in.
Wind shakes the edges of its yellow being.
Gasping for breath.
Living for the instant.
Climbing up the black border of the window.
Why do you want out.
I sit in pain. ·
A red robe amid debris.
You bend and climb, extending antennae.

I know the butterfly is my soul
grown weak from battle.

A Giant fan on the back of
                    a beetle.
A caterpillar chrysalis that seeks
a new home apart from this room.

And will disappear from sight
at the pulling of invisible strings.
Yet so tenuous, so fine
   this thing is, I am
   sitting on the hard bed, we could
            vanish from sight like the puff
               off an invisible cigarette.
Furred chest, ragged silk under
         wings beating against the glass

         no one will open.

The blue diamonds on your back
are too beautiful to do
            away with.

I watch you
  all morning
    long.
With my hand over my mouth.

blackbody

> "An ideal body is now defined, called a *blackbody* . . .
> the *blackbody* is a *perfect absorber* . . . "
>
> —Robert Siegel and John R. Howell,
> *Thermal Radiation Heat Transfer; Volume 1*

A body can be perfectly black meaning it absorbs all radiance—all heat and light waves that fall upon it. A blackbody is perfect because it is a perfect absorber—all waves that strike its surface pass into the body and the body absorbs them internally. Nothing striking the blackbody passes through the body's edge. Nothing striking the blackbody is reflected back into the environment. The blackbody is perfect. It is opaque. It is not defined by its size or shape. It might not be black at all. The color black absorbs all wavelengths of light that fall upon it. The blackbody is named for its presumed blackness to the naked eye but a blackbody can be red or blue or another color. The blackness is theoretical. The blackbody is theoretical—a device used to give body to abstractions. Perfect black is a theoretical ideal—it has not been observed but exists for the sake of comparison. For the sake of comparison, the opposite of a blackbody is a white body. A white body reflects all waves perfectly in all directions. The white body is also an abstraction that exists for the sake of comparison. The albedo scale compares white bodies and blackbodies. Albedo comes from Arabic's *albayad. Albayad* roughly translates to "whiteness." In physics, albedo is a measure of reflectivity and brightness. Scientists say the albedo effect is warming our planet beyond safety. Said another way, the whiteness effect is warming our planet beyond safety. 91% of Fortune 500 CEOs are white men. Outdoor air pollution has risen 8% in the past five years. The arctic is melting—the white ice is falling into the dark sea turning reflective surfaces into heat absorbers. It's getting warmer. By "it's getting warmer," I mean that it was 129.2° in Iran last week. By "it's getting warmer," I mean that in 2010, 10,000 scorched to death in Moscow. By "it's getting warmer", I mean that by 2080, 3,300 will scorch to death on the streets of New York City, and half of those buried will be black. It's getting warmer and I wonder about white men in boardrooms. I wonder about the PowerPoint presentations and profit diagrams. On the diagram, the blue line is profit. The black bodies pile under the blue line over the axis of time and the blue line rises. In the boardroom, the black body is the ideal—we absorb perfectly.

First Words

A storm and so a gift.
    Its swift approach
        lifts gravel from the road.
A fence is flattened in
    the course of the storm's
        worse attempt at language—
thunder's umbrage. A tree
    is torn apart,
        blown upward through a bedroom
window. A boy winnows
    through the pile
        of shards for the sharpest parts
from the blown-apart
    glass. He has
        a bag that holds found edges
jagged as a stag's
    horns or smooth as
        a single pane smashed into
smaller panes that he sticks
    his hand inside
        to make blood web across
his acheless skin flexing
    like fish gills
        O-lipped for a scream
it cannot make.
    He wants to feel
        what his friends have felt,
the slant of fear on their faces
    he could never
        recreate, his body born
without pain. When his skin's
    pouting welts
        don't rake a whimper
from his mouth, he runs

outside, arms up
      for the storm, aluminum
baseball bat held out
    to the sky
      until lightning, with an electric
tongue, makes his viscera
    luminescent;
      the boy's first word for pain
   is the light's
      new word for home.

Root Sutra

Take the square root
of home, an infinite progression
of willow tangles
and corn stalks,
of soybeans grown for nitrogen.
Add shadow self of alfalfa and timothy,
of cocklebur and button weed,
the deep tug of royal Canadian thistle,
the white heart
of an Englishman's dandelion.
Break into the matted core
of early prairie.

Root, O my soul, dug out,
transplanted, water logged,
hung to dry, resurrected.
Bed for acorn.
Home to the makers of soil.
Propagator of forests
waiting for the fire of grasses.
Wind-defying net.
Breaker of stone.
Fascia beneath the planet's skin.

O Root, perfect beauty,
wither us backward in time,
down and into the indivisible
tapestry of seasons.
Road out of history.
Tunnel to the afterlife.

Turing's Theories Regarding Homosexuality

If anything, we are this: hive, industry, insistent tales of fairy rings, all-chemical, penetrable, snow-drifted, darkling, that evening Murray stopped me outside the show, the amber of bourbon, windblown, sigil, lips tight, diurnal, lockstep, some future Velcro, conjured to the door, the way he took my hat and my platitudes, inserting look, opening, breaking open, knocking impatiently, clever sleight, clever ruse, standing by the window, weak blue like approaching light, clean, brandishing, he wanted us to have tea, leafy green, over-flowery, air, mist, he said he wanted to talk to a real scientist, entryway, hairline, disorganized, slick fabrications, the black line we ignore between speaking lips, eclipse, angles, blitzed, top to bottom, he held me in his hand like a kiss, Panama-brimmed, blinking, circuitry-sawing, sweating, the safest way to convey is from behind, lantern bearers, the word *water* in French, turbines, turbines waking up, the open-ask, how to subtract the man from his signs, his wide smile like a bridge to paradise, nightstands, the swell of morning behind heavy curtains, all those collections of O's, archipelagos, like planetary accretions, this swirling in, we press to spread wide, swallowed, discordant, gravity's only compromise, yes, relentlessly pressed, spreading, I opened, uncomplicated, unacknowledged, that the last time must needs remain memory, staccato of no applause, shoes on walls, fabric, bruise, a blast, helix-like in irony, fabulous liquids, his face increases in detail daily, unrevealable, that low smell of him.

The Trick

I made love with a man—hugely muscled, lean—the body
I always wished for myself. He kept pulling my arms
up over my head, pinning them there, pressing me down

with his entire weight, grinding into me roughly,
but then asked, begged, in a whisper of such sweetness,
Please kiss me. Earlier that evening, he told me

he'd watched a program about lions, admired
how they took their prey—menacing the herds at the water hole
before choosing the misfit, the broken one.

What surprised him was the wildebeests' calm
after the calf had been downed, how they returned to their grazing
with a dumb switching of tails. Nearby the lions looked up

from their meal, eyed the hopping storks and vultures,
before burying their faces, again, in the bloody ribs.
As a teenager, I wished to be consumed,

to be pressed into oblivion by a big forceful man.
It never happened. Instead I denied myself nourishment—
each un-filled plate staring back satisfied me, deprivation

reduced to a kind of bliss I could lie down in
where I remained unmoved, untouched.
Early on I was taught that the body was a cage,

that illness was a battle fought with chaos,
the viruses themselves unnatural; that sex lived
in some pastel chamber that gave way to infants,

first cousins, the handing down of names.
No one ever mentioned being taken in the dark,
or wanting to be broken open, pushed beyond words,

tongue thickening in another human mouth,
or how a person could be humiliated and like it.
To my surprise, I found myself struggling under this man,

pushing me chest up against his chest, arms straining
against the bed, until some younger, hungrier
version of myself lay back on top of me and took it—

the heaving back, the beard, the teeth at the throat.

The Kiss

I guided these fires
from a body of islands
burning and unable
to reach each other

Every day of needing
bends the waters closer
to the unseen flame who
moves to have anatomy

whose sudden heat will
open snow's first eyelid
to violet iris
and pupal stone

like the sprig of air
between our cheeks
and the whole pink birds
first writhing for it

The Gods among Us

One of them grants you the ability
to forecast the future; another wrenches
your tongue from your mouth, changes you
into a bird precisely because you have been
given this gift. The gods are generous

in this way. I learned to avoid danger, avoid fear,
avoid excitement, these the very triggers that prompt
my wings from their resting place deep inside.
And so, I avoided fights, avoided everything really.
In the locker room, I avoided other boys,

all the while intently studying that space
between their shoulder blades, patiently looking
for the tell-tale signs, looking to find even
one other boy like me, the wings buried but
there nonetheless. I studied them from a distance.

When people challenge a god, the gods curse them
with the label of madness. It is all very convenient.
And meanwhile, a god took the form of a swan
and raped a girl by the school gates. Another
took the shape of an eagle to abduct a boy

from the football field. Mad world.
And what about our teachers? Our teachers
expected us to sit and listen. In Theology, there was
a demon inside each of us; in History,
the demons among us. So many demons

in this world. Who among us could have spoken up
against the gods, the gods who continued living
among us? They granted wishes and punishments
much the way they always had. Very few noticed them
casually taking the shape of one thing or another.

Flora and Fauna

The girl I was
distrusted flowers
for their weakness,
for opening,
        the easy bruise.

I would hunt even if it broke stems,
blood among tattered instants of fragrance.

But this was before a Matisse tree

        was scissor-cut by sun

        and shadowcrack around me.

To prompt the change.

    What I mean is:
    all desire is apotheosis.

        Pull my head back by the hair-hank,
        demand my eyes,
        and I will more than submit to softening,
        to flush in rose, cleave to the dusk interior
        of clematis, draw nectar
        into my cuntly sepal and flourish.

    The story goes,
    "On the flesh playground
    (as every body is)
    a swing creaks
    like a heart valve
    letting a plume
    of blood slip out.

Under the mulberry bush,
two boys knocked me onto the dirt
and tried to discover the difference."

    One held me
    and one lay heavy
    on me. And I squirmed
    getting dirty,
    native to the fact
    struggling made me hot.

(mulberry juice sticky on my thighs.)

The dog in me sniffed its way home.

    Does that make me jump
    from where the girl drowned?

Alive and always growing, "queer nature" is a vast poetic subject. I'd like to thank and honor the geniuses featured in this anthology, with a deep appreciation of their talents and for allowing me to include them in these pages. While this anthology gathers together approximately two hundred poets, four times that number—in American poetry alone—could easily be recognized for their approaches and contributions, so I also want to recognize all the other equally ingenious poets whose work, whether historical or contemporary, engages with the theme of queer nature.

I couldn't have done the editorial work, which required thousands of hours of donated personal time over the last seven years, without the assistance of a poet whom I implicitly trust, my friend and collaborator: James Crews. As I was conceiving of the anthology, James was the sounding board for all of my ideas and brought his own to my wild vision. The array of early conceptual and administrative tasks was enormous, including, but not limited to, reading known work with a new lens, researching and discovering historical and contemporary work, typing poems, creating submission calls, soliciting work, and contacting potential publishers. The anthology wouldn't exist in its current form without James's many vital and structural contributions. His kindness broadened the communities of poets found in these pages, which his editorial strengths fortified. Getting *Queer Nature* to a stable state and finding the right publisher took longer than either of us imagined. I remain deeply thankful to James for all the heart he contributed as well as the time he donated in literary service to this essential resource.

In addition, I am equally grateful to Christine Stroud, editor in chief of Autumn House Press, for her generosity and willingness to take on a project of this size and scope. I am particularly thankful for the National Endowment for the Arts and Amazon Literary Partnership grants that Autumn House proposed and received in support of this book. *Queer Nature* couldn't have found a more hardworking and ideal champion in publishing than Christine.

Finally, I would like to express my profound gratitude to the National Endowment for the Arts, the Amazon Literary Partnership, and the Academy of American Poets for supporting this publication, which this editor intends as a resource for so many, especially queer and trans youth thinking about their places in the world.

Judith Barrington, "The Dyke with No Name Thinks About Landscape" from *Horses and the Human Soul* (Story Line Press, 2004). Reprinted with the permission of the author.

Samiya Bashir, "Ground State" from *Field Theories*. Copyright © 2020 by Samiya Bashir. Reprinted with the permission of The Permissions Company, LLC on behalf of Nightboat Books, Inc., nightboat.org.

Ellen Bass, "Kissing after Illness," Copyright © 2019 Ellen Bass.

Robin Becker, "Prairie Dogs" from *Tiger Heron*. Copyright © 2014 by Robin Becker. Reprinted by permission of the University of Pittsburgh Press.

Rosebud Ben-Oni, "Poet Wrestling with Why the Heart Feels So Bad" from *The Missouri Review* (2019). Copyright © 2019 by Rosebud Ben-Oni. Reprinted with the permission of the author.

Oliver Baez Bendorf, "Outing, Iowa" from *The Spectral Wilderness*. Copyright © 2014 by Oliver Baez Bendorf. Reprinted with the permission of The Kent State University Press.

Lillian-Yvonne Bertram, "Pastoral for Effective Teaching" from *But a Storm Is Blowing from Paradise*. Copyright © 2017 by Lillian-Yvonne Bertram. Reprinted with the permission of The Permissions Company, LLC on behalf of Red Hen Press, redhen.org.

Sophie Cabot Black, "Break Me to Prove I Am Unbroken" from *The Descent*. Copyright © 2004 by Sophie Cabot Black. Reprinted with the permission of The Permissions Company, LLC on behalf of Graywolf Press, graywolfpress.org.

Richard Blanco, "Burning in the Rain" from *Looking for the Gulf Motel*. Copyright © 2012 by Richard Blanco. Reprinted by permission of the University of Pittsburgh Press.

Elizabeth Bradfield, "Regarding the Absent Heat of Your Skin on Letters I Receive While at Sea" was originally published in *Alaska Quarterly Review* (Volume 27, No. 3 & 4).

Jari Bradley, "Unruly." Copyright © 2020 by Jari Bradley. Originally published in Poem-a-Day on January 8, 2020, by the Academy of American Poets. Reprinted with the permission of the author.

Julian Talamantez Brolaski, "in the cut" from *Of Mongrelitude*. Copyright © 2017 by Julian Talamantez Brolaski. Reprinted with the permission of The Permissions Company, LLC on behalf of Wave Books, wavepoetry.com.

Olga Broumas, "Fast" from *Rave: Poems 1975-1999*. Copyright © 1979 by Olga Broumas. Reprinted with the permission of The Permissions Company, LLC on behalf of Copper Canyon Press, coppercanyonpress.org.

Jericho Brown, "Lion" from *Please*. Copyright © 2009 by Jericho Brown. Reprinted with the permission of New Issues Poetry & Prose.

Nickole Brown, "Self-Portrait as Land Snail" from *To Those Who Were Our First Gods* (Rattle, 2018). Copyright © 2018 by Nickole Brown. Reprinted with the permission of the author.

Matthew Burgess, "Hurricane Lyric" originally appeared in *Court Green* (Issue 13, 2017).

Stephanie Burt, "Hermit Crab" from *Advice from the Lights*. Copyright © 2017 by Stephanie Burt. Reprinted with the permission of The Permissions Company, LLC on behalf of Graywolf Press, graywolfpress.org.

CAConrad, "For the Feral Splendor That Remains" from *Poetry* (January 2020). Copyright © 2020 by CAConrad. Reprinted with the permission of the author.

Gabrielle Calvocoressi, "Who Holds the Stag's Head Gets to Speak" from *Rocket Fantastic*. Copyright © 2017 by Gabrielle Calvocoressi. Reprinted with the permission of Persea Books (New York). All rights reserved.

Rafael Campo, "What I Would Give" from *Landscape with Human Figure*. Copyright © 2002 by

Rafael Campo. Reprinted with the permission of The Permissions Company, LLC on behalf of Copper Canyon Press, coppercanyonpress.org.

Kayleb Rae Candrilli, "On Harvesting Oneself" from *All the Gay Saints*. Copyright © 2019 by Kayleb Rae Candrilli. Reprinted with the permission of Saturnalia Books.

Cyrus Cassells, "The Hummingbird" from *Beautiful Signor*. Copyright © 1997 by Cyrus Cassells. Reprinted with the permission of The Permissions Company, LLC on behalf of Copper Canyon Press, coppercanyonpress.org.

Marcelo Hernandez Castillo, "Drown" from *Cenzontle*. Copyright © 2018 by Marcelo Hernandez Castillo. Reprinted with the permission of The Permissions Company, LLC on behalf of BOA Editions, Ltd., boaeditions.org.

Jerah Chadwick, "Lesson of Bread" from *Story Hunger*. Copyright © 1999 by Jerah Chadwick. Reprinted with the permission of Salmon Publishing.

Judith Chalmer, "Post Op" from *Minnow*. Originally in *Nimrod International Journal* (2013). Reprinted with the permission of the author and Kelsay Books.

Jos Charles, "XXIV." from *feeld*. Copyright © 2018 by Jos Charles. Reprinted with the permission of The Permissions Company, LLC on behalf of Milkweed Editions, milkweed.org.

Chen Chen, "Elegy to Be Exhaled at Dusk" from *When I Grow Up I Want to Be a List of Further Possibilities*. Copyright © 2017 by Chen Chen. Reprinted with the permission of The Permissions Company, LLC on behalf of BOA Editions, Ltd., boaeditions.org.

Ching-In Chen, "Dear O" from *Rumpus* (2018). Copyright © 2018 by Ching-In Chen. Reprinted with the permission of the author.

Justin Chin, "Magnified" from *Justin Chin: Selected Works*. Copyright © 2016 by Justin Chin. Reprinted with the permission of Manic D Press.

Franny Choi, "Wildlife" from *Under a Warm Green Linden*, Issue 2 (Winter 2016). Reprinted with the permission of the author.

Chrystos, "Desire as Blue Fog" from *In Her I Am* (Press Gang Publishers, 1999). Copyright © 1999 by Chrystos. Reprinted with the permission of the author.

Cody-Rose Clevidence, "[this the forest]" from *Beast-Feast* (Boise, Idaho: Ahsahta Press, 2014). Copyright © 2014 by Cody-Rose Clevidence. Reprinted with the permission of the author.

Henri Cole, "The Rock" from *Nothing to Declare*. Copyright © 2015 by Henri Cole. Reprinted by permission of Farrar, Straus & Giroux, LLC.

Flower Conroy, "Welcome to the Fall" from *Snake Breaking Medusa Disorder* (NSFPS Press, 2019). Reprinted with the permission of the author.

S. Brook Corfman, "(An Orchid)" from *Luxury, Blue Lace*. Copyright © 2018 by S. Brook Corfman. Reprinted with the permission of Autumn House Press, autumnhouse.org.

Eduardo C. Corral, "To a Straight Man" from *Guillotine*. Copyright © 2020 by Eduardo C. Corral. Reprinted with the permission of The Permissions Company, LLC on behalf of Graywolf Press, graywolfpress.org.

James Crews, "First Date, Hawk Mountain" from *Bluebird* (Green Writers Press, 2020). Reprinted by permission of the author.

Meg Day, "Once All the Hounds Had Been Called Home" from *Last Psalm at Sea Level*. Copyright © 2014 by Meg Day. Reprinted with the permission of Barrow Street Press.

tatiana de la tierra, "The Art of Butterflying" from *For the Hard Ones: A Lesbian Phenomenology* (A Midsummer Night's Press and Sinister Wisdom, 2018). Copyright © 2018 by tatiana de la tierra. Reprinted with the permission of the Estate of tatiana de la tierra.

Rae Gouirand, "You Form" from *Open Winter* (Bellday Books, 2011). Copyright © 2011 by Rae Gouirand. Reprinted with the permission of the author.

Jan-Henry Gray, "A Migration" from *Documents*. Copyright © 2019 by Jan-Henry Gray. Reprinted with the permission of The Permissions Company, LLC on behalf of BOA Editions, Ltd., boaeditions.org.

Miriam Bird Greenberg, "Heaven and Earth" from *In the Volcano's Mouth*. Copyright © 2016 by Miriam Bird Greenberg. Reprinted by permission of the University of Pittsburgh Press.

Rachel Eliza Griffiths, "A Kingdom of Longing" from *The Requited Distance*. Copyright © 2011 by Rachel Eliza Griffiths. Reprinted with the permission of Sheep Meadow Press.

Benjamin S. Grossberg, "Not Children" from *Sweet Core Orchard*. Copyright © 2009. Reprinted by permission of the author and the University of Tampa Press.

Thom Gunn, "Words for Some Ash" from *Collected Poems*. Copyright © 1994 by Thom Gunn. Reprinted by permission of Farrar, Straus & Giroux, LLC.

Roy G. Guzmán, "Queerodactyl" from *Catrachos*. Copyright © 2010 by Roy G. Guzmán. Reprinted with the permission of The Permissions Company, LLC on behalf of Graywolf Press, graywolfpress.org.

Marilyn Hacker, "Nearly a Valediction" from *Winter Numbers* (New York: W.W. Norton, 1994). Copyright © 1994 by Marilyn Hacker. Used by permission of Frances Collin Literary Agent.

Eloise Klein Healy, "The Valley of the Amazons" from *A Wild Surmise: New and Selected Poems*. Copyright © 2013 by Eloise Klein Healy. Reprinted with the permission of The Permissions Company, LLC on behalf of Red Hen Press, redhen.org.

Christopher Hennessy, "The Kiss" from *Love-in-Idleness*. Copyright © 2011 by Christopher Hennessy. Reprinted with the permission of Brooklyn Arts Press.

KateLynn Hibbard, "Bottle Gentian" originally appeared in *Simples* (Howling Bird Press, 2018). Reprinted by permission of the author.

Jane Hilberry, "Shadows, Saddle Canyon" from *Still the Animals Enter*. Copyright © 2016 by Jane Hilberry. Reprinted with the permission of The Permissions Company, LLC on behalf of Red Hen Press, redhen.org.

Matthew Hittinger, "Grafted" from *The Erotic Postulate* (Sibling Rivalry Press, 2014). Reprinted with the permission of the author.

Richie Hofmann, "Idyll" from *Second Empire*. Copyright © 2015 by Richie Hofmann. Reprinted with the permission of The Permissions Company, LLC on behalf of Alice James Books, alicejamesbooks.org.

Langston Hughes, "Demand" from *Collected Poems*. Copyright © 1994 by the Estate of Langston Hughes. Used by permission of Alfred A. Knopf, an imprint of the Knopf Doubleday Publishing Group, a division of Penguin Random House LLC. All rights reserved.

Luther Hughes, "Tenor" from *A Shiver in the Trees*. Originally in *Poetry* (December 2018). Copyright © 2018, 2022 by Luther Hughes. Reprinted with the permission of The Permissions Company, LLC on behalf of BOA Editions, Ltd., boaeditions.org.

Christina Hutchins, "Elementary Departures" from *The Stranger Dissolves* (San Francisco: Sixteen Rivers Press, 2011). Copyright © 2011 by Christina Hutchins. Reprinted with the permission of the author.

Jessica Jacobs, "Primer" from *Take Me with You, Wherever You're Going*. Copyright © 2019 by Jessica Jacobs. Reprinted with the permission of The Permissions Company, LLC on behalf of Four Way Books, fourwaybooks.com. All rights reserved.

"A Stranger Asks Where I Am From" by Charles Jensen first appeared in *Smartish Pace* Issue 24, released April 2017.

Joe Jiménez, "Mesquites" from *Rattlesnake Allegory*. Copyright © 2019 by Joe Jiménez. Reprinted with the permission of The Permissions Company, LLC on behalf of Red Hen Press, redhen. org.

Jenny Johnson, "Late Bloom" from *In Full Velvet*. Copyright © 2017 by Jenny Johnson. Reprinted with the permission of The Permissions Company, LLC on behalf of Sarabande Books, sarabandebooks.com.

Stephen Jonas, "To a Strayed Cat" from *Arcana: A Stephen Jonas Reader*. Copyright © 2019 by The Estate of Stephen Jonas. Reprinted with the permission of The Permissions Company, LLC on behalf of City Lights Books, citylights.com.

Ever Jones, "Golden Egg" from *Wilderness Lessons* (Future Cycle Press, 2016). Reprinted with the permission of the author.

Saeed Jones, "Drag" from *Prelude to Bruise*. Copyright © 2014 by Saeed Jones. Reprinted with the permission of The Permissions Company, LLC on behalf of Coffee House Press, coffeehousepress.org.

June Jordan, "Letter to the Local Police" from *Directed by Desire: Collected Poems* (Port Townsend, Wash.: Copper Canyon Press, 2005*)*. Copyright by The June M. Jordan Literary Trust. Reprinted by permission, www.junejordan.com.

Britteney Black Rose Kapri, "purple" from *Black Queer Hoe* (Chicago: Haymarket Books, 2018). Copyright © 2018 by Britteney Black Rose Kapri. Reprinted with the permission of the author.

Donika Kelly, "Love Poem: Chimera" from *Bestiary*. Copyright © 2016 by Donika Kelly. Reprinted with the permission of The Permissions Company, LLC on behalf of Graywolf Press, graywolfpress.org.

Maurice Kenny, "Young Male" from *Carving Hawk: New and Selected Poems*. Copyright © 2002 by Maurice Kenny. Reprinted with the permission of The Permissions Company, LLC on behalf of White Pine Press, whitepine.org.

Alyse Knorr, "Conservation & Rehabilitation" from *Building Fires in the Snow: A Collection of Alaska LBTQ Short Fiction and Poetry*. Copyright © 2016 by Alyse Knorr. Reprinted with the permission of the author.

Melissa Kwasny, "Sweet Briar" from *The Nine Senses*. Copyright © 2011 by Melissa Kwasny. Reprinted with the permission of The Permissions Company, LLC on behalf of Milkweed Editions, milkweed.org.

Joy Ladin, "A Little Bit of Ocean" from *The Future Is Trying to Tell Us Something: New and Selected Poems*. Copyright © by Joy Ladin. Reprinted with the permission of Sheep Meadow Press.

Gerrit Lansing, "Perianth" from *Heavenly Tree, Northern Earth*, published by North Atlantic Books. Copyright © 2009 by Gerrit Lansing. Reprinted by permission of the publisher.

Joan Larkin, "Breathing You In" from *My Body: New and Selected Poems*. Copyright © 2007 by Joan Larkin. Reprinted with the permission of Hanging Loose Press.

Travis Chi Wing Lau, "Self-Portrait with Scoliosis (II)" from *From Impossible Beasts: Queer Erotic Poems*. Copyright © 2020 by Travis Chi Wing Lau. Reprinted with the permission of the author and Damaged Goods Press.

Rickey Laurentiis, "A Southern Wind" from *Boy with Thorn*. Copyright © 2015 by Rickey Laurentiis. Reprinted by permission of the University of Pittsburgh Press.

Joseph O. Legaspi, "Amphibians" from *The Quarry: A Social Justice Poetry Justice Database*. Reprinted with the permission of the author.

Muriel Leung, "Love Two Times" Copyright © 2015 by Muriel Leung. As first published by *The Margins* the digital magazine of the Asian American Writers' Workshop. Reprinted with the permission of the author.

Timothy Liu, "I Came" from *Burnt Offerings*. Copyright © 1995 by Timothy Liu. Reprinted with the permission of The Permissions Company, LLC on behalf of Copper Canyon Press, coppercanyonpress.org.

Chip Livingston, "poem to my boyfriend's human immunodeficiency virus" from *Crow Blue, Crow Black*. Copyright © 2012 by Chip Livingston. Reprinted with the permission of the author and NYQ Books.

Audre Lorde, "Coal." Copyright © 1968, 1970, 1973 by Audre Lorde. Copyright © 1997 by The Audre Lorde Estate., from the *Collected Poems of Audre Lorde* by Audre Lorde. Used by permission of W. W. Norton & Company, Inc.

Su Smallen Love, "Falling, Falling, Then Rain, Then Snow" from *Kinds of Snow* (Brattleboro, Vermont: Green Writers Press, 2016). Copyright © 2016 by Su Smallen Love. Reprinted with the permission of the author, www.sulove.org.

Ed Madden, "Viscous" from *Prodigal: Variations* (Lethe Press, 2011). Copyright © 2011 by Ed Madden. Reprinted with the permission of the author.

Dawn Lundy Martin, "[Dear one, the sea . . .]" from *Life in a Box is a Pretty Life*. Copyright © 2014 by Dawn Lundy Martin. Reprinted with the permission of The Permissions Company, LLC on behalf of Nightboat Books, Inc., nightboat.org.

Janet McAdams, "The Way the World Comes Back" from *Feral* (Cambridge, United Kingdom: Salt Publishing, 2007). Copyright © 2007 by Janet McAdams. Reprinted with the permission of the author.

J. D. McClatchy, "My Sideshow" from *Plundered Hearts: New and Selected Poems*. Copyright © 2014 by J. D. McClatchy. Used by permission of Alfred A. Knopf, an imprint of the Knopf Doubleday Publishing Group, a division of Penguin Random House LLC. All rights reserved.

Anne Haven McDonnell, "Coming Out in the Ozarks," previously published in *The Fourth River*, the "Queering Nature" issue.

Kevin McLellan, "Dear Canaries" from *Ornitheology* (WordWorks, 2018). Reprinted with the permission of the author.

Sarah María Medina, "América" from *Poetry* (November 2019). Copyright © 2019 by Sarah María Medina. Reprinted with the permission of the author.

William Meredith, "For Two Lovers in the Year 2075 in the Canadian Woods" from *Effort at Speech: New and Selected Poems*. Copyright © 1997 by William Meredith. Published 1997 by TriQuarterly Books/Northwestern University Press. All rights reserved.

James Merrill, "The Lovers" from *Collected Poems*. Copyright © 2001 by the Literary Estate of James Merrill at Washington University. Used by permission of Alfred A. Knopf, an imprint of the Knopf Doubleday Publishing Group, a division of Penguin Random House LLC. All rights reserved.

Deborah Miranda, "Eating a Mountain" from *Raised by Humans*. Copyright © 2015 by Deborah Miranda. Reprinted with the permission of Tia Chucha Press.

Susanna J. Mishler, "Hemispheres" from *Termination Dust*. Copyright © 2014 by Susanna Mishler. Reprinted with the permission of The Permissions Company, LLC on behalf of Red Hen Press, redhen.org.

Rajiv Mohabir, "The Complete Tracker" from *The Taxidermist's Cut*. Copyright © 2016 by Rajiv Mohabir, Reprinted with the permission of The Permissions Company, LLC on behalf of Four Way Books, fourwaybooks.com.

Kamilah Aisha Moon, "Shared Plight" from *Starshine & Clay*. Copyright © 2017 by Kamilah Aisha Moon. Reprinted with the permission of The Permissions Company, LLC on behalf of Four Way Books, fourwaybooks.com.

Rachel Moritz, "Real Curvature" from *Borrowed Wave* (Kore Press, 2015). Copyright © 2015 by Rachel Moritz. Reprinted with the permission of the author.

Alicia Mountain, "Hawk like a Steeple" from *High Ground Coward*. Copyright © 2018 by Alicia Mountain. Reprinted with the permission of the University of Iowa Press.

Miguel Murphy, "He Says, Oyster" from *Detainee*. Copyright © 2016 by Miguel Murphy. Reprinted with the permission of Barrow Street Press.

Eileen Myles, "[I always put my pussy]" from *I Must Be Living Twice: New and Selected Poems*. Copyright © 2015 by Eileen Myles. Reprinted by permission of HarperCollins Publishers.

Hieu Minh Nguyen, "Changeling" from *Not Here*. Copyright © 2018 by Hieu Minh Nguyen. Reprinted with the permission of The Permissions Company, LLC on behalf of Coffee House Press, coffeehousepress.org.

Miller Oberman, "On Trans" from *The Unstill Ones*. Copyright © 2017 by Princeton University Press. Reprinted by permission of Princeton University Press.

Frank O'Hara, "To You" from *The Collected Poems of Frank O'Hara*. Copyright © 1971 by Maureen Granville-Smith, Administratrix of the Estate of Frank O'Hara, copyright renewed 1999 by Maureen O'Hara Granville-Smith and Donald Allen. Used by permission of Alfred A. Knopf, an imprint of the Knopf Doubleday Publishing Group, a division of Penguin Random House LLC. All rights reserved.

Mary Oliver, "Wild Geese" from *Dream Work*. Copyright © 1992 by Mary Oliver. Used by permission of Grove/Atlantic, Inc. Any third party use of this material, outside of this publication, is prohibited.

Kate Partridge, "Three times on the trail, I looked back for you," from *Ends of the Earth*. Copyright © 2017 by the University of Alaska Press. Reprinted by permission.

Juliet Patterson, "Toward" from *Threnody*. Copyright © 2016 by Juliet Patterson. Reprinted with the permission of The Permissions Company, LLC on behalf of Nightboat Books, Inc., nightboat.org.

Gerry Gomez Pearlberg, "Thrush" from *Marianne Faithfull's Cigarette* (San Francisco: Cleis Press, 1998). Copyright © 1998 by Gerry Gomez Pearlberg. Reprinted with the permission of the author.

Carl Phillips, "Radiance versus Ordinary Light" from *Riding Westward*. Copyright © 2006 by Carl Phillips. Reprinted by permission of Farrar, Straus & Giroux, LLC.

Xan Phillips, "Nature Poem with a Compulsive Attraction to the Shark" from *Hull*. Copyright © 2019 by Xan Phillips. Reprinted with the permission of The Permissions Company, LLC on behalf of Nightboat Books, Inc., nightboat.org.

Tommy Pico, "[This white guy asks do I feel more connected to nature]" from *Nature Poem*. Copyright © 2017 by Tommy Pico. Reprinted with the permission of Tin House Press.

Carol Potter, "Migration" from *Otherwise Obedient*. Copyright © 2008 by Carol Potter. Reprinted with the permission of The Permissions Company, LLC on behalf of Red Hen Press, redhen.org.

Eric Tran, "Garden" from *The Gutter Spread Guide to Prayer*. Copyright © 2020 by Eric Tran. Reprinted with the permission of Autumn House Press, autumnhouse.org.

Arianne True, "the aftermath of what" from *New Poetry by Queer Indigenous Women* (Literary Hub, 2017). Copyright © 2017 by Arianne True. Reprinted with the permission of the author.

Vanessa Angélica Villarreal, "Beast Meridian" from *Beast Meridian*. Copyright © 2017 by Vanessa Angélica Villarreal. Reprinted with the permission of Noemi Press.

Irene Villaseñor, "Instructions for Opening up the Heart" from *Tayo Literary Magazine* (June 2019). Copyright © 2019 by Irene Villaseñor. Reprinted with the permission of the author.

Ocean Vuong, "Torso of Air" from *Night Sky with Exit Wounds*. Copyright © 2016 by Ocean Vuong. Reprinted with the permission of The Permissions Company, LLC on behalf of Copper Canyon Press, coppercanyonpress.org.

Stacey Waite, "Butch Geography" from *Butch Geography*. Copyright © 2014 by Stacey Waite. Reprinted with the permission of The Permissions Company, LLC on behalf of Tupelo Press, tupelopress.org.

Michael Walsh, "A Natural History of Gay Love" was originally published in *Flyway: Journal of Writing & Environment* (Winter 2021-2022 Issue).

Michael Wasson, "The Third Measure Paused & Set to Your Breathing" from *The Rumpus* (2018). Copyright © 2018 by Michael Wasson. Reprinted with the permission of the author.

Valerie Wetlaufer, "Iowa" from *When We Become Weavers: Queer Female Poets on the Midwestern Experience* (Squares and Rebels Press, 2012). Copyright © 2012 by Valerie Wetlaufer. Reprinted with the permission of the author.

Arisa White, "Tail" from *You're the Most Beautiful Thing That Happened*. Copyright © 2016 by Arisa White. Reprinted with the permission of Augury Books.

James L. White, "Skin Movers" from *The Salt Ecstasies*. Copyright © 2010 by James L. White. Reprinted with the permission of The Permissions Company, LLC on behalf of Graywolf Press, graywolfpress.org.

Jim Whiteside, "Parable." Previously published in the chapbook: *Writing Your Name on the Glass* (Bull City Press, 2019). Reprinted by permission of the author.

Amie Whittemore, "Juneberry" from *Glass Harvest*. Copyright © 2016 by Amie Whittemore. Reprinted with the permission of Autumn House Press, autumnhouse.org.

John Wieners, "A Poem for Trapped Things" from *Supplication: Selected Poems*, edited by Joshua Beckman, CA Conrad, and Robert Dewhurst. Copyright © 1964 by John Wieners. Reprinted with the permission of The Literary Estate of John Wieners, Raymond Foye, Executor.

Candace Williams, "blackbody" from *Prelude* Issue 4 (2018). Reprinted with the permission of the author.

Phillip B. Williams, "First Words" from *Thief in the Interior*. Copyright © 2016 by Phillip B. Williams. Reprinted with the permission of The Permissions Company, LLC on behalf of Alice James Books, alicejamesbooks.org.

Morgan Grayce Willow, "Root Sutra" from *Dodge & Scramble* (Ice Cube Press, 2013). Copyright © 2013 by Morgan Grayce Willow. Reprinted with the permission of the author.

Tobias Wray, "Turing's Theories Regarding Homosexuality" appeared in *The Texas Review* (Fall/Winter 2017).

Mark Wunderlich, "The Trick" from *The Anchorage*. Copyright © 2013 by Mark Wunderlich. Published by the University of Massachusetts Press.

Tory Adkisson is the author of *The Flesh Between Us* (SIU Press), winner of the Crab Orchard Open Book competition. A native of Southern California, he currently lives in Oakland, California, with his husband and two cats while teaching writing at UC Berkeley.

Kaveh Akbar is the author of *Calling a Wolf a Wolf* as well as *Pilgrim Bell* and has received honors such as a Levis Reading Prize and multiple Pushcart Prizes. Born in Tehran, Iran, he teaches at Purdue University and in low-residency programs at Warren Wilson and Randolph Colleges.

Kazim Ali has published numerous books in multiple genres, including most recently the collection of poetry *The Voice of Sheila Chandra*, a nonfiction book *Northern Light: Power, Land, and the Memory of Water*, and a young adult interactive fantasy novel *The Citadel of Whispers*. He is also a translator and editor, most recently of the anthology *New Moons: Contemporary Writing by North American Muslims*. Founder of Nightboat Books, Ali is currently a professor and chair of the Department of Literature at the University of California, San Diego.

A renowned scholar of Native American literature, **Paula Gunn Allen** (1939-2008) was a professor as well as the author of many important books, including *The Sacred Hoop: Recovering the Feminine in American Indian Traditions* as well as *Life Is a Fatal Disease: Collected Poems 1962-1995*.

Ally Ang is a gaysian poet living on the occupied Duwamish & Coast Salish lands known as Seattle. Ally's work appears in *Foglifter, Muzzle Magazine, The Journal, Nepantla: An Anthology Dedicated to Queer Poets of Color,* and elsewhere. Find them at allysonang.com.

Antler, former poet laureate of Milwaukee, is author of *Exclamation Points ad Infinitum!, Factory, Last Words, Selected Poems, Subterranean Rivulet,* and *Touch Each Other*. His poems have been anthologized in *American Poets Say Goodbye to the 20th Century, Atomic Ghost: Poets Respond to the Nuclear Age, Nobody Gets Off the Bus: the Viet Nam Generation Big Book, Poetic Voices without Borders, Poets against the War, Reclaiming the Heartland: Lesbian & Gay Voices from the Midwest,* and *The Soul Unearthed: Celebrating Wildness & Personal Renewal through Nature*.

Gloria Anzaldúa (1942-2004) was an internationally acclaimed independent scholar and creative writer. She was the author of several books of poetry, nonfiction, and children's fiction. As the author of *Borderlands/La Frontera: The New Mestiza*, Anzaldúa played a major role in shaping contemporary Chicano/a and lesbian/queer theories and identities.

Aaron Apps is the author of *Intersex* (Tarpaulin Sky Press, 2015) and *Dear Herculine*, winner of the 2014 Sawtooth Poetry Prize from Ahsahta Press. His writing has appeared in numerous journals, including *Pleiades, LIT, Washington Square Review, Puerto del Sol, Columbia Poetry Review*, and *Blackbird*.

Francisco Aragón is the son of Nicaraguan immigrants. His books include *After Rubén* (2020), *Glow of Our Sweat* (2010), and *Puerta del Sol* (2005). His poetry has appeared in over twenty anthologies. A native of San Francisco, California, he's on the faculty of the University of Notre Dame's Institute for Latino Studies (ILS), where he teaches courses in Latinx poetry and creative writing. He directs the ILS literary initiative, Letras Latinas. He's read his work widely, including at universities, bookstores, art galleries, the Dodge Poetry Festival, and the Split This Rock Poetry Festival. For more information, visit: http://franciscoaragon.net.

Brent Armendinger is the author of *Street Gloss* (The Operating System, 2019) and *The Ghost in Us Was Multiplying* (Noemi Press, 2015), both of which were finalists for the California Book Award in Poetry. His poems and translations have appeared in many journals, including *Asymptote, Bennington Review, Colorado Review, Conjunctions, Denver Quarterly, DIAGRAM, The Georgia Review, Ghost Proposal, Interim*, and *Sporklet*. Brent has been awarded residencies and fellowships at Mineral School, Blue Mountain Center, Headlands Center for the Arts, and the Community of Writers. He teaches creative writing at Pitzer College and lives in Los Angeles with his husband, Joseph Gallucci.

Jubi Arriola-Headley (he/him) is a Blacqueer poet, a storyteller, a first-generation United Statesian, and author of the poetry collection *original kink* (Sibling Rivalry Press), recipient of the 2021 Housatonic Book Award. Jubi's received support from PEN America, Millay Arts, Lambda Literary, and the Atlantic Center for the Arts, among others, and he and his work have been featured in *Literary Hub, The Rumpus, Beloit Poetry Journal, Nimrod, Southern Humanities Review*, PBS NewsHour's *Brief But Spectacular*, and elsewhere. Jubi lives with his husband in South Florida, on Tequesta and Seminole lands.

John Ashbery (1927-2017) was a poet, professor, and art critic. The author of many collections of poetry, he received the Pulitzer Prize for Poetry, the National Book Award, and the National Book Critics Circle Award for *Self-Portrait in a Convex Mirror*.

Derrick Austin is the author of *Tenderness* and *Trouble the Water* (BOA Editions). *Black Sand*, his first chapbook, will be published by Foundlings Press in early 2022.

Ruth Awad is a 2021 NEA Poetry Fellow and the author of *Set to Music a Wildfire* (Southern Indiana Review Press, 2017), winner of the 2016 Michael Waters Poetry Prize and the 2018 Ohioana Book Award for Poetry. Alongside Rachel Mennies, she is the coeditor of *The Familiar Wild: On Dogs & Poetry* (Sundress Publications, 2020).

Cameron Awkward-Rich is the author of two collections of poetry: *Sympathetic Little Monster* (Ricochet Editions, 2016) and *Dispatch* (Persea Books, 2019). His creative work has been supported by fellowships from Cave Canem, The Watering Hole, and the Lannan Foundation. His more critical writing can be found in *Signs, Transgender Studies Quarterly, American Quarterly*, and elsewhere, and has been supported by fellowships from Duke University and the American Council of Learned Societies. Presently, he is an assistant professor of Women, Gender, and Sexuality Studies at the University of Massachusetts Amherst.

Rick Barot's most recent book of poems, *The Galleons*, was published by Milkweed Editions and was longlisted for the National Book Award. His work has appeared in numerous publications, including *Poetry, The New Republic, Tin House, Kenyon Review*, and *The New Yorker*. He has received fellowships from the Guggenheim Foundation, the National Endowment for the Arts, and Stanford University. He lives in Tacoma, Washington, and directs The Rainier Writing Workshop, the low-residency MFA program in creative writing at Pacific Lutheran University.

Judith Barrington's sixth collection, *Long Love: New & Selected Poems*, came out from Salmon Poetry in 2018. In 2013 she was awarded the Gregory O'Donoghue International Poetry Prize at the Cork Poetry Festival. Poems have appeared in many literary journals including *Prairie Schooner, Americas Review, Kenyon Review, ZYZZYVA, The American Voice*, and *Poetry London*. Her *Lifesaving: A Memoir* was the winner of the Lambda Book Award and a finalist for the PEN/Martha Albrand Award for the Art of the Memoir. She is cofounder of Soapstone Inc., an organization offering study groups on women writers in Portland, Oregon. More at www.judithbarrington.com.

Samiya Bashir is a poet, writer, librettist, performer, and multimedia poetry maker whose work, both solo and collaborative, has been widely published, performed, installed, printed, screened, experienced, and Oxford comma'd from Berlin to Düsseldorf, Amsterdam to Accra, Florence to Rome, and across the United States. An associate professor at Reed College in Portland, Oregon, Bashir works to create, employ, and teach—within and without traditional academic setting—a restorative poetics which can acknowledge the despair often bred by isolation and turn it towards a poetics of light and its potential for witness, for healing, and for change.

Ellen Bass's most recent book is *Indigo* (Copper Canyon Press, 2020). She coedited the first major anthology of women's poetry, *No More Masks!* (Doubleday, 1973), and co-wrote the groundbreaking *The Courage to Heal* (HarperCollins, 1988, 2008). Her awards include fellowships from the Guggenheim Foundation, the NEA, California Arts Council, three Pushcart Prizes, and The Lambda Literary Award. Her poems frequently appear in *The New Yorker* and many other magazines. A Chancellor of the Academy of American Poets, Bass founded poetry workshops at Salinas Valley State Prison and Santa Cruz, California jails, and teaches in the MFA program at Pacific University.

Robin Becker's books of poems include *The Black Bear Inside Me* (2018), *Tiger Heron* (2014), *Domain of Perfect Affection* (2006), and *All-American Girl* (1996), all published in the Pitt Poetry Series. Her poems and book reviews have appeared in the *American Poetry Review*, *The Georgia Review*, *Prairie Schooner*, *The New Yorker*, *The New York Times Magazine*, and many other journals. For two decades, Becker served as Poetry and Contributing Editor for the *Women's Review of Books*. Pennsylvania State University Liberal Arts Research Professor Emerita, in English and Women's Studies, Becker served as the 2010-2011 Penn State Laureate.

Rosebud Ben-Oni is the winner of 2019 Alice James Award for *If This Is the Age We End Discovery* (2021), and author of *turn around, BRXGHT XYXS* (Get Fresh Books, 2019) and *20 Atomic Sonnets* (*Black Warrior Review,* 2020). She has received fellowships from the New York Foundation for the Arts, CantoMundo, and Queens Council on the Arts. Her work appears in *Poetry, American Poetry Review, Academy of American Poets, Poetry Society of America, The Poetry Review* (UK), *Tin House*, and *Guernica*, among others. Her poem "Poet Wrestling with Angels in the Dark" was commissioned by the National September 11 Memorial in NYC.

Oliver Baez Bendorf is the author of *Advantages of Being Evergreen* and *The Spectral Wilderness*. A recipient of fellowships from the National Endowment for the Arts,

Vermont Studio Center, and University of Wisconsin-Madison, he teaches as poetry faculty for the MFA Program for Writers at Warren Wilson College. He lives in Olympia, Washington, and founded and directs Spellworks, a fun and welcoming portal for anyone working with the magic of poetry.

Lillian-Yvonne Bertram is the author of *Travesty Generator* (Noemi Press), *How Narrow My Escapes* (DIAGRAM/New Michigan Press), *Personal Science* (Tupelo Press), *a slice from the cake made of air* (Red Hen Press), and *But a Storm is Blowing From Paradise* (Red Hen Press).

Tamiko Beyer is the author of the poetry collections *Last Days* and *We Come Elemental*, both from Alice James Books. Her writing has been published widely, including by *Denver Quarterly*, *Idaho Review*, *Black Warrior Review*, and *The Georgia Review*. She has received awards from PEN America and the Astraea Lesbian Writers Fund. She publishes *Starlight and Strategy*, a monthly newsletter for shaping change. She is a queer, multiracial (Japanese and white), cisgender woman and femme, living and writing in on Massachusett, Wampanoag, and Pawtucket land. A social justice communications writer and strategist, she spends her days writing truth to power. (tamikobeyer.com)

Elizabeth Bishop (1911-1979) was a poet who published sparingly as well as a painter. In 1956, she received the Pulitzer Prize for Poetry for *Poems: North & South: A Cold Spring*.

Sophie Cabot Black has three poetry collections from Graywolf Press, *The Misunderstanding of Nature*, which received the Poetry Society of America's First Book Award; *The Descent*, which received the 2005 Connecticut Book Award; and most recently, *The Exchange*. Her poetry has appeared in numerous magazines, including *The Atlantic Monthly*, *The New Republic*, *The New Yorker*, and *The Paris Review*.

Selected by President Obama as the fifth Presidential Inaugural Poet in U.S. history, **Richard Blanco** was the youngest and the first Latino, immigrant, and gay person to serve in such a role. Born in Madrid to Cuban exile parents and raised in Miami, cultural identity characterizes his many collections of award-winning poetry, including his most recent, *How to Love a Country*, and his memoir *The Prince of Los Cocuyos: A Miami Childhood*. Blanco is a Woodrow Wilson Fellow, has received numerous honorary doctorates, serves as Education Ambassador for the Academy of American Poets, and is an Associate Professor at Florida International University.

Sam Bonosevich (she/they) is a queer, nonbinary poet, musician, and storyteller currently based in Philadelphia [unceded Lenni-Lenape land]. Growing up in the woodlands of Vermont and New Hampshire [unceded Abenaki land], she quickly became fascinated by both the beauty and darkness she saw in nature. They have performed their work on stages, in basements, and everywhere in between.

Elizabeth Bradfield is the author of *Toward Antarctica, Once Removed, Approaching Ice, Interpretive Work*, and *Theorem*, a collaboration with artist Antonia Contro. *Cascadia: A Field Guide Through Art, Ecology and Poetry*, which Bradfield is co-editing with Derek Sheffield and CMarie Fuhrman, will be published in 2023. Her work has been published in *The New Yorker, Atlantic Monthly, Poetry*, and her honors include the Audre Lorde Prize and a Stegner Fellowship. Founder of Broadsided Press, Liz works as a naturalist/guide and teaches creative writing at Brandeis University. (ebradfield.com)

Jari Bradley is a Black, genderqueer poet and scholar from San Francisco, California. They have received fellowships and support from Callaloo, Cave Canem, Tin House, The Pittsburgh Foundation, and The Heinz Endowments. They are currently a PhD candidate in Poetry at the University of Houston, and an Inprint C. Glenn Cambor Fellow.

Julian Talamantez Brolaski is the author of *Of Mongrelitude* (Wave Books, 2017), *Advice for Lovers* (City Lights, 2012), and *gowanusatropolis* (Ugly Duckling Presse, 2011), as well the recipient of the 2020 Cy Twombly Award for Poetry and a 2021 Pew Foundation Fellowship. Julian is also the lead singer and songwriter for Juan & the Pines, whose albums include *Glittering Forest* (2019) and *Saddest Songs* (forthcoming). Julian's poetry was recently included in *When the Light of the World was Subdued, Our Songs Came Through: A Norton Anthology of Native Nations Poetry* (2020) and *We Want It All: An Anthology of Radical Trans Poetics* (Nightboat, 2020).

The recipient of fellowships from the National Endowment for the Arts and the Guggenheim Foundation, **Olga Broumas** is a Professor Emerita at Brandeis University, where she chaired the creative writing department for twenty years. Her first book in English, *Beginning with O*, was selected by Stanley Kunitz for the Yale Younger Poets prize in 1977. Since then, she has published seven volumes of solo and collaborative poetry (with T Begley and Jane Miller) and translated three volumes of poems and a volume of essays by Odysseas Elytis. She lives on Cape Cod and teaches yoga.

Jericho Brown is the author of the collection *The Tradition* (2019), which was a finalist for the 2019 National Book Award and the winner of the 2020 Pulitzer Prize for Poetry.

Nickole Brown is the author of *Sister: A Novel-in-Poems* (Red Hen Press, Sibling Rivalry Press) and *Fanny Says: A Biography-in-Poems* (BOA Editions). Currently, she lives in Asheville, North Carolina, where she volunteers at several animal sanctuaries. Since 2016, she's been writing about these animals, and *To Those Who Were Our First Gods*, a chapbook of these first poems, won the 2018 Rattle Prize. Her essay-in-poems, *The Donkey Elegies*, was published by Sibling Rivalry Press in 2020. In 2021, Spruce Books of Penguin Random House published *Write It! 100 Poetry Prompts to Inspire*, a book co-authored with her wife Jessica Jacobs, and they regularly teach together as part of their SunJune Literary Collaborative. Every summer, she teaches at the low-residency MFA at the Sewanee School of Letters.

Matthew Burgess is an Assistant Professor at Brooklyn College. He is the author of a poetry collection, *Slippers for Elsewhere*, and six children's books, including *Enormous Smallness: A Story of E. E. Cummings*, *Drawing on Walls: A Story of Keith Haring*, and *Make Meatballs Sing: The Life & Art of Corita Kent*. Matthew has edited an anthology titled *Dream Closet: Meditations on Childhood Space*, as well as a collection of essays titled *Spellbound: The Art of Teaching Poetry*. A poet-in-residence in NYC public schools since 2001, he also serves as a contributing editor of *Teachers & Writers Magazine*.

Tara Shea Burke is a queer writer and educator from the Blue Ridge Mountains of Virginia. Her book *Animal Like Any Other* was published in 2019. She is currently Assistant Professor of writing and poetry at Virginia Commonwealth University, but she's worn many worker hats in and outside of academia and the arts, has served as a board member for *Sinister Wisdom*, an editor for journals, contests, and anthologies, and is now happily working on a professional development award centered on alternative grading and anti-racist teaching and feedback practices in writing classrooms.

Stephanie Burt is Professor of English at Harvard. Her most recent books include *After Callimachus* (Princeton UP, 2020) and *Don't Read Poetry: A Book About How to Read Poems* (Basic Books, 2019). A new full-length collection of her own poems will appear from Graywolf Press in late 2022.

CAConrad has been working with the ancient technologies of poetry and ritual since 1975. They are the author of *AMANDA PARADISE: Resurrect Extinct Vibration* (Wave

Books, 2021). Other titles include *While Standing in Line for Death* and *Ecodeviance*. *The Book of Frank* is now available in nine different languages. They have received a Creative Capital grant, a Pew Fellowship, a Lambda Literary Award, and a Believer Magazine Book Award. They teach at Columbia University in New York City and Sandberg Art Institute in Amsterdam. Please visit their website: https://linktr.ee/CAConrad88.

Gabrielle Calvocoressi is the author of *The Last Time I Saw Amelia Earhart*, *Apocalyptic Swing* (a finalist for the LA Times Book Prize), and *Rocket Fantastic*, winner of the Audre Lorde Award for Lesbian Poetry. Calvocoressi teaches at UNC Chapel Hill and lives in Old East Durham, North Carolina, where joy, compassion, and social justice are at the center of their personal and poetic practice.

Dr. Rafael Campo teaches and practices internal medicine at Beth Israel Deaconess Medical Center and Harvard Medical School, where he also directs the Art and Humanities Initiative's Literature and Writing Program. He is also the Poetry Section Editor for *JAMA*, the *Journal of the American Medical Association*. His poetry and essays have appeared in numerous periodicals, including *The Nation*, *The New Republic*, *The New York Times*, *Poetry*, *Scientific American*, and elsewhere. He lectures widely, with recent appearances at TEDx Cambridge, the Folger Shakespeare Library, and the Library of Congress. His new and selected volume of poems, *Comfort Measures Only*, is now available from Duke University Press. For more information, please visit www.rafaelcampo.com.

Kayleb Rae Candrilli is the recipient of a Whiting Award, a Pew Fellowship, and a fellowship from the National Endowment of the Arts. They are the author of *Water I Won't Touch*, *All the Gay Saints*, and *What Runs Over*. Candrilli's work is published in *Poetry*, *American Poetry Review*, *Ploughshares*, among others.

Cyrus Cassells is the 2021 Texas Poet Laureate. Among his honors: a Guggenheim fellowship, a Lambda Literary Award, and a Lannan Literary Award. His 2018 volume, *The Gospel according to Wild Indigo*, was a finalist for the NAACP Image Award. *Still Life with Children: Selected Poems of Francesc Parcerisas*, translated from the Catalan, was awarded the Texas Institute of Letters' Soeurette Diehl Fraser Award for Best Translated Book of 2018 and 2019. His latest volume is *The World That the Shooter Left Us* (Four Way Books, 2022).

Marcelo Hernandez Castillo is the author of *Children of the Land: a Memoir* (Harper Collins), *Cenzontle,* winner of the A. Poulin, Jr. Prize (BOA Editions), and

Dulce, winner of the Drinking Gourd Prize (Northwestern University Press). He is a founding member of the Undocupoets, which eliminated citizenship requirements from all major poetry book prizes in the US, and was recognized with the Barnes & Noble Writers for Writers Award. He lives in Northern California where he teaches at St. Mary's College and the Ashland University Low-Res MFA program.

The Alaska Poet Laureate from 2004-2006, **Jerah Chadwick** (1956-2016) was a resident of the Aleutian Island of Unalaska, where he raised goats and wrote poetry while living in an abandoned World War II military compound.

Judith Chalmer is a listener, learner, paddler, walker, camper, gardener, thinker, lover of conversation, of color, of winter woods, of dusk and water, introvert, and the author of two books of poetry. Her most recent book, *Minnow* (Kelsay Books, 2020), is an examination of queer love in natural spaces. She lives in Vermont.

Jos Charles is author of *a Year & other poems* (Milkweed Editions, 2022), *feeld*, a Pulitzer finalist and winner of the 2017 National Poetry Series selected by Fady Joudah (Milkweed Editions, 2018), and *Safe Space* (Ahsahta Press, 2016). She is a PhD candidate at UC Irvine and currently resides in Long Beach, California.

Chen Chen's second book of poetry, *Your Emergency Contact Has Experienced an Emergency,* is forthcoming from BOA Editions and Bloodaxe Books (UK) in fall 2022. His debut, *When I Grow Up I Want to Be a List of Further Possibilities* (BOA Editions, 2017; Bloodaxe Books, 2019), was long-listed for the National Book Award and won the Thom Gunn Award, among other honors. He is the 2018-2022 Jacob Ziskind Poet-in-Residence at Brandeis University and also teaches for the low-residency MFA programs at New England College and Stonecoast.

Ching-In Chen is a genderqueer Chinese American hybrid writer, community organizer, and teacher. They are author of *The Heart's Traffic* and *recombinant* (2018 Lambda Literary Award for Transgender Poetry) as well as the chapbooks *how to make black paper sing* and *Kundiman for Kin :: Information Retrieval for Monsters* (Finalist for the Leslie Scalapino Award). Chen is also co-editor of *The Revolution Starts at Home: Confronting Intimate Violence Within Activist Communities* and *Here Is a Pen: An Anthology of West Coast Kundiman Poets.* They are a Kundiman, Lambda, Watering Hole, Can Serrat, and Imagining America Fellow. (chinginchen.com)

A prose writer, poet, and performer, **Justin Chin** (1969-2015) interrogated the personal and political aspects of queer Asian-American identities. In 2007, his poetry collection *Gutted* won the Publishing Triangle's Thom Gunn Award for Poetry.

Franny Choi is the author of *Floating, Brilliant, Gone* (Write Bloody Publishing) and *Soft Science* (Alice James Books), winner of the Science Fiction Poetry Association's Elgin Award. Other honors include a Ruth Lilly and Dorothy Sargent Rosenberg Poetry Fellowship, a Holmes National Poetry Prize, and a Rhode Island State Council on the Arts Fellowship. Founder of the Brew & Forge project, she has two books forthcoming from Ecco.

Chrystos has been the recipient of the Sappho Award of Distinction from the Astraea Lesbian Foundation for Justice, NEA, and Barbara Deming Grants, and the Human Rights Freedom of Expression Award, in addition to winning the Audre Lorde International Poetry Competition. Chrystos's work as a poet and activist spans Native land and treaty rights; freedom for imprisoned Indigenous activists; and feminist, two-spirit, and lesbian solidarity. A proudly self-educated poet, Chrystos's powerful work celebrates sovereignty and desire as counterforces against colonialism, genocide, patriarchy, and hegemony. She is the author of *Not Vanishing, Dream On, Fugitive Colors, Fire Power,* and *Red Rollercoaster.* She is a resident of Ocean Shores, Washington.

James Cihlar's most recent book is *The Shadowgraph,* published by the University of New Mexico Press in 2020. His previous books include *Rancho Nostalgia* and *Undoing.* His poetry chapbooks are *A Conversation with My Imaginary Daughter, What My Family Used,* and *Metaphysical Bailout.* His writing has appeared in the *American Poetry Review, The Threepenny Review, Lambda Literary Review,* and *The Gay and Lesbian Review.* He lives in Saint Paul, Minnesota, with his husband.

Cody-Rose Clevidence is the author of *Beast Feast* (2014) and *Flung Throne* (2018), both from Ahsahta Press; *Perverse, All Monstrous* (Nion Editions, 2017); *Listen My Friend, This Is the Dream I Dreamed Last Night* (The Song Cave, 2021); and *Aux/Arc Trypt Ich* (Nightboat, 2021) as well as several handsome chapbooks. They live in the Arkansas Ozarks with their medium-sized but lion-hearted dog, Birdie.

Henri Cole was born in Fukuoka, Japan. He has published ten collections of poetry, including *Middle Earth,* which was a finalist for the Pulitzer. His most recent collection is *Blizzard* (Farrar, Straus & Giroux) and a memoir *Orphic Paris* (New York Review Books). He teaches at Claremont McKenna College and lives in Boston.

LGBTQ+ writer, NEA and MacDowell Fellow, and former Key West Poet Laureate, **Flower Conroy**'s the author of *Snake Breaking Medusa Disorder* (winner of the Stevens Manuscript Competition), *A Sentimental Hairpin* (a Small Press Distribution Bestseller), and *Greenest Grass (or You Can't Keep Killing Yourself & Not Expect to Die)* (winner of the Blue Lynx Poetry prize, forthcoming). Her poetry will/has appeared in *American Poetry Review, American Literary Review, New England Review, Prairie Schooner*, and others.

S. Brook Corfman is the author of the poetry collections *Luxury, Blue Lace*, chosen by Richard Siken for the Autumn House Rising Writer Prize, and *My Daily Actions, or The Meteorites*, one of *The New York Times* Best Poetry Books of 2020, finalist for the Publishing Triangle Award for Trans and Gender Variant Literature, and winner of the Fordham University Press POL Prize, chosen by Cathy Park Hong. They are also the author of several chapbooks including *Frames* (Belladonna* Books). (sbrookcorfman. com)

Eduardo C. Corral is the son of Mexican immigrants. He's the author of *Guillotine*, published by Graywolf Press, and *Slow Lightning*, which won the 2011 Yale Series of Younger Poets Competition. He's the recipient of a Lannan Foundation Literary Fellowship, a Whiting Writers' Award, a National Endowment for the Arts Fellowship, and a Hodder Fellowship from Princeton University. He teaches in the MFA program at North Carolina State University.

One of the most influential poets of his generation, **Hart Crane** (1899-1932) is best known for *The Bridge*.

James Crews is editor of the bestselling anthology, *How to Love the World*, featured on NPR's *Morning Edition*, as well as in *The Boston Globe* and *The Washington Post*. He is also the author of four prize-winning collections of poetry: *The Book of What Stays, Telling My Father, Bluebird*, and *Every Waking Moment*, and his poems have appeared in *The New York Times Magazine, Ploughshares*, and *The Sun*. Crews teaches in the Poetry of Resilience seminars and lives with his husband in Shaftsbury, Vermont. To sign up for weekly poems and prompts, visit: www.jamescrews.net.

A major voice of the Harlem Renaissance, **Countee Cullen** (1903-1946) was a poet, novelist, children's writer, and playwright, particularly known for his poetry books *Color* and *The Black Christ*.

Deaf, genderqueer poet **Meg Day** is the author of *Last Psalm at Sea Level* (Barrow Street, 2014), winner of the Publishing Triangle's Audre Lorde Award, and a finalist for the 2016 Kate Tufts Discovery Award, and the co-editor of *Laura Hershey: On the Life & Work of an American Master* (Pleiades, 2019). The 2015-2016 recipient of the Amy Lowell Poetry Travelling Scholarship and a 2013 recipient of an NEA Fellowship in Poetry, Day's work can be found in, or forthcoming from, *Best American Poetry 2020*, *The New York Times*, *Poetry*, and elsewhere. Day is Assistant Professor of English & Creative Writing at Franklin & Marshall College. (www.megday.com)

A librarian and unapologetic writer, **tatiana de la tierra** (1961-2012) was the creator of the first international Latina lesbian magazine *esto no tiene nombre*.

Natalie Diaz is Mojave and an enrolled member of the Gila River Indian Tribe. Her first poetry collection, *When My Brother Was an Aztec*, was published by Copper Canyon Press, and her second book, *Postcolonial Love Poem*, was published by Graywolf Press in March 2020, for which she won the Pulitzer Prize for Poetry in 2021. She is a MacArthur Fellow, a Lannan Literary Fellow, a United States Artists Ford Fellow, and a Native Arts Council Foundation Artist Fellow. Diaz is Director of the Center for Imagination in the Borderlands and is the Maxine and Jonathan Marshall Chair in Modern and Contemporary Poetry at Arizona State University. She lives in Phoenix, Arizona.

William Dickey (1928-1994) was a professor and poet who wrote fifteen collections, including his final, posthumously published collection *The Education of Desire*.

Little-known during her life, **Emily Dickinson** (1830-1886) has since been regarded as one of the most important figures in American poetry.

A brilliant poet, novelist, translator, and critic, **Melvin Dixon** (1950-1992) was the author of *Change of Territory* and the posthumous collection *Love's Instruments*.

Lynn Domina is the author of several books, including two collections of poetry, *Corporal Works* and *Framed in Silence*. She currently serves as Head of the English Department at Northern Michigan University and as Creative Writing Editor of *The Other Journal*. She lives with her family in Marquette, Michigan, along the beautiful shores of Lake Superior. Read more here: www.lynndomina.com.

Mark Doty is the author of nine books of poetry, including *Deep Lane* (April 2015), *Fire to Fire: New and Selected Poems*, which won the 2008 National Book Award, and *My Alexandria*, winner of the *Los Angeles Times* Book Prize, the National Book Critics Circle Award, and the T.S. Eliot Prize in the UK. Doty has received fellowships from the Guggenheim Foundation, the Ingram Merrill Foundation, the National Endowment for the Arts, the Rockefeller Foundation, and the Whiting Foundation.

Qwo-Li Driskill is an associate professor of Women, Gender, and Sexuality Studies and Queer Studies at Oregon State University and the author of *Walking with Ghosts: Poems and Asegi Stories: Cherokee Queer and Two-Spirit Memory.*

Cheryl Dumesnil's books include the poetry collections *Showtime at the Ministry of Lost Causes* and *In Praise of Falling* (University of Pittsburgh Press); a memoir, *Love Song for Baby X* (Ig Publishing); and the anthologies *We Got This: Solo Mom Stories of Grit, Heart, and Humor* (SheWrites Press) and *Dorothy Parker's Elbow: Tattoos on Writers, Writers on Tattoos* (Warner Books). A freelance writer, editor, and writing coach, she lives in the San Francisco Bay Area with her two children and her wife, Sarah. Learn more about her work at www.cheryldumesnil.com.

A writer, educator, editor, and political activist during the Harlem Renaissance, **Alice Moore Dunbar-Nelson** (1875-1935) provided us with the collections *Violets and Other Tales* as well as *The Goodness of St. Rocque and Other Stories.*

A poet, public intellectual, and historical figure in the history of pre-Stonewall gay culture, **Robert Duncan** (1919-1988) was the author of more than two dozen poetry collections.

Julie R. Enszer, PhD, is the author of four poetry collections, including *Avowed*, and the editor of *OutWrite: The Speeches that Shaped LGBTQ Literary Culture, Fire-Rimmed Eden: Selected Poems by Lynn Lonidier, The Complete Works of Pat Parker,* and *Sister Love: The Letters of Audre Lorde and Pat Parker 1974-1989.* Enszer edits and publishes *Sinister Wisdom*, a multicultural lesbian literary and art journal. You can read more of her work at www.JulieREnszer.com.

Jenny Factor's first book, *Unraveling at the Name* (Copper Canyon Press), was a finalist for the Lambda Literary Award. Her new book, *Want, the Lake* will be published by Red Hen Press in 2023. Jenny serves as Lecturer in Poetry at Caltech. She divides her time between Pasadena, California, and Marblehead, Massachusetts.

Nikky Finney was born by the sea in South Carolina and raised during the Civil Rights, Black Power, and Black Arts Movements. She is the author of *On Wings Made of Gauze*; *Rice*; *The World Is Round*; and *Head Off & Split*, which won the National Book Award for Poetry in 2011. Her new collection of poems, *Love Child's Hotbed of Occasional Poetry*, was released in 2020 from TriQuarterly Books/Northwestern University Press.

Denice Frohman is a poet, performer, and educator from New York City. A CantoMundo Fellow, she's received residencies and awards from the National Association of Latino Arts & Cultures, Leeway Foundation, Millay Colony, and Blue Mountain Center. Her work has appeared in *The New York Times, The BreakBeat Poets: LatiNext, Nepantla: An Anthology for Queer Poets of Color,* ESPNW, and elsewhere. A former Women of the World Poetry Slam Champion, she's featured on hundreds of stages from The White House to The Apollo, and co-organized #PoetsforPuertoRico. She lives in Philadelphia.

Benjamin Garcia's first collection, *Thrown in the Throat* (Milkweed Editions), was selected by Kazim Ali for the 2019 National Poetry Series. A CantoMundo and Lambda Literary fellow, he serves as core faculty at Alma College's low-residency MFA program. His poems and essays have recently appeared or are forthcoming in: *AGNI, American Poetry Review, Quarterly West, Kenyon Review,* and *New England Review*. His video poem "Ode to the Corpse Flower" is available for viewing at the Broad Museum's website as part of *El Poder de la Poesia: Latinx Voices in Response to HIV/AIDS*.

R. J. Gibson lives and works in West Virginia. His poems have appeared in *Court Green, The Cortland Review, Waxwing, Columbia Poetry Review,* and other journals. He is the author of two chapbooks: *Scavenge* and *You Could Learn a Lot*. His essays and poems have been anthologized in *My Diva: 65 Gay Men on the Women Who Inspire Them, Collective Brightness: LGBTIQ Poets on Faith, Religion & Spirituality,* and *Walk Till the Dogs Get Mean: Meditations on the Forbidden from Contemporary Appalachia*.

aeon ginsberg is a tranfeminine agender writer and bitch from Baltimore City. Eir book *Greyhound* was published through Noemi Press.

Tried in 1957 for obscenity for his poem "Howl," **Allen Ginsberg** (1926-1997) founded, along with Anne Waldman, The Jack Kerouac School for Disembodied Poetics.

Sarah Giragosian is the author of the poetry collection *Queer Fish*, a winner of the *American Poetry Journal* Book Prize (Dream Horse Press, 2017) and *The Death Spiral* (Black Lawrence Press, 2020). The craft anthology, *Marbles on the Floor: How to Assemble a Book of Poems*, which is coedited by Sarah and Virginia Konchan, is forthcoming from the University of Akron Press. Sarah's writing has appeared in journals such as *Orion*, *Ecotone*, *Tin House*, and *Prairie Schooner*, among others. She teaches at the University at Albany-SUNY.

Matty Layne Glasgow is the author of *deciduous qween* (Red Hen Press), winner of the Benjamin Saltman Award. His poems have appeared in or are forthcoming from *Copper Nickel*, *Crazyhorse*, *Ecotone*, *Houston Public Media*, *Gulf Coast*, *Missouri Review*, *Pleiades*, *Poetry Daily*, and elsewhere. Matty is a PhD student and the Jeff Metcalf Humanities in the Community Fellow at the University of Utah, where he serves as the Writers in the Schools Coordinator and the Editor of *Quarterly West*.

Rigoberto González is Distinguished Professor of English and director of the MFA Program in Creative Writing at Rutgers-Newark.

Rae Gouirand is the author of two collections of poetry, *Glass is Glass Water is Water* (Spork Press, 2018) and *Open Winter* (winner of the Bellday Prize, Bellday Books, 2011), the chapbooks *Little Hour* (winner of the Swan Scythe Chapbook Contest, Swan Scythe Press, 2022), *Jinx* (winner of the Summer Kitchen Competition, Seven Kitchens Press, 2019) and *Must Apple* (winner of the Oro Fino Competition, Educe Press, 2018), and a short work of nonfiction, *The History of Art* (winner of the Open Reading Competition, *The Atlas Review*, 2019). She leads several long-running independent workshops in Northern California and online, including the cross-genre workshop Scribe Lab, and lectures in the Department of English at UC-Davis.

Jan-Henry Gray is the author of *Documents* (BOA Editions, Ltd.), selected by D.A. Powell as the winner of the A. Poulin Jr. Poetry Prize and the chapbook *Selected Emails* (speCt! Books). Born in the Philippines and raised in California where he worked as a chef, Jan lived undocumented in the U.S. for more than 32 years. A Cooke Foundation Scholar and Kundiman Fellow, he is an assistant professor at Adelphi University in New York.

Miriam Bird Greenberg is a poet with a fieldwork-derived practice. The author of *In the Volcano's Mouth* (University of Pittsburgh, 2016), which won the Agnes Lynch Starrett Poetry Prize, her work on economic migrants, hitchhikers, and hobos living on society's margins has appeared in *Granta, Poetry, Kenyon Review,* and elsewhere. A high school dropout and former hitchhiker herself, she's held fellowships from the National Endowment for the Arts, the Poetry Foundation, and the Jan Michalski Foundation. Her limited-edition letterpress artist book *The Other World* was published by the Center for Book Arts in 2019.

Rachel Eliza Griffiths is a poet, novelist, and visual artist. Her most recent collection, *Seeing the Body* (W.W. Norton), was selected as the winner of the 2021 Hurston/Wright Legacy Award in Poetry, the 2020 winner of the Paterson Poetry Prize, and nominated for the 2020 NAACP Image Award. Her literary and visual work has appeared widely, including *The New Yorker, The Paris Review, Kenyon Review,* and *Best American Poetry* (2020, 2021). She is the recipient of fellowships including Yaddo and the Robert Rauschenberg Foundation. Her debut novel is forthcoming from Random House. She lives in New York City.

A journalist, teacher, playwright, short story writer, and poet, **Angelina Weld Grimké** (1880-1958) was one of the first women of color to have a play publicly performed in America.

Benjamin S. Grossberg is Director of Creative Writing at the University of Hartford. His books include *My Husband Would* (University of Tampa Press, 2020), winner of the 2021 Connecticut Book Award; *Space Traveler* (University of Tampa Press, 2014); and *Sweet Core Orchard* (University of Tampa Press, 2009), winner of a Lambda Literary Award.

A resident alien of San Francisco for much of his life, **Thom Gunn** (1929-2004) wrote many collections of poetry, including *The Man with Night Sweats,* an elegy composed during the HIV pandemic.

Roy G. Guzmán was born in Tegucigalpa, Honduras, and grew up in Miami, Florida. Their debut collection, *Catrachos* (Graywolf Press, 2020), was named a finalist for the Minnesota Book Award in Poetry as well as a finalist for the 2021 Kate Tufts Poetry Award. Roy is a 2019 National Endowment for the Arts fellow and a 2017 Ruth Lilly and Dorothy Sargent Rosenberg poetry fellow. They are currently pursuing a PhD in Cultural Studies and Comparative Literature from the University of Minnesota, Twin Cities, where they also received their MFA in creative writing. (www.roygguzman.com)

A novelist, memoirist, and poet, **H. D.** (1886-1961) was the author of many books of poetry and prose, including *Notes on Thought and Vision*, in which she articulates a theory of "jellyfish consciousness."

Marilyn Hacker is the author of fourteen books of poems, including *A Stranger's Mirror* (Norton, 2015) and *Blazons* (Carcanet, 2019), two collaborative books, *Diaspo/Renga*, written with Deema K. Shehabi (Holland Park Press,2014) and *A Different Distance*, written with Karthika Naïr (Milkweed Editions, 2021), and an essay collection, *Unauthorized Voices* (Michigan, 2010), as well as eighteen books of poems translated from the French.

Eloise Klein Healy, the author of nine books of poetry, was named the first Poet Laureate of Los Angeles in 2012. She was the founding chair of the MFA in Creative Writing Program at Antioch University Los Angeles where she is Distinguished Professor of Creative Writing Emerita. Healy directed the Women's Studies Program at California State University Northridge and taught in the Feminist Studio Workshop at The Woman's Building in Los Angeles. She is the founding editor of ARKTOI BOOKS, an imprint of Red Hen Press specializing in the work of lesbian authors. *A Wild Surmise: New & Selected Poems & Recordings* was published in 2013 and *Another Phase* in 2018. Her forthcoming book is *A Brilliant Loss* and will be published in 2022.

Christopher Hennessy, PhD, is the author of *Love-in-Idleness* (Brooklyn Arts Press), a finalist for the Thom Gunn Award. His other books include *Outside the Lines: Talking with Contemporary Gay Poets* (University of Michigan Press) and *Our Deep Gossip: Conversations with Gay Writers on Poetry and Desire* (University of Wisconsin Press).

KateLynn Hibbard's books include *Sleeping Upside Down* (Silverfish Review Press), *Sweet Weight* (Tiger Bark Press), and *Simples* (Howling Bird Press), and she is editor of *When We Become Weavers: Queer Female Poets on the Midwest Experience* (Squares & Rebels Press). A professor of writing and women's history at Minneapolis College, she lives with many pets and her spouse Jan in Saint Paul, Minnesota.

Jane Hilberry writes a body-centered poetry that combines elements of spirituality and sexuality. Her books of poetry include *Still the Animals Enter* and *Body Painting*, which won the Colorado Book Award for Poetry. Her poems have appeared in *The Sun*, *The Hudson Review*, *Denver Quarterly*, and many other places. She facilitates arts-based leadership workshops in the US and Canada and serves as Professor of Creativity and Innovation at Colorado College.

Matthew Hittinger is the author of *The Masque of Marilyn* (GOSS183, 2017), *The Erotic Postulate* (2014) and *Skin Shift* (2012), both from Sibling Rivalry Press, and the chapbooks *Platos de Sal* (Seven Kitchens Press, 2009), *Narcissus Resists* (GOSS183, 2009), and *Pear Slip* (Spire Press, 2007). Named a Debut Poet by *Poets & Writers Magazine*, his work has appeared in many journals and anthologies, has been adapted into art songs, and has been featured on Verse Daily and the Academy of American Poets' Poem-a-Day.

Richie Hofmann is the author of two collections of poems, *Second Empire* and *A Hundred Lovers*.

A key figure in the Harlem Renaissance, **Langston Hughes** (1901-1967) published numerous novels, plays, and poetry collections, beginning with *The Weary Blues*.

Luther Hughes is the author of the debut poetry collection, *A Shiver in the Leaves*, forthcoming from BOA Editions in September 2022, and the chapbook *Touched* (Sibling Rivalry Press, 2018). He is the founder of Shade Literary Arts, a literary organization for queer writers of color, and co-hosts The Poet Salon podcast with Gabrielle Bates and Dujie Tahat. Recipient of the Ruth Lilly and Dorothy Sargent Rosenberg Fellowship and 92Y Discovery Poetry Prize, his writing has been published in various magazines, journals, and newspapers. Luther was born and raised in Seattle, where he currently lives.

Christina Hutchins's poetry collections are *Tender the Maker* (May Swenson Award, Utah State) and *The Stranger Dissolves*, finalist for Lambda Literary and Publishing Triangle Awards. Poems appear in *The Antioch Review*, *The New Republic*, *Prairie Schooner*, *Salmagundi*, *The Southern Review*, and *Women's Review of Books*, with essays on queer theory and philosophy in volumes by Columbia, Ashgate, and Fordham. Awards include the Missouri Review Editors' Prize and Dartmouth Poet in Residence at the Frost Place. Christina holds degrees from UC Davis, Harvard, and Graduate Theological Union, and she's worked as a biochemist, congregational minister, and professor of poetry and literary arts.

Jessica Jacobs is the author of *Take Me with You, Wherever You're Going* (Four Way Books), winner of the Devil's Kitchen and Goldie Awards, and *Pelvis with Distance* (White Pine Press), winner of the New Mexico Book Award and a finalist for the Lambda Literary Award. She serves as Chapbook Editor for *Beloit Poetry Journal* and lives in Asheville, North Carolina, with her wife, the poet Nickole Brown, with whom she co-authored *Write It! 100 Poetry Prompts to Inspire* (Spruce Books/Penguin Random House). Her collection of poems in conversation with the Book of Genesis will be out from Four Way Books in 2024.

Charles Jensen is the author of three poetry collections, most recently *Instructions between Takeoff and Landing*, and seven chapbooks. He has received the Frank O'Hara Chapbook Award, Zócalo Poetry Prize, Dorothy Sargent Rosenberg Prize, and a grant from the Arizona Commission on the Arts. His poetry appears in *American Poetry Review*, *Crab Orchard Review*, *Prairie Schooner*, *New England Review*, and elsewhere. He directs the Writers' Program at UCLA Extension. He hosts the podcast *The Write Process* and co-hosts *You Wanna Be On Top?*, a retrospective of America's Next Top Model.

Joe Jiménez is the author of the poetry collections *The Possibilities of Mud* and *Rattlesnake Allegory*, as well as *Bloodline*, a young adult novel. Jiménez is the recipient of the 2016 Letras Latinas/Red Hen Press Poetry Prize. His poems have appeared on the PBS NewsHour and Lambda Literary sites. Jiménez was awarded a Lucas Artists Literary Artists Fellowship from 2017 to 2020. He lives in San Antonio, Texas, and is a member of the Macondo Writers Workshop.

Jenny Johnson is the author of *In Full Velvet* (Sarabande Books, 2017). Her honors include a Whiting Award, a Hodder Fellowship at Princeton University, and a NEA Fellowship. Her poems have appeared in *The New York Times*, *New England Review*, *Waxwing*, and elsewhere. She is an Assistant Professor of Creative Writing at West Virginia University, and she is on the faculty of the Rainier Writing Workshop, Pacific Lutheran University's low-residency MFA program. She lives in Pittsburgh.

Of self-obscured origins, **Stephen Jonas** (1921-1970) was an influential, if underground, figure in the Boston poetry scene during the '50s and '60s.

Ever Jones (formerly JM Miller) is a queer/trans writer, artist & instructor. Their poetry collections include *nightsong* (Sundress Publications, 2020) and *Wilderness Lessons* (FutureCycle Press, 2016). Their chapbook, *Primitive Elegy*, was printed by alice blue books. Ever won the Grand Prize for the Eco Arts Awards in 2014 & was a finalist for terrain.org's 2013 poetry contest. Their work can be found at *Tupelo Quarterly*, *Bellingham Review*, *Poecology*, terrain.org, *CURA*, *Cimarron Review*, *Written River: A Journal of Eco-Poetics* & others. Ever is a Professor of Creative Writing at the University of Washington in Tacoma & teaches at Richard Hugo House.

Saeed Jones is the author of the memoir *How We Fight for Our Lives*, winner of the 2019 Kirkus Prize for Nonfiction, and the poetry collection *Prelude to a Bruise*, winner for the 2015 PEN/Joyce Osterweil Award for Poetry. His work has appeared in *The New Yorker*, *The New York Times*, and *GQ*, among other publications.

June Jordan (1936-2002) was a poet, activist, journalist, essayist, and teacher. Prolific and passionate, she was an influential voice who lived and wrote on the frontlines of American poetry, international political vision, and human moral witness.

Britteney Black Rose Kapri is a semi-retired teaching artist, writer, performance poet, and playwright from Chicago. She has been published in *Poetry*, *Vinyl*, *Day One*, *Seven Scribes*, *The Offing*, and *Kinfolks Quarterly*. She is a 2015 Rona Jaffe Writers Award Recipient. Her debut book *Black Queer Hoe* was released September 4th, 2018, through Haymarket Books.

Donika Kelly is the author of *The Renunciations* and *Bestiary*. *Bestiary* is the winner of the Cave Canem Poetry Prize, a Hurston/Wright Legacy Award, and the Kate Tufts Discovery Award. She is a Cave Canem graduate fellow and a founding member of the collective Poets at the End of the World. Her poems have been published in *The New Yorker*, *The Atlantic*, *The Paris Review*, and *Foglifter*.

Maurice Kenny (1929-2016) was the author of more than two dozen collections of poetry, including *Carving Hawk: New and Selected Poems 1956-2000*.

Alyse Knorr is an associate professor of English at Regis University and coeditor of Switchback Books. She is the author of three collections of poetry and four chapbooks—most recently, *Mega-City Redux* (Green Mountains Review, 2017). Her work has appeared in *The New Republic*, *Poetry*, *The Georgia Review*, and *Alaska Quarterly Review*, among others.

Melissa Kwasny is the author of six books of poetry, including *Where Outside the Body is the Soul Today* (University of Washington Press); *Pictograph*; *The Nine Senses*; and *Reading Novalis in Montana* (all from Milkweed Editions), as well as a collection of essays *Earth Recitals: Essays on Image and Vision* (Lynx House). She is also the editor of two anthologies: *Toward the Open Field: Poets on the Art of Poetry 1800-1950* (Wesleyan University Press) and, with M.L. Smoker, *I Go to the Ruined Place: Contemporary Poets in Defense of Global Human Rights* (Lost Horse Press).

Joy Ladin is the author of nine books of poetry, including recently reissued *The Book of Anna*; two Lambda Literary Award finalists, *Impersonation* and *Transmigration*; the National Jewish Book Award finalist *Through the Door of Life*; and *The Soul of the Stranger: Reading God and Torah from a Transgender Perspective*, a finalist for a Lambda Literary Award and a Triangle Award. A new collection, *Shekhinah Speaks*, is forthcoming in 2022. Links to her poems and essays are available at wordpress.joyladin.com.

A poet and esoteric bookseller, **Gerrit Lansing** (1928-2018) refined his book *Heavenly Tree, Northern Earth* many times over the years until it reached its final form in 2009.

Joan Larkin is the author of five collections of poetry, most recently *Blue Hanuman*, published by Hanging Loose Press in 2014. Among her many honors are two Lambda Literary Awards and the Audre Lorde Award for Lesbian Poetry; fellowships in poetry and playwriting from the Massachusetts Cultural Council, the New York Foundation for the Arts, and the National Endowment for the Arts; and the 2011 Academy of American Poets Fellowship.

Travis Chi Wing Lau (he/him/his) is Assistant Professor of English at Kenyon College. His research and teaching focus on eighteenth- and nineteenth-century British literature and culture, health humanities, and disability studies. Alongside his scholarship, Lau frequently writes for venues of public scholarship like *Synapsis: A Journal of Health Humanities*, *Public Books, Lapham's Quarterly*, and *The Los Angeles Review of Books*. His poetry has appeared in *Wordgathering*, *Glass, South Carolina Review, Foglifter,* and *Hypertext,* as well as in two chapbooks, *The Bone Setter* (Damaged Goods Press, 2019) and *Paring* (Finishing Line Press, 2020). (travisclau.com)

Rickey Laurentiis is the author of *Boy with Thorn*, winner of the Cave Canem Poetry Prize and the Levis Reading Prize. Their poems have appeared in *Boston Review,* the *Los Angeles Review of Books Quarterly*, *New Republic*, *The New York Times*, and *Poetry*.

Joseph O. Legaspi, a Fulbright and NYFA fellow, is the author of the poetry collections *Threshold* and *Imago* (CavanKerry Press), and the chapbooks *Postcards* (Ghost Bird Press), *Aviary, Bestiary* (Organic Weapon Arts), and *Subways* (Thrush Press). He co-founded Kundiman, a national nonprofit serving writers and readers of Asian American literature. He lives with his husband in Queens, New York.

Muriel Leung is the author of *Imagine Us, The Swarm* (Nightboat Books), *Bone Confetti* (Noemi Press), and *Images Seen to Images Felt* (Antenna) in collaboration with artist

Kristine Thompson. She is a recipient of fellowships to Kundiman, VONA/Voices Workshop, and the Community of Writers. She is the Poetry Co-Editor of *Apogee Journal* and co-hosts The Blood-Jet Writing Hour Podcast with Rachelle Cruz and MT Vallarta. Currently, she is an Andrew W. Mellon Humanities in a Digital World fellow at the University of Southern California where she is completing her PhD in Creative Writing and Literature. She is from Queens, New York.

Dr. Mel Michelle Lewis is Vice President of Diversity, Equity, Inclusion, and Justice, offering strategic guidance to American Rivers, the most trusted and influential river conservation organization in the United States. Previously, Dr. Mel served as Associate Professor and Director of the Ecosystems, Sustainability, and Justice Program and Co-Founder of The Space for Creative Black Imagination at Maryland Institute College of Art and Associate Professor and Director of the Center for Geographies of Justice at Goucher College. Originally from Bayou la Batre, Alabama, their creative work explores queer of color themes in rural coastal settings.

Timothy Liu is the author of twelve books of poems, most recently *Let It Ride* and *Luminous Debris: New & Selected Legerdemain (1992-2017)*. A reader of occult esoterica, he lives in Manhattan and Woodstock, New York. (www.timothyliu.net)

Chip Livingston is the author of two books of poetry, *Museum of False Starts* and *Crow-Blue, Crow-Black*; a novel; and a story/essay collection. He edited *Love Loosha: The Letters of Lucia Berlin and Kenward Elmslie*. Chip teaches in the low-rez MFA program at Institute of American Indian Arts in Santa Fe, New Mexico. He lives in Montevideo, Uruguay.

A professor, prose writer, and poet, **Audre Lorde** (1934-1992) published fourteen essential books of prose and poetry, including *Coal* and *The Black Unicorn*.

Su Smallen Love is the author of six collections of poetry, including *Buddha, Proof*, a Minnesota Book Award finalist, *Weight of Light*, a Pushcart Press Editors' Book Award nominee, and *The Memoir of Mona Lisa and Other Poems*. Her work has been recognized internationally with residencies and publications, most recently by the Unamuno Author Series in Madrid, Spain, and Salmon Literary Centre in County Clare, Ireland. Su was a professional dancer and choreographer, and her poetry has served as scores for dance and film. You can find some films, poems, and interviews of Su at sulove.org.

Amy Lowell (1874-1925) was a dedicated poet, publicity agent, collector, critic, and lecturer. She posthumously received the Pulitzer Prize for Poetry for *What's a Clock* in 1926.

Ed Madden is the author of four books of poetry, most recently *Ark*, a poetry memoir about his father's last months in hospice care. He is a professor of English and director of the Women's and Gender Studies Program at the University of South Carolina. His poems have appeared in *Hard Lines: Rough South Poetry*, the *Forward Book of Poetry 2021*, and elsewhere. In 2015, Ed was named poet laureate for the City of Columbia. In 2019, he was named a Poet Laureate Fellow of the Academy of American Poets and a visiting artist at the Instituto Sacatar in Brazil.

Michael Martella earned an MFA from the University of Mississippi. His poems have appeared in *Rattle*, *Rust + Moth*, and the *Virginia Quarterly Review*. He lives in Jackson, where he works for the University Press of Mississippi.

Dawn Lundy Martin, an American poet, essayist, and memoirist, is the author of four books of poetry: *A Gathering of Matter /A Matter of Gathering*; *DISCIPLINE*; *Life in a Box is a Pretty Life*; and *Good Stock Strange Blood*, which won the prestigious Kingsley Tufts Poetry Award in 2019. Her essays can be found in *The New Yorker*, *n+1*, *The Believer*, and *Best American Essays 2019* and *2021*. *The Laceration: Poems* is forthcoming from Nightboat Books. *When a Person Goes Missing: A Memoir* is forthcoming from Pantheon Books. Martin is the Toi Derricotte Endowed Chair in English at the University of Pittsburgh.

Janet McAdams is a writer, editor, and translator. Her books include *The Island of Lost Luggage, Feral, Red Weather*, and the chapbook *Seven Boxes for the Country After*. A bilingual edition of her new and selected poems, *Buffalo in Six Directions / Búfalo en seis direciones*, with translations by Katherine M. Hedeen and Victór Rodríguez Núñez, was recently published in Mexico City (Editorial Aldus) and in Patagonia (Espacio Hudson). She lives in San Miguel de Allende, Mexico.

A critic, editor, librettist, and poet, **J. D. McClatchy** (1945-2018) was the author of many collections of poetry, including *Plundered Hearts: New and Selected Poems*.

Anne Haven McDonnell lives in Santa Fe, New Mexico, where she teaches as associate professor in English and Creative Writing at the Institute of American Indian Arts. Her poetry has been published in *Orion Magazine, The Georgia Review, The*

American Journal of Poetry, Nimrod International Journal of Prose and Poetry, Alpinist Magazine, Terrain.org, and elsewhere. Anne Haven's chapbook, *Living With Wolves*, was published by Split Rock Press in Fall 2020.

A central figure in the Harlem Renaissance, **Claude McKay** (1889-1948) was a writer of fiction, nonfiction, and poetry, particularly *Harlem Shadows*, known today for its queer subtext.

Kevin McLellan authored the full-length poetry collections, *Ornitheology* (2019 Massachusetts Book Awards recipient) and *Tributary*. He also authored the book objects, *Hemispheres* (which resides in the Poetry Center at the University of Arizona and other special collections) and *[box]* (which resides in the Blue Star Collection at Harvard University and other special collections), and the chapbook *Round Trip*. Kevin is also *Duck Hunting with the Grammarian*—his video, *Dick* showed in the Flickers' Rhode Island Film Festival, the Tag! Queer Film Festival, the Berlin Short Film Festival, and the Vancouver Queer Film Festival. He lives in Cambridge, Massachusetts. (kevmclellan.com)

Sarah María Medina is a poet, translator, and fiction writer from the American Northwest. Her writing has been published in *Poetry, Prelude, Black Warrior Review, The Offing, Poetry Northwest,* and elsewhere. Her work is also found in *Nepantla: An Anthology Dedicated to Queer Poets of Color*. She is the recipient of an ARTIST UP Grant LAB, a Jack Straw Writer fellowship, and a Caldera AIR. At Washington University, she received her MFA in Poetry, and she is currently pursuing her PhD in Comparative Literature, the International Writers Track, in Saint Louis, Missouri.

William Meredith (1919-2007) was an American poet whose formal and unadorned verse was compared to that of Robert Frost. Meredith was awarded a Pulitzer Prize in 1988.

An essayist, novelist, playwright, and poet, **James Merrill** was the author of fifteen poetry collections. He received a Pulitzer Prize for Poetry in 1977 for *Divine Comedies*.

A poet and playwright, **Edna St. Vincent Millay** (1892-1950) received the second annual Pulitzer Prize in Poetry in 1923.

Deborah Miranda is an enrolled member of the Ohlone-Costanoan Esselen Nation, with Santa Ynez Chumash ancestry. She's also a Two Spirit mother, grandmother, and auntie. For 25 years, she taught mostly straight white university kids how to read mostly queer black and brown literature, and how to write poetry and memoir about interesting life choices, what it was like to come out to their parents as a Democrat, and why it's not okay to wear that Chief Illini T-shirt into Professor Miranda's classroom. Now retired, she writes full-time and joyfully follows the call of her demons. Her books include *Bad Indians: A Tribal Memoir*, and four poetry collections.

Susanna J. Mishler is the author of the poetry collection, *Termination Dust* (published by Boreal Books/Red Hen Press), which was a finalist for a 2015 Lambda Literary Award. She has received fellowships and awards from The Alaska Arts and Culture Foundation, the Kenyon Review Writers Workshop, the Rasmuson Foundation, and the University of Arizona. Her poems appear in journals such as *Alaska Quarterly Review, The Iowa Review, Kenyon Review Online, Mid-American Review*, and *Michigan Quarterly Review*, among others. She lives in Alaska, is a licensed electrician, and teaches electrical trades work to apprentices in her local union.

Rajiv Mohabir is the author of three collections of poetry including *Cutlish* (Four Way Books, 2021) and *Antiman: A Hybrid Memoir* (Restless Books, 2021). His translation of *I Even Regret Night: Holi Songs of Demerara* (Kaya, 2019) won the Harold Morton Landon Translation Award from the Academy of American Poets in 2020. He teaches in the MFA program at Emerson College and lives in the Boston area.

Resting in power, **Kamilah Aisha Moon** (1973-2021) was the author of *She Has a Name* and *Starshine and Clay*.

Rachel Moritz is the author of *Sweet Velocity* (Lost Roads Press, 2017), *Borrowed Wave* (Kore Press, 2015), and five poetry chapbooks. Her work has appeared in Academy of American Poets' Poem-a-Day, *American Letters and Commentary, Colorado Review, Iowa Review, Tupelo Quarterly, VOLT, Water~Stone Review*, and other journals. She's been honored with a Best American Essay Notable Mention and Artist Initiative Grant in poetry and prose from the Minnesota State Arts Board. Rachel lives in Minneapolis with her partner, the writer Juliet Patterson, and their son.

Alicia Mountain is the author of *HIGH GROUND COWARD* (University Of Iowa Press), which won the Iowa Poetry Prize. She is also the author of the chapbook *THIN FIRE* (BOAAT Press) and the collection *FOUR IN HAND* (BOA Editions). She holds an MFA from the University of Montana and a PhD from the University of Denver. She is a lesbian poet, writer, and teacher.

Miguel Murphy is the author of *Shoreditch* and two previous collections of poetry. He lives in Southern California where he teaches at Santa Monica College.

Eileen Myles (they/them) came to New York from Boston in 1974 to be a poet. Their books include *For Now* (an essay/talk about writing), *I Must Be Living Twice/new and selected poems*, and *Chelsea Girls*. They showed their photographs in 2019 at Bridget Donahue, NYC. Eileen has received a Guggenheim Fellowship and an award from the American Academy of Arts and Letters. They live in New York and Marfa, Texas.

Jim Nawrocki's poetry has appeared in *Poetry, Kyoto Journal, Nimrod, Chroma Journal*, and *Mudfish*, among others. It has also been included in other anthologies such as *The Place That Inhabits Us: Poems of the San Francisco Bay Watershed* (Sixteen Rivers Press, 2010) and *Art & Understanding: Literature from the First Twenty Years* (Black Lawrence Press, 2014). He wrote for the *Gay & Lesbian Review Worldwide* and lived in San Francisco with his husband before passing away from cancer in 2018. A posthumous collection of his poems and short fiction, *House Fire*, will be published by 7.13 Books.

Hieu Minh Nguyen is the author of two collections of poetry, *Not Here* (Coffee House Press, 2018), and *This Way to the Sugar* (Write Bloody Press, 2014). His work has appeared in *The Atlantic, Hobart, BOAAT, Best American Poetry, The New York Times*, and elsewhere. He is a graduate of the MFA Program for Writers at Warren Wilson College. Originally from the Twin Cities, Hieu now lives in the Bay Area.

Miller Oberman is the author of *The Unstill Ones*, poems and translations, published as part of the Princeton Series of Contemporary Poets, 2017. He has received a number of awards for his poetry, including a Ruth Lilly Fellowship, a 92Y Discovery Prize, and *Poetry*'s John Frederick Nims Memorial Prize for Translation. Miller's poems have appeared in *Poetry, London Review of Books, The Nation, The New Yorker*, Poem-a-Day, and *Foglifter*. Miller teaches writing at Eugene Lang College at The New School.

Frank O'Hara (1926-1966) was an American poet who gathered images from an urban environment to represent personal experience. O'Hara was drawn to both poetry and the visual arts for much of his life.

Mary Oliver (1935-2019) was an American poet whose work reflects a deep communion with the natural world. Oliver held the Catharine Osgood Foster Chair for Distinguished Teaching at Bennington College until 2001. In addition to such major awards as the Pulitzer and National Book Award, Oliver received fellowships from the Guggenheim Foundation and the National Endowment for the Arts.

Kate Partridge is the author of two poetry collections, *THINE* (Tupelo, 2023) and *Ends of the Earth* (U. of Alaska, 2017). Her poems have appeared in *FIELD, Yale Review, Pleiades, Michigan Quarterly Review, Alaska Quarterly Review,* and other journals. She is a graduate of the MFA program at George Mason University and the PhD in Creative Writing and Literature at the University of Southern California. She lives in Denver, where she is an Assistant Professor of English at Regis University.

Juliet Patterson is the author of the memoir *Sinkhole: A Natural History of Suicide* (Milkweed Editions, September 2022) and two full-length poetry collections, *Threnody* (Nightboat, 2016) and *The Truant Lover* (Nightboat, 2006). She lives in Minneapolis on the west bank of the Mississippi near the Great River Road.

Gerry Gomez Pearlberg lives in the dynamic ecosystem of the Northwest Catskills—unceded lands of the Haudenosaunee peoples. Gerry wrote the award-winning poetry collections *Marianne Faithfull's Cigarette* (Cleis) and *Mr. Bluebird* (University of Wisconsin Press). Queerer than ever, she spends her days hanging out with beavers and rescuing insects from misadventures.

Carl Phillips is the author of sixteen books of poetry, including *Then the War: And Selected Poems 2007-2020* (Farrar, Straus & Giroux, and Carcanet/UK, 2022) and *Wild Is the Wind* (FSG, 2018), which won the Los Angeles Times Book Prize. Phillips has also written three prose books, most recently *My Trade Is Mystery: Seven Meditations from a Life in Writing* (Yale University Press, 2022); and he has translated the *Philoctetes* of Sophocles (Oxford University Press, 2004). He teaches at Washington University in St. Louis.

Xan Phillips is a poet and visual artist from rural Ohio. The recipient of a Whiting Award, Lambda Literary Award, and The Judith A. Markowitz Award, Xan is the author of *HULL* (Nightboat Books, 2019) and *Reasons for Smoking*, which won the 2016 Seattle Review Chapbook contest judged by Claudia Rankine. They have received fellowships from Brown University, Cave Canem, The Conversation Literary Festival, the Wisconsin Institute for Creative Writing, the Sewanee Writers' Conference, and the Center for African American Poetry and Poetics. Xan's poetry is featured in *Berlin Quarterly Review, Bomb Magazine, Crazyhorse, Poets.org,* and *Virginia Quarterly Review.*

Tommy Pico is the author of the books *IRL* (2016), winner of the 2017 Brooklyn Library Literary Prize and a finalist for the 2018 Kate Tufts Discovery Award; *Nature Poem* (2017), winner of a 2018 American Book Award and finalist for the 2018 Lambda Literary Award; *Junk* (2018), an NPR Best Book of the Year; and *Feed* (2019), a finalist for the Kingsley Tufts Award for Poetry and a *New York Times* Notable Book of the Year.

Author of six books of poems, **Carol Potter**'s latest book, *What Happens Next Is Anyone's Guess*, won the 2021 Pacific Coast Series Award from Beyond Baroque. She lives in Vermont and teaches for the Antioch University MFA low-residency program in Los Angeles.

D. A. Powell's books include *Chronic* and *Useless Landscape, or A Guide for Boys*. His honors include fellowships from the National Endowment for the Arts and the Guggenheim Foundation, the Kingsley Tufts Prize, the National Book Critics Circle Award in Poetry, and the John Updike Award from the American Academy of Arts and Letters. A former Briggs-Copeland Lecturer at Harvard, Powell teaches at University of San Francisco.

Minnie Bruce Pratt's poetry on being a lesbian mother, *Crime Against Nature*, was honored with the Lamont Poetry Selection of the Academy of American Poets. Her most recent book, *Magnified*—poems emerging from her life with trans activist and writer Leslie Feinberg—is available from the Wesleyan Poetry Series and through Charis Books & More. Her creative nonfiction essay, "The Queer South: Where the Past Is Not Past and the Future is Now," was lately published in *Scalawag*. More information on her work is at minniebrucepratt.net.

Alison Prine's debut collection of poems, *Steel* (Cider Press Review, 2016) was named a finalist for the 2017 Vermont Book Award. Her poems have appeared in *Ploughshares*, *Virginia Quarterly Review*, *Five Points*, *Harvard Review*, and *Prairie Schooner*, among others. She lives and works in Burlington, Vermont. Visit her at alisonprine. com.

Khalisa Rae is an award-winning poet, educator, and journalist based in Durham, NC. She is best known as the co-founder of Athenian Press—QPOC writer's collective. Khalisa is a four-time Best of the Net nominee, Pushcart Prize nominee, and the author of the debut collection *Ghost in a Black Girl's Throat* from Red Hen Press 2021. Notably, she was the Gen Z Culture Editor of Blavity News. As a champion for Black queer narratives, her articles appear in Fodor's, *Autostraddle*, *Catapult*, *LitHub*, *Bitch Media*, NBC-BLK, and others. Her work appears in *Electric Lit*, *Southern Humanities Review*, *Pinch*, *Tishman Review*, *Frontier Poetry*, *Rust + Moth*, *PANK*, *Hobart*, among countless others. Currently, she serves as Assistant Editor of Glass Poetry, co-founder of Think in Ink and the WOC Speak reading series. Her YA novel in verse, *Unlearning Eden,* is forthcoming in 2022. Follow her at khalisarae.com.

Jacques J. Rancourt is the author of two full-length poetry collections, *Brocken Spectre* (Alice James Books, 2021) and *Novena* (Pleiades Press, 2017), as well as a chapbook, *In the Time of PrEP* (*Beloit Poetry Journal,* 2018). His poems have appeared in the *Boston Review, Kenyon Review, New England Review, Southern Review,* and *Virginia Quarterly Review,* among others. A former Stegner Fellow at Stanford University, he lives now in San Francisco.

Varun Ravindran was born and lives.

Justin Phillip Reed is an American writer and amateur bass guitarist. His preoccupations include horror cinema, poetic form, morphological transgressions, and uses of the grotesque. He is the author of two poetry collections, *The Malevolent Volume* (2020) and *Indecency* (2018), both published by Coffee House Press. He studies traditional martial arts and participates in alternative rock music cultures. He was born and raised in the Pee Dee region of South Carolina and enjoys smelling like outside.

Rita Mae Reese is the author of *The Book of Hulga.* Her work has won numerous awards, including a Rona Jaffe Foundation Writers' Award, a Stegner Fellowship, and a "Discovery"/*The Nation* award. She designs Lesbian Poet Trading Cards for Headmistress Press, is in the bluegrass band Coulee Creek, and serves as the Co-Director at Arts + Literature Laboratory in Madison, Wisconsin.

William Reichard is a writer, editor, and educator. His most recent books are *Our Delicate Barricades Downed* (Broadstone Books, 2021) and *The Night Horse: New and Selected Poems* (Brighthorse Books, 2020).

Noʻu Revilla is a queer ʻŌiwi (Hawaiian) poet, performer, and educator. She won the 2021 National Poetry Series and her debut book of poems, *Ask the Brindled,* will be published by Milkweed Editions. She is an assistant professor of creative writing at the University of Hawaiʻi-Mānoa, where she teaches ʻŌiwi literature, spoken word, and decolonial poetics. Read her work at www.nourevilla.com/.

heidi andrea restrepo rhodes is a poet, feminist scholar, and cultural worker. Her poetry collection *The Inheritance of Haunting* (University of Notre Dame Press, 2019) won the 2018 Andrés Montoya Poetry Prize and explores intergenerational memory and postcolonial trauma. She has received poetry fellowships from CantoMundo, Radar, and Yale's Center for the Study of Race, Indigeneity, and Transnational

Migration. Her work has been published in *Poetry*, the Academy of American Poets' Poem-a-Day, *Nat. Brut*, *Foglifter*, and *Waxwing*, among other places. She currently lives in Cambridge, Massachusetts.

An essayist and poet, **Adrienne Rich** (1929–2012) published poetry for fifty years and is especially well known for her collection *Diving into the Wreck*.

Elizabeth Lindsey Rogers is the author of two poetry collections: *The Tilt Torn Away from the Seasons* (2020) and *Chord Box* (2013). Recent poems appear in *Poetry*, *Waxwing*, *Pleiades*, *Bennington Review*, and elsewhere. Her essays appear in *Best American Nonrequired Reading*, *Best American Travel Writing*, *The Missouri Review*, *The Rumpus*, and elsewhere. Rogers is a Visiting Assistant Professor of Creative Writing at Oberlin College.

Dakota R. Rottino-Garilli (she/they) is an educator, social worker, and writer. She holds an MFA in poetry, creative nonfiction, and pedagogy from Chatham University and an MSW from the University of Pittsburgh. Dakota has taught creative writing to adults and youth in schools, the carceral system, the public health system, and elsewhere. Dakota's chapbook, *Call it Something Different*, was published by Seven Kitchens Press, and her poems and book reviews have appeared in *Homology Lit*, *Pretty Owl Poetry*, and *Coal Hill Review*, among others. Her current work focuses on creating affirming educational environments for LGBTQ+ youth of color.

Kay Ryan, US Poet Laureate and Pulitzer Prize winner, was born in California in 1945 and grew up in the small towns of the San Joaquin Valley and the Mojave Desert. She has lived in Marin County in Northern California since 1971. Ryan's collections of poetry include the 2011 Pulitzer Prize-winning *The Best of It*, *New and Selected Poems* (2010); *The Niagara River* (2005); *Say Uncle* (2000); *Elephant Rocks* (1996); *Flamingo Watching* (1994); and *Erratic Facts* (2015). Her newest book, *Synthesizing Gravity: Selected Prose* (Grove, 2020), is an essay collection of critical prose, book reviews, and thoughts on poetry.

sam sax is a queer, Jewish writer and educator. They're the author of *Madness*, winner of the National Poetry Series and *Bury It* winner of the James Laughlin Award from the Academy of American Poets. They're the two-time Bay Area Grand Slam Champion with poems published in *The New York Times*, *The Atlantic*, *Granta*, and elsewhere. Sam's received fellowships from the NEA, The Poetry Foundation, MacDowell, and is currently serving as an ITALIC Lecturer at Stanford University.

A poet and playwright, **James Schuyler** (1923-1991) received the Pulitzer Prize in Poetry for *The Morning of the Poem* in 1981.

Ruth L. Schwartz has received many national poetry awards, including grants from the NEA, the Ohio Arts Council, and the Astraea Foundation for Lesbian Rights, and book prizes from the National Poetry Series, the Association of Writers and Writing Programs, Autumn House Press, and Anhinga Press. She is the author of five books of poems and three nonfiction books, including the self-help classic *Conscious Lesbian Dating & Love*. Ruth has taught at eight colleges and universities and is the founder and director of the Conscious Girlfriend Academy, the #1 global resource for dating, love, and sex education for lesbians and queer women worldwide.

Maureen Seaton has authored over two dozen poetry collections, both solo and collaborative—most recently, *Undersea* (JackLeg Press, 2021); *Myth America* (Anhinga Press, 2020), co-authored with Carolina Hospital, Nicole Hospital-Medina, and Holly Iglesias; and *Sweet World* (CavanKerry Press, 2019), winner of the 2019 Florida Book Award for Poetry. Her honors include the Lambda Literary Award for both Lesbian Poetry and Lesbian Memoir, Publishing Triangle's Audre Lorde Award, a National Endowment for the Arts Fellowship, and a Pushcart Prize. Seaton is Professor Emerita of English at the University of Miami. She was voted Miami's Best Poet 2020 by *The Miami New Times*.

Charif Shanahan is the author of *Into Each Room We Enter without Knowing* (SIU Press, 2017), which was winner of the Crab Orchard Series in Poetry First Book Award, and a finalist for the Lambda Literary Award for Gay Poetry and the Publishing Triangle's Thom Gunn Award. He is currently an Assistant Professor of English and Creative Writing at Northwestern University, where he teaches poetry in the undergraduate and Litowitz MFA+MA graduate creative writing programs.

Brenda Shaughnessy was born in Okinawa and raised in Southern California. She's the author of five poetry collections, most recently *The Octopus Museum*. A sixth collection, *Tanya*, is forthcoming (Knopf, 2023). Her work's been a finalist for the Griffin International Prize, the PEN/Open Book Award, the Kingsley Tufts Prize, a NBCC award, and a Lambda Literary Award. She's been recognized with a Literature Award from the American Academy of Arts and Letters, a Guggenheim Fellowship, and the James McLaughlin Award. She is a professor of English and Creative Writing at Rutgers University-Newark and lives in West Orange, New Jersey.

A critic and poet, **Reginald Shepherd** (1963-2008) was the author of six collections of poetry, all published by the University of Pittsburgh Press.

Ely Shipley is the author of *Some Animal* (Nightboat Books), winner of the Publishing Triangle's Trans and Gender Variant Literature Award and finalist for a Lambda Literary Award; *Boy with Flowers*, winner of the Barrow Street Press book prize judged by Carl Phillips, the Thom Gunn Award, and finalist for a Lambda Literary Award; and *On Beards: A Memoir of Passing*, a letterpress chapbook from speCt! Books. He holds an MFA from Purdue University and a PhD from the University of Utah. He taught for many years in NYC and currently lives and teaches in Washington.

Cedar Sigo was raised on the Suquamish Reservation in the Pacific Northwest and studied at the Jack Kerouac School of Disembodied Poetics at the Naropa Institute. He is the author of eight books and pamphlets of poetry, including *Language Arts* (Wave Books, 2014), *Stranger in Town* (City Lights, 2010), *Expensive Magic* (House Press, 2008), and two editions of *Selected Writings* (Ugly Duckling Presse, 2003 and 2005). He lives in San Francisco.

Richard Siken is a poet, painter, and filmmaker. His book *Crush* won the 2004 Yale Series of Younger Poets Prize, selected by Louise Glück. His second collection of poems, *War of the Foxes* (Copper Canyon Press), was released in 2015. Siken has received fellowships from the National Endowment for the Arts and the Lannan Foundation. His third collection of poems is forthcoming from Copper Canyon Press.

Jake Skeets is the author of *Eyes Bottle Dark with a Mouthful of Flowers*, winner of the National Poetry Series, Kate Tufts Discovery Award, American Book Award, and Whiting Award. He is from the Navajo Nation and teaches at Diné College.

Aaron Smith is the author of four books of poetry: *Blue on Blue Ground*, winner of the Agnes Lynch Starrett Prize, *Appetite, Primer*, and, most recently, *The Book of Daniel*. He is associate professor of creative writing at Lesley University in Cambridge, Massachusetts.

Danez Smith is the author of three collections including *Homie* and *Don't Call Us Dead*. Their work has been awarded the UK's Forward Prize for Best Collection, the Minnesota Book Award in Poetry, the Kate Tufts Discovery Award, and has been a finalist for the NAACP Image Award in Poetry, the National Book Critic Circle Award, and the National Book Award. Former host of the VS Podcast, they live in Minneapolis near their people.

Bruce Snider is the author of three poetry collections—*Fruit, The Year We Studied Women*, and *Paradise, Indiana*. He is co-editor of *The Poem's Country: Place and Poetic Practice*, and his poems and essays have appeared in the *American Poetry Review, Iowa Review, Kenyon Review, Poetry, New England Review*, and *Best American Poetry*, among others. He is currently the chair of the Department of English at the University of San Francisco.

Jess X. Snow is a non-binary writer/director, public artist, poet, children's book author, and arts educator who creates genre-defying queer Asian immigrant stories. Through merging eastern modalities of healing with community arts activism and film directing, their stories explore intimacy, intergenerational trauma, time travel, and abolitionist futures. They are the author and illustrator of *We Always Had Wings*, (Make Me a World / Random House) forthcoming in Fall 2023. They also illustrated *The Ocean Calls* (Kokila / Penguin Young Readers). Their artwork has been featured in the *New York Times*, international protests, billboards, bus shelters, Broadway theaters, and museums.

Christopher Soto is a writer and abolitionist based in Los Angeles, California.

A research linguist and poet, **Jack Spicer** (1925-1965) refused to sign a "loyalty oath" to the United States and lost his teaching assistantship at the University of California. *My Vocabulary Did This To Me: The Collected Poetry of Jack Spicer* is his most recent posthumous collection.

An art collector, novelist, playwright, and poet, **Gertrude Stein** (1874-1946) was the author of numerous collections, including *Tender Buttons*.

James Thomas Stevens—Aronhió:ta's (Akwesasne Mohawk) was born in Niagara Falls, New York. He attended the Institute of American Indian Arts, Naropa University's Jack Kerouac School of Disembodied Poetics, and Brown University's graduate creative writing program. Stevens has authored eight books of poetry, including, *Combing the Snakes from His Hair, Mohawk/Samoa: Transmigrations, A Bridge Dead in the Water, The Mutual Life, Bulle/Chimere, DisOrient*, and *The Golden Book* (SplitLevel Texts). He is a 2000 Whiting Award recipient and Full Professor in IAIA's undergraduate Creative Writing Program. He teaches poetry, Native American literature, and world survey courses. He lives in Cañoncito, New Mexico.

Will Stockton's work has appeared in journals including *Hotel Amerika, Bennington Review*, and *Tupelo Quarterly*. He teaches English at Clemson University.

The eldest of ten children in a Mormon family in Utah, **May Swenson** (1913-1989) was a stenographer, ghostwriter, and secretary as well as the author of nine collections of poetry.

Lehua M. Taitano is a queer CHamoru writer and interdisciplinary artist from Yigu, Guåhan (Guam), familian Kabesa yan Kuetu, and co-founder of Art 25: Art in the Twenty-fifth Century. She is the author of *Inside Me an Island* and *A Bell Made of Stones*. Taitano's work investigates modern Indigeneity, decolonization, and cultural identity in the context of diaspora.

Brian Teare is the author of six critically acclaimed books, most recently *Companion Grasses, The Empty Form Goes All the Way to Heaven*, and *Doomstead Days*, winner of the Four Quartets Prize. His honors include the Brittingham Prize and Lambda Literary and Publishing Triangle Awards, as well as Guggenheim, Pew Foundation, and NEA fellowships. After over a decade of teaching and writing in the San Francisco Bay Area, and eight years in Philadelphia, he's now an Associate Professor at the University of Virginia, and lives in Charlottesville, where he makes books by hand for his micropress, Albion Books.

Amber Flora Thomas is the author of *Eye of Water: Poems* which was selected by Harryette Mullen as the winner of the Cave Canem Poetry Prize for a first book by a Black writer of African descent. Her other poetry books include *The Rabbits Could Sing* (University of Alaska Press, 2012) and *Red Channel in the Rupture* (Red Hen Press, 2018). She has received fellowships from Yaddo, Atlantic Center for the Arts, Bread Loaf Writers' Conference, and Sewanee Writers' Conference. She earned an MFA at Washington University in St. Louis, Missouri. She was born and raised in Northern California.

Bradford Tice is the author of two books of poetry: *Rare Earth* (New Rivers Press, 2013), which was named the winner of the 2011 Many Voices Project and a 2014 Debut-litzer finalist, and *What the Night Numbered* (Trio House Press, 2015), winner of the 2014 Trio Award. His poetry and fiction have appeared in such periodicals as *The Atlantic Monthly, North American Review, The American Scholar, Epoch*, as well as in *Best American Short Stories 2008*. His poetry was also selected as the winner of *Prairie Schooner*'s 2009 Edward Stanley Award. He currently teaches at Nebraska Wesleyan University in Lincoln.

Eric Tran is a queer Vietnamese poet and the author of *Mouth, Sugar, and Smoke* (Diode Editions) and *The Gutter Spread Guide to Prayer* (Autumn House Press). He serves

as an associate editor for Orison Press and a poetry reader for the *Los Angeles Review.*
He has received awards and recognition from *Prairie Schooner, New Delta Review, Best of
the Net,* and others. His work appears in *RHINO, 32 Poems,* the *Missouri Review,* and
elsewhere. He is a resident physician in psychiatry in Asheville, North Carolina.

Arianne True (Choctaw, Chickasaw) is a raging homosexual, poet, and folk artist
from Seattle. She's received writing fellowships from Jack Straw and the Hugo House
and is a proud alum of Hedgebrook and of the MFA program at the Institute of
American Indian Arts. Arianne teaches and mentors youth poets around Puget Sound
and moonlights as a copyeditor. She's the Seattle Repertory Theater's inaugural Native
Artist-in-Residence, and through her residency is finishing her first manuscript,
exhibits. You can find more of her work online at ariannetrue.com.

Vanessa Angélica Villarreal is the author of *Beast Meridian* (Noemi Press, Akrilica
Series, 2017), a recipient of a 2019 Whiting Award, a Kate Tufts Discovery Award
nomination, and winner of the John A. Robertson Award for Best First Book of Poetry
from the Texas Institute of Letters. She is a 2021 National Endowment for the Arts
poetry fellow, and has appeared in *The New York Times, Harper's Bazaar, Oxford American,
The Cut, Poetry,* and elsewhere. She is working on a poetry and essay collection while
raising her son in Los Angeles with the help of a loyal dog.

Irene Villaseñor (Aeta, Chinese, Ifugao, and Purépecha) examines art and culture,
bi-societal experiences, Indigeneity, injustice, community-building, care, and trauma.
Her writing appears in *My Phone Lies to Me: Fake News Poetry Workshops as Radical Digital
Media Literacy* (Punctum Books), *Nepantla: An Anthology Dedicated to Queer Poets of Color*
(Nightboat Books, 2018), *TAYO Literary Magazine, The Santa Fe Writers Project's Quarterly
Journal, Nat. Brut,* and *The Yellow Medicine Review: A Journal of Indigenous Literature, Art,
and Thought.* She contributed to *Heart On Your Sleeve,* a project with Saint Flashlight and
The Poetry Project that features six short poems on coffee sleeves.

Ocean Vuong is the author of *Night Sky with Exit Wounds* (Copper Canyon Press,
2016), *On Earth We're Briefly Gorgeous* (Penguin Press, 2019), and *Time Is a Mother*
(Penguin Press, 2022). He was awarded a 2019 MacArthur "Genius" Grant.

Stacey Waite is Associate Professor of English and Graduate Chair at the University
of Nebraska—Lincoln and is the author of four collections of poetry: *Choke* (winner
of the Frank O'Hara Prize for Poetry), *Love Poem to Androgyny, the lake has no saint*
(Winner of the Snowbound Prize), and *Butch Geography* (Tupelo Press, 2013). Waite is
also the author of *Teaching Queer: Radical Possibilities for Writing and Knowing* (University

of Pittsburgh Press, 2017) and co-editor of a forthcoming book from Parlor Press, *Inventing the Discipline: Student Work in Composition Studies.*

Michael Walsh is the author of two poetry collections, *The Dirt Riddles* (University of Arkansas Press) and *Creep Love* (Autumn House Press), as well as two chapbooks, *Adam Walking the Garden* and *Sleepwalks* (Red Dragonfly Press).

Michael Wasson is Nimíipuu from the Nez Perce Reservation in Idaho. He is the author of *Swallowed Light* (Copper Canyon, 2021) and *This American Ghost* (YesYes Books, 2017). In 2019 he was awarded a Ruth Lilly and Dorothy Sargent Rosenberg Poetry Fellowship from the Poetry Foundation.

Valerie Wetlaufer is the author of the Lambda Award-winning collection *Mysterious Acts by My People* (Sibling Rivalry Press, 2014), and *Call Me by My Other Name* (Sibling Rivalry Press, 2016). Valerie lives in Cedar Rapids, Iowa.

Arisa White is an assistant professor of English and Creative Writing at Colby College. Her recent poetic memoir *Who's Your Daddy* was published by Augury Books; she co-edited the anthology *Home Is Where You Queer Your Heart* and co-authored *Biddy Mason Speaks Up*, the second book in the Fighting for Justice Series for young readers. Arisa's work has been widely published and nominated for a Lambda Literary Book Award, California Book Award, and an NAACP Image Award. As the creator of the Beautiful Things Project, Arisa curates poetic collaborations that center queer BIPOC narratives. She is a Cave Canem fellow and serves on the board of directors for Foglifter and Nomadic Press and is a community advisory board member for Maine Writers & Publishers Alliance. (arisawhite.com)

James L. White (1936-1981) was the author of four poetry collections, including *The Salt Ecstasies*, published posthumously in 1982.

Jim Whiteside is the author of a chapbook, *Writing Your Name on the Glass* (Bull City Press, 2019), and is a former Wallace Stegner Fellow in Poetry. His work has received support from the Sewanee Writers' Conference, The Virginia Center for the Creative Arts, and The University of North Carolina at Greensboro, where he earned his MFA. His poems have appeared in *The New York Times*, *Poetry*, *Ploughshares*, *The Southern Review*, and *Boston Review*. Originally from Cookeville, Tennessee, he lives in Brooklyn, New York.

An essayist, journalist and poet, **Walt Whitman** (1819-1892) is renowned for *Leaves of Grass*, seven editions of which appeared between 1855 and 1891.

Amie Whittemore is the author of the poetry collections *Glass Harvest* (Autumn House Press), *Star-tent: A Triptych* (Tolsun Books, 2023), and *Nest of Matches* (Autumn House, 2024). She was the 2020-2021 Poet Laureate of Murfreesboro, Tennessee, and an Academy of American Poets Laureate Fellow. Her poems have won multiple awards, including a Dorothy Sargent Rosenberg Prize, and her poems and prose have appeared in *The Gettysburg Review, Nashville Review, Smartish Pace, Pleiades*, and elsewhere. She is the Reviews Editor for *Southern Indiana Review* and teaches English at Middle Tennessee State University.

A lesser-known Beat poet, **John Wieners** (1934-2002) was the author of more than a dozen poetry collections, including *Asylum Poems*.

Candace Williams is a Black, queer nerd living a double life. By day, they are a middle school English teacher. By night, they're a poet. Candace's work has appeared in *Hyperallergic, Foglifter, Bennington Review*, the *Brooklyn Poets Anthology* (Brooklyn Arts Press, 2017), *Bettering American Poetry 2016* (Bettering Books, 2017), and *Nepantla: An Anthology Dedicated to Queer Poets of Color* (Nightboat Books, 2018) among other places. Their chapbook, *Spells for Black Wizards*, was a 2017 TAR Chapbook Series winner published by the Atlas Review. *FUTURE/BLACK* (formerly *futureblack*), their first full-length poetry manuscript, was a 2018 National Poetry Series finalist.

Phillip B. Williams is a Chicago, Illinois native and author of *Thief in the Interior*, winner of the 2017 Kate Tufts Discovery Award and a 2017 Lambda Literary award; and *Mutiny* (Penguin Poetry, 2021). He received a 2017 Whiting Award and fellowship from the Radcliffe Institute for Advanced Study. He currently teaches at Bennington College and Randolph College low-residency MFA.

Morgan Grayce Willow has published several poetry collections and chapbooks, including: *Dodge & Scramble, Between, Silk, Oddly Enough, The Maps are Words*. As essayist, Morgan's work has appeared in *Third Coast, Imagination & Place: Cartography*, and the anthology *Riding Shotgun: Women Write About Their Mothers* (Borealis Books). Her essay "(Un)Document(ing)" from *Water~Stone Review* #22 was nominated for a Pushcart Prize. As a book artist, Morgan exhibited her artist's book *Collage for Mina Loy* at the Minnesota Center for Book Arts (2016) and contributed poetry and visual art to the Quilt, Not Quilt exhibition and its accompanying chapbook *Stitch by Stitch* (2018).

Tobias Wray's *No Doubt I Will Return a Different Man* won the CSU Poetry Center's Lighthouse Poetry Series Competition. Poems and other writing have found homes in *The Arkansas International*, *Blackbird*, *Bellingham Review*, *Hunger Mountain*, *Meridian*, and *The Georgia Review*. Poems will also appear in *The Queer Movement Anthology of Literatures* (Seagull Books). After some years directing the University of Idaho's Creative Writing Programs, he now lives in Los Angeles.

Mark Wunderlich is the author of four books of poems, the most recent of which is *God of Nothingness*, published by Graywolf Press. His other titles include *The Earth Avails*, which received the Rilke Prize, *Voluntary Servitude*, and *The Anchorage*, which received the Lambda Literary Award. He has received fellowships from the Guggenheim Foundation, the NEA, Civitella Ranieri Foundation, and his poems have appeared in *The New Yorker, The New Republic, The Nation, The New York Times Magazine,* and numerous anthologies. He is the director of the Bennington Writing Seminars graduate writing program and lives in New York's Hudson Valley.

Yanyi is the author of *Dream of the Divided Field* (One World Random House, 2022) and *The Year of Blue Water* (Yale University Press, 2019), winner of the 2018 Yale Series of Younger Poets Prize. His work has been featured in or at NPR's *All Things Considered*, New York Public Library, *Tin House, Granta,* and *A Public Space*, and he is the recipient of fellowships from Asian American Writers' Workshop and Poets House. He holds an MFA in Poetry from New York University. He was most recently poetry editor at *Foundry*. Currently, he teaches creative writing at large and gives creative advice at *The Reading*.

C. Dale Young is the author of the novel *The Affliction* (2018) and five collections of poetry, including *The Halo* (2016) and *Prometeo* (2021). A recipient of fellowships from the National Endowment for the Arts, The John Simon Guggenheim Memorial Foundation, and the Rockefeller Foundation, he practices medicine full-time and teaches for the Warren Wilson MFA Program for Writers. He lives in San Francisco.

Amanda Yskamp is a writer and collage artist living on the banks of the Russian River. With degrees from UC Berkeley and NYU, she teaches writing and literary analysis from her online classroom, Wordwise Instruction, and is the librarian of the Guerneville School. She has published her work in such magazines as *Threepenny Review*, *Hayden's Ferry Review, The Georgia Review,* and *Caketrain*.

An independent scholar, creative writing instructor, and writer, **Michael Walsh** received his BA in Creative Writing from Knox College and his MFA in Creative and Professional Writing from the University of Minnesota—Twin Cities. His awards include a Minnesota State Arts Board Fellowship in Poetry, a Jerome Foundation Emerging Artist Fellowship, The Miller Williams Prize in Poetry, and The Publishing Triangle's Thom Gunn Award for Gay Poetry. His poetry books include *The Dirt Riddles* (University of Arkansas Press) and *Creep Love* (Autumn House Press) as well as two chapbooks, *Adam Walking the Garden* and *Sleepwalks* (Red Dragonfly Press). His poems and stories have appeared in anthologies and journals such as *Alaska Quarterly Review, Birmingham Poetry Review, Borderlands: Texas Poetry Review, Blue Mesa Review, The Chattahoochee Review, Cherry Tree, Cimarron Review, Crab Creek Review, Crab Orchard Review, Cream City Review, Fiction on a Stick, Fiddleblack, Flyway Literary Review, The Fourth River, Great River Review, The Journal, The Midwest Quarterly, Midwestern Gothic, Mudfish, the museum of americana, Natural Bridge, North American Review, North Dakota Quarterly, Pangyrus, Permafrost, Prairie Schooner, Quiddity International Journal, South Dakota Review,* and *Southern Poetry Review.* As a curriculum administrator at the University of Minnesota, Michael has worked in social sciences and humanities departments, including English, to which he recently returned, as well as Psychology, where he augmented his literary thinking with psychological thinking. After residing in Minneapolis for more than two decades, Michael now lives in a valley among coulees and springs in the Driftless region of southwest Wisconsin, where his eco-queer and literary teachings are taking shape. Connect with him at michaeltwalsh.com.